Crossing the Kingdom

Crossing the Kingdom

PORTRAITS OF SAUDI ARABIA

Loring M. Danforth

UNIVERSITY OF CALIFORNIA PRESS

University of California Press, one of the most distinguished university presses in the United States, enriches lives around the world by advancing scholarship in the humanities, social sciences, and natural sciences. Its activities are supported by the UC Press Foundation and by philanthropic contributions from individuals and institutions. For more information, visit www.ucpress.edu.

University of California Press
Oakland, California

Library of Congress Cataloging-in-Publication Data

Danforth, Loring, author.
    Crossing the kingdom : portraits of Saudi Arabia /
    Loring M. Danforth.
        p.   cm.
    Includes bibliographical references and index.
    ISBN 978-0-520-29028-0 (cloth, alk. paper) —
      ISBN 0-520-29027-5 (pbk., alk. paper) —
    ISBN 978-0-520-96451-8 (electronic)
    1. Saudi Arabia—Description and travel.   I. Title.
DS208.D36   2016
953.805´4—dc23   2015034605

Manufactured in the United States of America

25   24   23   22   21   20   19   18   17   16
10   9   8   7   6   5   4   3   2   1

In keeping with a commitment to support environmentally responsible and sustainable printing practices, UC Press has printed this book on Natures Natural, a fiber that contains 30% post-consumer waste and meets the minimum requirements of ansi/niso z39.48-1992 (r 1997) (*Permanence of Paper*).

For Peggy, Nicholas, and Ann

CONTENTS

ACKNOWLEDGMENTS

It was a great privilege to have had the opportunity to spend a month traveling and learning in Saudi Arabia. I owe my greatest debt of gratitude to Leena, whose initiative, creativity, and determination made the trip possible. I would also like to thank the sixteen Bates College students who joined us on the trip; they were great company. All of us, I know, would like to express our appreciation to Halah and Ahmed, who helped guide us on our journey across the Kingdom, and to all the Saudis we met, both those who are named in this book and those who are not. Finally, I want to thank the company where Leena's father works for its support, as well as Leena's entire family for their warm hospitality.

I have been fortunate to have taught at Bates College for over thirty-five years. Bates has always encouraged its faculty to maintain what, in my opinion, is an ideal balance between scholarship and teaching. The College has always been very supportive of my research, and the Bates faculty has provided me with a wonderful group of colleagues and friends. While I was writing this book, Steve Kemper, Tom Tracy, and other members of the Religious Studies Department provided me with much valuable advice, as did Rashed al-Munajjim, a Saudi student who arrived at Bates after our trip. Sylvia Hawks has been unfailingly helpful in preparing the many drafts of this book. Reed Malcolm, Stacy Eisenstark, and Cindy Fulton at the University of California Press have been a pleasure to work with, as has my copy editor, Andrew Frisardi. I would also like to thank Bill Nelson for the map of Saudi Arabia and the Arabian Peninsula.

Over the course of my education, I have benefited from the support of many fine teachers: John Davey and Dennis Kratz at the Roxbury Latin School; Frederick Errington, Anne Lebeck, and Donald Pitkin at Amherst

College; and Vincent Crapanzano, Hildred Geertz, and Peter Seitel at Princeton University.

My parents, John and Judy Danforth, nurtured in me a passion for language and learning. My wife, Peggy Rotundo, has always inspired me with her commitment to social justice, her patience, and her love. And finally, my children, Ann and Nicholas Danforth, are never-ending sources of joy and pride.

PREFACE

Strange paths lead to unexpected places, and sometimes the world opens up.[1]

One afternoon in the spring of 2011, a student from Saudi Arabia stopped by my office at Bates College, where I teach. She asked me a question that would change my life. Leena asked if I would be interested in taking a group of Bates students to Saudi Arabia for a month-long educational program. I was stunned. Leena had offered me a priceless gift: the opportunity to travel to a new part of the world and begin to try to understand a new culture.

I am an anthropologist; conducting fieldwork, immersing myself in other cultures, is what I do. The joy of exploring a different culture is what I live for. I'm enthralled with the complexity, the power, and the beauty of human diversity. Listening to a language I don't understand is—for me at least—a spiritual experience. Encountering a new culture, which literally involves entering a new world, is for me a kind of conversion experience. But it's not a conversion experience in the usual sense. It's not a *religious* conversion experience; it's a *secular* one. When I encounter a new culture, it's as if I am possessed—not by a new god, but by a new culture, a new way of being human.

I've spent most of my adult life, my entire career as an anthropologist, conducting ethnographic fieldwork in northern Greece and writing about different aspects of modern Greek culture—death rituals, spirit possession, nationalism, and the experiences of refugee children from the Greek Civil War. Now Leena was offering me the opportunity to travel to the Middle East, to the Arabian Peninsula, to the Kingdom of Saudi Arabia. I was being offered the chance to learn about Islam, the oil industry, and what it's like to live under an absolute monarchy.

I knew that I did not have time to learn Arabic, as I had modern Greek, or to acquire the depth of knowledge of Saudi culture that I had of modern Greek culture. But I was confident that my abilities as an ethnographer and a writer would enable me to gain valuable insights into Saudi culture and communicate them effectively to a wide audience. I was looking forward to reexperiencing the excitement of encountering a new culture for the first time, as I had when I was a young graduate student living in small village in northern Greece.

As soon as I told Leena that I would be delighted to join her in taking a group of Bates students to Saudi Arabia, we began planning the trip. The Kingdom of Saudi Arabia is a difficult country to visit; the Saudi government does not issue tourist visas. Our program, which came to be known as #Bates2Saudi, was made possible by the kindness and generosity of Leena's family and the multinational corporation where her father works. I have been asked to maintain the confidentiality of Leena's family and her father's company, and I feel obligated to honor that request.

Leena and I spent the 2011–12 academic year designing the course. We met regularly to decide on the general topics we wanted to cover and the specific aspects of Saudi society and culture we hoped to explore. We also began planning our itinerary: the places we hoped to visit and the kinds of people we wanted to meet.

Over sixty students applied for the course, but I could only take sixteen. The students I chose were a wonderful group of young people. They were smart, enthusiastic, and fully committed to learning as much as they could about Saudi Arabia. During the semester that preceded the trip, we all met weekly to discuss the readings I had selected: books and articles on Islam, the oil industry, the role of women in Arab cultures, and the history, politics, and culture of Saudi Arabia. We also watched several documentary films, including one about a trip Harvard Business School students had taken to the Kingdom in 2007. Finally, we devoted several meetings to learning how to conduct ethnographic fieldwork, with a focus on interviews, participant observation, and the ethical and political issues that often arise during anthropological research.

Our itinerary was subject to certain constraints. The U.S. State Department has a long-standing travel warning on travel to Saudi Arabia. The corporation that sponsored our trip also had concerns, which imposed some limits on our plans. For example, we were not able to visit Qatif, a city north of Dhahran on the Persian Gulf, whose population is predominantly Shia and which has been the site of protests and political violence.

As a result of Leena's hard work and careful planning, as well as that of her extensive network of friends and colleagues, we enjoyed considerably more freedom and access to a much wider range of people, than I had anticipated. Among the Saudis we met were a historian who had been banned from teaching at King Saud University, a well-known religious and cultural leader who has been a sharp critic of the Saudi government, a human rights activist who shortly after our trip was sentenced to a long prison term, and women's rights activists who had been persecuted by the government for protesting the ban against women driving.

With only two exceptions where we had a translator (noted in the text), all the people we interviewed spoke English with near-native fluency. Our inability to speak Arabic clearly limited the people we were able to meet, but it did not interfere with our ability to communicate with the people we did meet. Most of the Saudis we spoke with had received undergraduate or graduate degrees from American universities and were members of the Saudi elite. This constitutes a significant limitation on our experiences that I am well aware of and fully acknowledge.

Throughout the trip, we were accompanied by Leena's close female friend, Halah, and a young male colleague of theirs, Ahmed. Leena and Halah were constantly on their smart phones making last minute arrangements for our next meetings, while Ahmed accompanied the male members of our group when we were in public and needed to maintain strict gender segregation. Both Halah and Ahmed did an excellent job explaining different aspects of their culture to us, and they became our good friends. They also gained valuable insights into their own culture as they worked hard to share it with us. Such is the joy of anthropology.

We arrived at the King Fahd International Airport in Dammam on April 28, 2012 and spent the first ten days of our trip in Dhahran, where the headquarters of Saudi Aramco, the Saudi national oil company, are located (see map 1). We spent time on the Aramco compound visiting Aramco's administrative center and research facilities, as well as meeting with Aramco executives, engineers, and scientists. In the immediate vicinity of Dhahran, we visited an art gallery, a local mosque, and a private folklore museum; a private secondary school, Prince Mohammad bin Fahd University, and a job fair for nontraditional occupations; and a mall, a luxury beach resort, and the twenty-five-kilometer-long causeway linking Saudi Arabia and Bahrain. In addition, we interviewed artists, journalists, and educators; religious officials, professional women, and social entrepreneurs; women's rights activists, students from local universities,

MAP I. Saudi Arabia and the Arabian Peninsula.

and a member of the royal family. During this part of our program, we also visited the city of Hofuf in the al-Hasa Oasis region about seventy-five kilometers southwest of Dhahran. There we visited a museum, a historic castle, and, yes, a camel market.

On May 8, we traveled by bus 380 kilometers across the desert of the Eastern Province to Riyadh, the Saudi capital, located in the conservative Najd region in the center of the country. There we visited important museums, historical buildings, and archaeological sites. We also met with lawyers, human rights activists, and a group of young comedians, filmmakers, and social media specialists.

After a short trip to Madain Saleh, a spectacular pre-Islamic archaeological site in the northwest of the country, which has recently been declared a UNESCO World Heritage Site, we traveled to Jeddah on the Red Sea coast for the final ten days of the course. There we spoke with the Saudi minister of education, the mayor of Jeddah, and a female surgeon internationally known for her work on breast cancer. We also met with local artists, architects, journalists, medical students, historic preservationists, and other civic leaders. In addition, we visited Effat, a private women's university, and King Abdullah University of Science and Technology (KAUST), a new coeducational, graduate research university specializing in math, science, and engineering. Throughout our stay in Jeddah, the students traveling with us lived in the homes of Saudi host families.

On May 21, the last night of our journey across Saudi Arabia, I sent the following email message to all the students on the trip. It was my attempt to convey to them what the trip had meant to me—and what I hoped it had meant to them.

This trip has been one of the most amazing experiences of my life. I want to thank you all for sharing it with me. It has been a privilege and a pleasure to have had the opportunity to bring you to Saudi Arabia.

I expect our departure and our return to the United States may be difficult for you. If you find yourself depressed, disoriented, or alienated from other people—if you find yourself trapped between the world in which you have lived for the past month and the world you are returning to—welcome to culture shock. Just know that it may take you a while to return to normal. Maybe, if you're lucky, you will never return to normal, if that means the way you were before your experiences in Saudi Arabia.

You may also find it hard to share what you've experienced here with others. That's because what we've experienced here is ineffable. That means it can't be expressed. "Ineffable" is a term people often apply to transcendent religious experiences of the divine. I would also apply it to transcendent experiences of other religions and other cultures. Hang on to this feeling as long as you can. It will enrich your lives forever.

Loring M. Danforth
Bates College
Lewiston, Maine
June 2015

Introduction

People in the West don't understand the Middle East. They come
with Bin Laden in their heads.[1]

THE IMAGES MOST AMERICANS HAVE OF SAUDI ARABIA are fright-
eningly predictable—deserts, camels, and oil; Sharia law, Islamic fundamentalism, and jihad; rich sheikhs in white robes, oppressed women in black
veils, and terrorists. Many Americans know Saudi Arabia only as a medieval
monarchy, an ultraconservative theocracy, and a breeding ground for religious extremism; a country whose feudal system of justice is responsible for a
never-ending parade of floggings, amputations, and beheadings.

These images are largely the product of the coverage Saudi Arabia receives
in the American media, coverage that often highlights the exotic, the sensational, and the violent. A Saudi poet is charged with blasphemy and apostasy
for posting short poems about the Prophet Muhammad on Twitter; a Saudi
woman who had been gang raped is sentenced to two hundred lashes and six
months in jail; another Saudi woman is beheaded for practicing witchcraft
and sorcery; and fifteen Saudi school girls die when the religious police prevent them from leaving their burning school because they are not wearing
proper Islamic dress.[2]

A major goal of this book is to challenge these destructive Orientalist
stereotypes of Saudi Arabia by offering alternative images of its people, their
society, and their culture. I present here more nuanced and more complex
portraits of Saudi Arabia than those that circulate in the American media. I
describe a Saudi woman who has been jailed for protesting the government
ban on women driving, a Saudi architect who encourages Muslims and
Christians to struggle together with love to know God, and a Saudi artist

who uses metal gears and chains to celebrate the diversity of the pilgrims who come as "guests of God" to the holy city of Mecca. And there are many other Saudis I met whose portraits are not included in this book: a Saudi comedian who makes his fellow countrymen laugh with his biting social commentary, a Saudi high school student who moves his teacher to tears with a mournful Saudi folk song, and a young Saudi lesbian eager to learn about the lives of gay women in the United States.

I recognize that many of the basic facts that Americans know about Saudi Arabia are true. It *is* an absolute monarchy, there *is* strict media censorship, political parties *are* banned, the lives of women *are* very restricted, the practice of any religion other than Islam *is* prohibited, democratic freedoms and human rights *are* virtually nonexistent, and, yes, Osama bin Laden and fifteen of the nineteen 9/11 hijackers *were* Saudi citizens.

But there is much more to learn about Saudi Arabia before it is possible to form a more balanced, more complete, understanding of this complicated and rapidly changing country. A striking example of the challenge facing anyone trying to present a perceptive account of Saudi culture involves making sense of the *abaya,* the long black robe that Saudi women wear when they're out in public. One American journalist has described wearing an *abaya* as an "indignity" imposed on Saudi women; another as a practice that renders Saudi women "invisible."[3] These comments are insensitive, inaccurate, and misleading. Contrast them with the much more nuanced observation offered by a young Saudi woman, a medical student I met at a Jeddah hospital, who told me what wearing an *abaya* meant to her: "It represents respect for my community and preserving my culture. It's restricting, suffocating, fashionable, and comfortable. I know my answers are contradictory, but that's how it feels." Needless to say, this Saudi woman was definitely not invisible.

◆　◆　◆

Crossing the Kingdom: Portraits of Saudi Arabia was inspired by, and is in part based on, the month I spent traveling through Saudi Arabia with a group of undergraduates from Bates College, where I teach. The trip, which took place in May 2012, was for me a transformative experience. It introduced me to Islam, to the Middle East, and to one of the most important countries in the Arab world. As a specialist on modern Greece and the Balkans, I had a lot to learn in preparation for our program, but the reading

I did the year before the trip was only a scratch on the surface of what I needed to know in order to understand even partially the many experiences we had.

The year immediately following our journey across Saudi Arabia, I was on sabbatical leave. I had planned to begin a new research project in northern Greece, but I couldn't stop thinking about the amazing places we'd visited and the extraordinary people we'd met. I couldn't let go of Saudi Arabia. Or to put it another way, Saudi Arabia wouldn't let go of me. So at that point, I made what seems now to have been a somewhat rash decision. I decided to spend my sabbatical writing a book about Saudi Arabia.

I needed to learn a lot more about Saudi culture in order to understand more fully the different experiences we had been privileged to have. I wanted to learn more about Islam, the pilgrimage to Mecca, the oil industry, the position of women, and the roles of art and science in Saudi culture. I simply wanted to keep thinking about Saudi Arabia; I wanted to keep my experiences there alive.

I had been given an extraordinary opportunity to travel for a month in a country that is difficult to visit, and to speak with members of a very influential segment of Saudi society. As an anthropologist, I felt an obligation to prove worthy of this opportunity. I knew that the only way to do this was to learn more about Saudi culture and share my insights with as wide an audience as possible. I wrote this book in an attempt to convey the complexity, the power, and the beauty of Saudi culture. I wrote it to show people that in Muslim countries the call to prayer, the *adhan,* is not musical background for acts of terrorism, as it is in many American films, but a ubiquitous, and to me and many others, beautiful expression of religious piety and devotion.

Crossing the Kingdom is not a traditional academic monograph. I am not a scholar of the Middle East, I don't read or speak Arabic, and I haven't conducted long-term ethnographic fieldwork in Saudi Arabia. As an experienced anthropologist who has done research in other parts of the world, however, I am confident in my ability to avoid the problems of ethnocentrism, oversimplification, and overgeneralization that characterize much popular writing on Saudi Arabia.

This book, however, does not belong to the genre of travel literature either. It is not about traveling; it's not a book *about* the journey I took across Saudi Arabia. It's a book that emerged *from* the journey. I have written a series of essays—I call them portraits—that are based *on* the experiences I had during the trip. Each of these portraits can stand alone; each deals with a separate and distinct topic. But they are all linked by a concern with common themes that are essential elements of contemporary Saudi culture. Together, I hope, these portraits offer a coherent contribution to our understanding of Saudi reality in the second decade of the twenty-first century.

◆ ◆ ◆

Clifford Geertz, one of the most influential anthropologists of the twentieth century, has written that human beings are animals "suspended in webs of significance" they have spun themselves. Each of the many cultures that human beings have constructed is a complex web woven from many different threads. For Geertz, anthropology—the study of human cultures—is an interpretive discipline, a discipline "in search of meaning."[4] This is the perspective that has guided me throughout my career as an anthropologist.

Islam is deeply woven into the fabric of Saudi life. It is the dominant discourse with which Saudis articulate the different positions they hold on the many issues that confront them in their rapidly changing and highly contested world. The portraits presented in the seven chapters of this book offer valuable insights into the dominant role Islam plays in contemporary Saudi life. More specifically, these portraits suggest the ways in which Islam is used to negotiate the role of women in Saudi society; to shape the fields of Saudi art, archaeology, history, and science; and to define the very boundaries of the Muslim world by deciding precisely who is—and who is not—allowed to join the Hajj and travel to Mecca, the most holy city in the Muslim world. Some of the subjects of the portraits presented here—art, archaeology, tourism, historic preservation, urban renewal, and Islamic creationism—have not received the attention they deserve. Others—the oil industry, the position of women, and the Hajj—have been the subject of much greater attention, but I have tried to offer a new perspective on these more familiar topics as well.

With this book I hope to contribute to an understanding of the relationships between traditional Saudi culture and more recent influences from the West that have so dramatically transformed the country. I explore how the threads of traditional Islamic beliefs and practices in Saudi Arabia have become interwoven with the global threads that have been introduced through ever more pervasive contact with the western world. This complex interplay is at work in the increasing impact that outsiders of many different kinds have had on Saudi culture: expatriate American oil executives; foreign workers from Pakistan, Bangladesh, and the Philippines; European and

American feminists, archaeologists, and museum consultants; and pilgrims from all over the world. The process of weaving together threads from a variety of different cultures is marked not only by conflict and tension, but also by innovation and creativity. This is why Saudi Arabia is such an interesting and important country, a country that deserves to be understood much better than it usually is.

In this book, I explore in considerable detail specific people, events, and issues. By concentrating on the micro level and analyzing particular topics in depth, I hope to achieve a concreteness that eliminates any hint of Orientalism. Rather than painting the Saudi landscape in broad strokes, I present a series of portraits, ethnographic miniatures, which taken together offer more revealing insights into the complexities of Saudi culture. To quote Clifford Geertz again, good interpretive anthropology "makes small facts speak to large issues."[5] That is precisely what I have tried to accomplish in this book.

Each of the portraits that make up *Crossing the Kingdom* is a "mixed-genre text."[6] Each portrait includes detailed first-person narratives of experiences I had, substantial quotations from people I interviewed, more general historical and cultural background material drawn from a variety of primary and secondary sources, as well as my own interpretations of what this all means. In each portrait, I adopt several different styles—I speak in several different voices—moving back and forth between the genres of ethnography, travel writing, and the literature of fact. I try to let individual Saudis speak for themselves, so that readers can hear their voices as clearly as possible. At times, I adopt the voice of the interpretive anthropologist engaged in the traditional task of ethnographic description and analysis. At other times, I adopt the voice of the travel writer trying to evoke as vividly as possible the everyday lives of the Saudis we met. And finally, on occasion, I adopt the more private voice of the individual student and teacher trying to understand the many moving and challenging encounters we had with members of a very different culture.

◆　◆　◆

After conquering most of the Arabian Peninsula, King Abdulaziz ibn Saud founded the Kingdom of Saudi Arabia in 1932.[7] The dominant position the Al Saud dynasty has occupied throughout the history of Saudi Arabia is suggested by a literal translation of the country's name, *al-Mamlaka al-Arabiyya al-Suudiyya,* the Arab Kingdom of the House of Saud. The longevity of the Al Saud dynasty can be attributed to the alliance, dating back to the mid-eighteenth century, between the Al Sauds, with their political and military power, on the one hand, and the descendants of Muhammad ibn Abd al-Wahhab, leaders of the conservative, fundamentalist form of Islam that has given legitimacy to Al Saud rule, on the other. The term *Wahhabism* is widely used to refer to this particularly literalist Saudi version of the larger reformist movement within Sunni Islam known as Salafism (from *salaf,* "predecessor" or "ancestor"). According to this strict, puritanical Wahhabi approach to Islam, the Muslim community, the ideal Muslim state, should be the living embodiment of the law of God.[8]

Soon after the establishment of the Kingdom, oil was discovered in the Eastern Province on the shores of the Persian Gulf. By the 1940s, Aramco, the Arabian American Oil Company, was in full-scale production, and by the 1960s oil wealth had begun to radically transform Saudi society through the entwined processes of industrialization, urbanization, and rapid, but unequal, economic development. In 1979, two decisive events seriously challenged this narrative of growth and progress. The Iranian Revolution, which overthrew the shah and established an Islamic republic ruled by Shia clerics, threatened to destabilize Saudi Arabia's Eastern Province by mobilizing the large Shia minority that lives there against the Sunni regime of the Al Sauds. And on November 20, 1979, a group of Wahhabi fundamentalists led by Juhayman al-Otaybi staged a violent takeover of the Holy Mosque in Mecca, the most sacred site in the Muslim world. Juhayman and his followers believed that the Mahdi (the "redeemer of Islam") had arrived in the person of one of their leaders. More significantly, they wanted to demonstrate in the most dramatic manner possible their dissatisfaction with the Al Saud regime, whose rule they considered materialistic, corrupt, and sacrilegiously subservient to the West.[9] During the two-week siege of the Holy Mosque, thousands of pilgrims were held hostage, and hundreds of Saudi troops were killed. After the siege was lifted—with the intervention, ironically, of French special forces—Juhayman and sixty-seven of his followers were beheaded by the Saudi government.

Both of these events seriously threatened the legitimacy of Al Saud rule. In response to pressure from conservative Wahhabi religious leaders, the Saudi government began to reverse the gradual process of liberalization that had been taking place during the preceding decades. The royal family grew increasingly deferential in its relationship with the *ulama,* the council of religious scholars, an appointed body that advises the king on the administration of sharia law and the interpretation of the Quran, which serves as the country's constitution. During this period, the royal family empowered the Committee for the Promotion of Virtue and the Prevention of Vice, a government agency known informally as the *hayah,* to use the "religious police" (the *mutawwa*), to enforce more severely the many restrictions on women's dress, mobility, and employment. In this way, the Saudi government sacrificed the rights of women in an effort to appease the country's conservative religious leaders and their many followers.

When Saddam Hussein invaded Kuwait in August 1990, the Saudi government asked the United States for protection and granted its request to station over a million American troops in the country during the 1990–91 Gulf War that followed. This request for foreign assistance was an embarrassing admission of military weakness in light of the billions of dollars worth of American arms the Saudi government had purchased over the years. To conservative religious leaders, the presence of American troops on Saudi soil was a desecration of the Land of the Two Holy Mosques, as Saudi Arabia is often referred to. The American presence in the Kingdom also provoked the anger and hostility of Osama bin Laden, a member of a wealthy Saudi family (originally from Yemen) with close ties to the royal family.

During the early years of the twenty-first century, the world has been scarred by tragic episodes of violence associated with the unrest and turmoil that engulfed the entire Middle East: the September 11, 2001, suicide attacks on the Twin Towers of the World Trade Center and the wars in Afghanistan and Iraq that followed. Less well known to many in the West, is the fact that between 2003 and 2006 over two hundred people were killed in Saudi Arabia by al-Qaeda terrorists. This campaign of violence, like the earlier siege of the Holy Mosque in Mecca, posed a significant threat to the stability of the Al Saud dynasty.

The Saudi government responded to these attacks by withdrawing some of its support from the conservative Wahhabi clerics who had exerted such great power over Saudi society during the previous decades. Crown Prince Abdullah, the de facto ruler of the country after King Fahd's 1995 stroke, began to exercise more control over the actions of the *ulama,* most importantly by limiting their ability to issue independent legal pronouncements known as fatwas. In this way Abdullah was able to assert greater independence from the country's religious leaders and move more freely to adopt the liberal social policies he thought were needed to keep the country on the path toward economic development and progress. This process has inevitably involved a significant degree of modernization and westernization of precisely the kind Wahhabi authorities so fiercely oppose.

When he assumed the throne in 2005, King Abdullah instituted a more substantial program of moderate reforms, and under his rule the Kingdom has experienced a period of very gradual liberalization. Abdullah has engaged in a careful balancing act between the conservative Wahhabi segments of society, on the one hand, and the more liberal, reform-minded segments, on the other. Abdullah, often referred to approvingly as the "king of dialogue," has released dissidents, restricted the freedom of action of the *mutawwa,* advocated better relationships between the country's Sunni majority and its Shia minority, expanded education and employment opportunities for women within the country, and increased the opportunities for qualified Saudi youth—both men and women—to study abroad. He has also appointed 30 women to the 150 member Shura Council, the king's advisory body, and has even promised that women will be allowed to vote *and* run for office in the municipal elections set for 2015.

Thuraya al-Arrayed, a well-known Saudi writer and public intellectual I spoke with at her home in Dhahran, characterized her country's recent history as a detour. "We had been on a highway headed straight toward our destination," she said. "Then you could feel we were going off the road. Now, under King Abdullah, we are turning again; we are back on the road toward a more forward, developing society." Many other Saudis I met spoke with approval about the path King Abdullah had chosen for their country. It was, they said, "a path of evolution, not revolution."

In spite of these positive developments, Saudi Arabia remains an absolute monarchy. According to the Basic Law of Governance issued by King Fahd in 1992—the closest thing the Kingdom has to a constitution other than the Quran—the purpose of the Saudi state is to promote Wahhabi Islam, not to protect the individual rights of its citizens. Many Saudis compare the Saudi state to "a giant family-owned corporation" in which the king is the "chief executive," the Al Saud family is the "board of directors," and the citizens are the employees. The loyalty and cooperation of the workers, who play no role in running the company, are secured through a generous package of welfare and entitlements, which includes heavily subsidized water, electricity, and gasoline, as well as interest-free loans, free university education, free health care, and a complete absence of taxes.[10]

More specifically, in Saudi Arabia there is no serious opposition to the royal family of any kind. Political parties do not exist, and no meaningful democratic elections for national office have ever been held. According to a recent Human Rights Watch report, Saudi authorities "continue to systematically suppress or fail to protect the rights of nine million Saudi women and girls, eight million foreign workers, and some two million Shia citizens."[11] Torture, arbitrary detention, and secret trials are common, while freedom of religion and freedom of expression are nonexistent. The Saudi government heavily censors both traditional media—print, film, and television—as well as Internet sites like Google and Wikipedia. YouTube, Facebook, and Twitter are extremely popular with Saudis, and have allowed them to escape many of the government's attempts to limit their ability to communicate with one another and with the outside world.

Despite its tremendous oil wealth, Saudi Arabia faces significant social and economic problems. The popular image of the country as one vast desert notwithstanding, Saudi Arabia is highly urbanized. Over 80 percent of the population of twenty eight million people live in the country's five largest cities, and these cities suffer from many of the same problems as cities in other developing countries around the world: poverty, drugs, violence, housing shortages, and illegal immigration. More than two million people depend for their livelihood on government handouts.

Saudi Arabia faces other, more idiosyncratic challenges as well. Its long-term economic well-being is heavily dependent on its vast, but finite, reserves of oil and gas. Food and water security also present possible threats to the future stability of the country. Another problem facing Saudi economic growth is its heavy dependence on foreign labor. Over four million workers from Yemen, Pakistan, India, Bangladesh, and the Philippines live and work in the country, doing unskilled and semiskilled work that many Saudis are unwilling to do. Even many skilled jobs are being done by foreign workers from Palestine, Egypt, and other countries in the Middle East. As a result, Saudi Arabia is virtually a country "without a national working class."[12]

The failure of sustained government efforts to replace foreign workers with Saudi citizens—a process known as "Saudization"—is suggested by the fact that in 2009 less than half the total labor force consisted of Saudis. This unusual employment pattern creates particular difficulties for Saudi women and young people. In 2009, women constituted only 14 percent of the Saudi labor force in spite of the fact that they made up 60 percent of university students in the country. In recent years the unemployment rate for Saudis between the ages of twenty and twenty-four has stood at about 40 percent.[13]

The Saudi educational system is at least partially responsible for the challenge that the Saudi government faces in effectively incorporating Saudi young people into the workforce. Its flaws are many. Rote learning and the conservative Wahhabi form of Islam occupy prominent places in the curriculum. Much emphasis is placed on teaching conformity and obedience to both religious and political authorities. And finally, creativity, tolerance, and individual initiative are often discouraged.[14]

Sectarian conflict is another significant problem facing the Saudi government. The Shia minority, which constitutes approximately 10 to 15 percent of the Saudi population, is concentrated in the Eastern Province along the Persian Gulf, where the bulk of Saudi oil reserves are located. The Shia in Saudi Arabia experience significant discrimination at the hands of the Sunni government. They are excluded from government employment and from the officer ranks in the military, and they are often accused of being polytheists, apostates, and foreign agents who serve the interests of Shia-dominated Iran. In spite of King Abdullah's efforts to promote reconciliation between the country's Sunni and Shia communities, unrest continues with riots, demonstrations, and protests, some of which have turned violent.[15]

The Arab Spring, which began in 2010 in Tunisia, has raised hopes for democratization and social change throughout the Arab world, but it has also been the cause of tragic unrest, violence, and civil war in Bahrain, Yemen, Syria, Egypt, and Libya. It has done nothing, however, to undermine the stability of the Al Saud regime and its autocratic control over the people of Saudi Arabia. In response to this recent unrest, Saudi religious authorities have issued fatwas ruling that antigovernment activity is unlawful and that demonstrations against the Al Saud regime constitute demonstrations against Islam itself.[16]

The Saudi government has also announced plans to continue its policy of trying to maintain the loyalty and support of its citizens—and in that way fight extremism—through its generous programs of welfare and state subsidies. For their part, the people of Saudi Arabia seem to have reached a consensus that the status quo is preferable to the violence and suffering that the people of other countries in the Middle East have endured. The Saudi upper class in particular seems to value the stability that the monarchy has been able to maintain; they prefer "the path of evolution" over "the path of revolution."

As they confront the implications that the Arab Spring has for their country, the government and the people of Saudi Arabia face many challenges;

they have many questions to answer. Throughout most of its history, the Saudi government has distributed its tremendous oil wealth in exchange for the political loyalty of its citizens. How much longer is this relationship tenable? How will the government manage the growing conflicts and tensions between different factions of Saudi society: wealthy and poor, urban and rural, Sunni and Shia? How will it meet the desire of many Saudis for more democratic political institutions? And most importantly, how will it balance the sharply conflicting demands of the conservative Wahhabi religious authorities and their supporters, on the one hand, and those of more liberal members of Saudi society with their call for modernization and dramatic social change, on the other?

In the final analysis, the struggle to meet these challenges, the struggle to answer these questions, is not a struggle between East and West; it is not a "clash of civilizations."[17] Rather, it is a struggle between different understandings, different interpretations, of Islam; between more narrow, intolerant, and hierarchical forms of Islam, on the one hand, and more open, tolerant, and egalitarian forms of Islam, on the other.

◆ ◆ ◆

Chapter 1 of this book presents an ethnographic and historical portrait of Saudi Aramco, the most valuable corporation and the largest producer of oil in the world. Saudi Aramco is also the dominant force in the Saudi economy. The chapter opens with a description of the Aramco residential compound in Dhahran. The "Aramco camp" is a strange fusion of a 1950s American suburb, on the one hand, and a twenty-first-century multicultural global community, on the other. As one Saudi put it, it's "a piece of the United States that just landed on Saudi Arabia." The company's impressive administrative and research center is also located on the Dhahran compound.

Two very different histories of Aramco follow. The first is the "Aramco story," a corporate history based on the company's own publications that illustrates what an Aramco employee called "the American dream, Saudi style." This story begins with a small group of brave Americans committed to transforming a poor and undeveloped desert land into a modern industrialized state. It ends when the Saudi government assumes full control of the company in a process characterized by cooperation and mutual respect. The second history is a more critical and a more accurate one, a narrative of neo-colonialism, racism, and economic exploitation that concludes with the grudging realization on the part of Aramco's American owners that complete Saudi control of the company is inevitable. The chapter ends with a glimpse into the community of "Aramco Brats," American expatriates who grew up on the Aramco compounds, a glimpse provided by a documentary film produced by members of the community themselves.

Chapter 2 examines the courageous attempts by a small group of Saudi women to repeal the infamous ban against women driving that imposes severe restrictions on the mobility of all Saudi women. *Bad Girls,* a 2012 music video by M.I.A., the controversial English singer of Sri Lankan Tamil descent, presents an exoticized and eroticized image of Muslim women engaged in "drifting," a dangerous and illegal practice in which young alienated Saudi men skid, slide, and spin their cars on the outskirts of Riyadh and other large cities. According to some critics—others disagree—the video is an expression of M.I.A.'s support for Saudi women's right to drive.

The position of women in Saudi society is heavily influenced by the system of guardianship according to which they remain legal minors all their lives, by cultural rules about "covering" and "mixing" that determine the way they dress and interact with others, and by their changing roles in the worlds of education and employment. This chapter focuses particularly on the history of the controversy surrounding women's right to drive. In 1990, a group of Saudi women who protested the ban by driving were arrested and lost both their passports and their jobs. Then in 2011, Manal al-Sharif, a young Saudi Aramco employee, engaged in a similar act of protest. She was arrested and spent nine days in prison. After posting on YouTube a video of herself driving, her #Women2Drive campaign attracted worldwide attention. Since then al-Sharif has continued to use Twitter and Facebook, as well as personal appearances at human rights conferences around the world, to continue her work on behalf of women's rights in Saudi Arabia.

Chapter 3 explores the relatively unknown world of contemporary Saudi art. After describing a visit to an art gallery in Dhahran, I place contemporary Saudi art in the historical context of Islamic and Arab art more broadly. Tacking back and forth again between the specific and the general, I examine the work of two Saudi artists that were on display at the Dhahran gallery. A survey of recent developments in Saudi art follows, which focuses specifically on the contributions of *Edge of Arabia,* a new London-based Saudi arts initiative.

The main emphasis of chapter 3 is on the work of three of the best-known contemporary Saudi artists, Manal al-Dowayan, Ahmed Mater, and

Abdulnasser Gharem, who are all affiliated with *Edge of Arabia*. I analyze specific examples of their work, drawing on comments by art critics and the artists themselves: a black-and-white photograph of a woman holding a car steering wheel that completely covers the lower part of her face; a black cube-shaped magnet—the Kaba at the Holy Mosque in Mecca—surrounded by concentric rings of tiny black iron filings—pilgrims—whirling around it; a series of four bright-blue x-ray images in which a gasoline pump morphs eerily into a man holding a pistol to his head; and the roadbed of a bridge over a ravine, destroyed in a flood, where the word *siraat*—the path, the straight path, the path of Islam—has been spray painted thousands of times. The chapter ends with an account of a moving experience I had during a work-shop at an art gallery in Jeddah that was led by Saddek Wasil, another well-known Saudi artist affiliated with *Edge of Arabia*.

Chapter 4 deals with the relationship between science and religion in the Muslim world. This relationship pervades two important new museums in Saudi Arabia, the National Museum in Riyadh and the Museum of Science and Technology in Islam at the King Abdullah University of Science and Technology north of Jeddah. Both museums juxtapose material from the world of science and the world of Islam in a way that is unfamiliar to people who have visited "science museums" in the United States or Europe. Verses from the Quran about the divine creation of the universe are displayed in front of a diorama depicting clouds of stellar gases produced by the Big Bang. A university-educated museum guide denies the scientific validity of Darwinian evolution.

After stepping back and discussing Stephen Jay Gould's insights into the relationship between science and religion, I offer a brief history of the rela-tionship between science and Islam. This is followed by more detailed por-traits of the work of Adnan Oktar (the leading Islamic creationist), the views of Muslim concordists (who use modern scientific discoveries to support their claim that the Quran is the product of divine revelation), and the work of the Mecca-based International Commission on Scientific Signs in the Quran and Sunnah. The chapter concludes with a description of a morning I spent at the Jeddah offices of the Ladies' Section of the Islamic Education Foundation, where one of the foundation's officers argued, much to the dis-may of some students, that anthropologists had proven scientifically that homosexuality is evil and immoral.

In Chapter 5, I consider the construction of Saudi national identity by examining two recent, but related, developments in Saudi society, the growth of archaeology as an academic discipline, and the birth—perhaps premature, perhaps stillborn, it's too early to tell—of a Saudi tourism industry. This chapter opens with a description of Madain Saleh, a spectacular archaeological site, which has been named a UNESCO World Heritage Site. Madain Saleh, however, receives very few visitors because Saudi Arabia does not issue tourist visas and because many Saudis consider the pre-Islamic tombs that dominate the site taboo.

After discussing the political implications of archaeological practice, I present an analysis of Roads of Arabia, the "groundbreaking" exhibition of "never before seen" artifacts from the pre-Islamic and early Islamic periods in Saudi Arabia, which appeared at the Sackler Gallery in Washington, D.C., from November 2012 through February 2013. The Roads of Arabia exhibition was an act of international diplomacy intended to "rebrand" Saudi Arabia as a culturally rich and diverse country lying at the center of both the ancient and the modern Middle East. The exhibition was also part of ongoing efforts to strengthen the "special relationship" that is said to link Saudi Arabia and the United States.

Chapter 6 presents a portrait of the city of Jeddah, Saudi Arabia's second largest city, which is also the country's principle port and the point of entry for millions of pilgrims on their way to Mecca to perform the Hajj. This chapter begins with a brief account of the city's history and geography drawing on interviews I conducted with the mayor of the city, as well as with local historians, civic leaders, and architectural preservationists. Then it explores in greater detail recent efforts to restore al-Balad, the old city of Jeddah, with its collection of remarkable four- and five-story Ottoman houses, and efforts to beautify the city with one of the largest collections of open-air monumental sculpture in the world.

The chapter concludes with an examination of the work of several local NGOs dedicated to improving the quality of life of Jeddah's poor, many of whom are undocumented immigrants from Somalia, Yemen, and other poor Muslim countries, who have "overstayed" their Saudi visas after traveling to Mecca to perform the Hajj. These NGOs, many of them led by women, are trying to create a more livable urban environment by helping victims of two recent floods that devastated large parts of the city and by providing clean, safe open spaces where poor children and young adults can gather to exercise and obtain job training.

The final chapter explores the relationship between the process of converting to Islam and the Hajj, the pilgrimage to Mecca, the holiest city in the

Muslim world and a city that only Muslims are allowed to enter. This chapter opens with a series of answers—some humorous, some provocative—offered online to the question: "Who can go to Mecca?" After describing the sequence of rituals performed by pilgrims who travel to Mecca on the Hajj, I present a brief survey of the fourteen-hundred-year history of the Hajj.

Chapter 7 continues with the experiences of two nineteenth-century British travelers, Sir Richard Burton and Arthur Wavell, both of them Christians who traveled to Mecca in disguise and performed the Hajj under false pretenses. Parallel accounts follow of two twentieth-century Westerners, one British, H. St. John Philby, and one American, Malcolm X, who each converted to Islam for complicated reasons and then traveled to Mecca to perform the Hajj. Then I describe the Hajj as it is performed in the early twenty-first century—two million pilgrims a year, luxury tours offered by international travel agencies, and the process of verifying that applicants for Hajj visas are really Muslims. The chapter—and the book—end with an account of the moral dilemma I faced when three of the students I was responsible for were offered the opportunity to visit Mecca even though they were not Muslims.

◆ ◆ ◆

As I write this introduction, many countries in the Arab world are convulsed in violence. Iraq is being dismembered by ethnic and sectarian conflict between Kurds and Arabs, Sunni and Shia. This warfare has been horribly exacerbated by American military intervention in the name of an ill-advised project of "nation building." In Syria, forces loyal to the government of Bashar al-Assad are engaged in a civil war against a range of opponents that include the Islamic State, an extremist group also known as ISIS or ISIL, which has occupied large portions of Syria and Iraq. During this war, the Islamic State has also destroyed many priceless cultural and religious monuments, killed thousands of civilians, and driven hundreds of thousands more from their homes. And Yemen, which borders Saudi Arabia to the southwest, is also on the verge of collapse, as Houthi rebels battle the forces of former president Hadi and al-Qaeda in the Arabian Peninsula. A Saudi-led campaign of airstrikes against Houthi targets has only increased the suffering of the civilian population of the country.

In the midst of all this chaos, the Kingdom of Saudi Arabia has enjoyed relative stability. As the world's largest producer of oil, the wealthiest country in the Arab world, and the home of two of the most holy sites in the Muslim world, Saudi Arabia is an extraordinarily important country to understand. It is my hope that *Crossing the Kingdom: Portraits of Saudi Arabia* will provide a wide audience with valuable insights into the lives of men and women who constitute an important segment of Saudi society. Many Saudis recognize the serious limitations that their government imposes on their rights and freedoms; many of these same Saudis are engaged in trying to build better lives for themselves and their fellow citizens at a difficult time in a very troubled part of the world.

ONE

———

Can Oil Bring Happiness?

ALTERNATE VISIONS OF SAUDI ARAMCO

A piece of the United States that just landed on Saudi Arabia.[1]

DHAHRAN IS HOME TO THE SAUDI ARABIAN OIL COMPANY, better known as Saudi Aramco, the national oil company of Saudi Arabia. With an estimated value of 10 trillion dollars, Saudi Aramco is the world's most valuable corporation. Saudi Arabia produces more oil and has more oil reserves than any other country in the world. In the words of a former president of the company, "Oil is a gift from God, but the recovery of oil is the work of men. What's good for the well-being of Saudi Aramco and Arabia is good for the well-being of the whole world."[2] Or as another Saudi Aramco executive put it much more simply: "Oil brings happiness."

Many international travelers approach Dhahran by flying into Bahrain and then driving twenty-five kilometers over the Persian Gulf on the King Fahd Causeway to Saudi Arabia. But Dhahran is also served by the King Fahd International Airport, which was completed in 1990, just in time to serve as a storage facility for American military aircraft during the First Gulf War. The route from King Fahd Airport to the Aramco camp in Dhahran follows King Fahd Road, a three-lane highway through the desert. At night bonfires cast flickering orange light on the SUVs and tents of Saudis camping in the sand. During the day, tall transmission lines can be seen running across the flat expanses of rock, gravel, and sand to the horizon. Along the highway are mounds of construction debris, parking lots filled with oil tankers and dump trucks, and storage yards lined with rows and rows of pipes stacked in neat triangular piles. Exit signs are marked "Desert Access," and off in the distance small herds of camels graze. A large sign at one construction site announces that the work there is being done by the Binladin Group, one of the largest construction companies in the world.

The Aramco camp in Dhahran is bordered on one side by the U.S. Consulate and the King Fahd University of Petroleum and Minerals, and on the other by King Abdulaziz Air Base. The sound of Royal Saudi Air Force jets taking off and landing often fills the air. The camp is a city unto itself with its own education and transportation systems, its own radio and television stations, its own banks and mosques, and its own library, hospital, and heliport. Security at the camp is high, because as an Aramco public relations officer put it: "There are ultraconservative people here who grate at the presence of foreigners and who are hostile to oil. They might do harm."

The Aramco compounds—there are several others nearby—have their own rules, their own culture. They aren't really a part of Saudi Arabia. Men and women work together; women are allowed to drive and are not required to wear ankle-length black *abayas* or *hijabs* covering their hair, as they must in public everywhere else in the country. It's as if Saudi culture itself can't penetrate the tight security—the fences, gates, and checkpoints—that surrounds the camps. People living in the camps are both isolated *and* protected from the Saudi Arabia that lies outside. The Aramco camps represent an unsettling fusion of two very different visions: an idealized American suburb of the 1950s, on the one hand, and a utopian community of cosmopolitanism and multiculturalism, on the other. In the difficult balancing act between the two, the scales are definitely weighted in favor of American suburbia.

Aramcons, as Saudi Aramco employees refer to themselves, can be quite explicit about the nature of the community they inhabit. When they try to describe life in the camps, they stress the same qualities they would if they were describing life in small-town America. The camps are safe; you know your neighbors; they're good places to raise a family. Publicly at least, Aramcons almost always speak positively about Saudi Arabia, but they really don't live there. They sound enthusiastic about Saudi culture, but they never really experience it. One American expatriate, who had worked for Aramco for twenty years but never learned Arabic, referred to "this place"—the Aramco camp in Dhahran, not Saudi Arabia—as the "fifty-second state." The fifty-first, she explained, was Israel.

In the nearby cities of Damman and al-Khobar, the streets have Saudi names: Prince Talal Street, Omar ibn al-Khattab Street, and Gulf Cooperation Council Road. Inside the Aramco camp, they have American names: Geode Lane, Apple Street, and Easter Avenue. The walls and fences that surround the camp, like the desert beyond, are hidden from view by large green hedges. At points along the hedges, stand grottos of artificial rock; from the top flow cascades of recycled wastewater. Wide sidewalks run along quiet streets laid out in a neat pattern of rectangular blocks. Green, well-watered lawns with stands of tall palms and imported shade trees lead up to the front doors of modest single-story homes.

Early one morning before the heat of the day in May 2012, people were out walking, jogging, and riding bicycles. An American woman wearing a large sun hat and running clothes, her face flushed from power walking, told me how much she enjoyed living in Saudi Arabia. A few minutes later a professionally dressed Saudi woman expressed a very different perspective: "Saudi Arabia is a difficult place to live," she said, "especially for a woman. I like my independence." She didn't have a driver, she explained, so she was walking to the next corner to catch a bus to work.

Foreign workers were also out in force—Filipinos, Bangladeshis, and Pakistanis—sweeping the streets with long palm fronds, cutting the grass with power mowers, and just sitting on the curb talking. Each group wore a different color uniform—orange jump suits, blue overalls, or khaki pants and yellow shirts. Few of them spoke Arabic or English. They worked for companies owned by Saudis and managed by Arabs from Egypt or Lebanon. One Saudi I spoke with explained what he called this "caste system" with no hint of awkwardness or embarrassment. "Arabs are more expensive than Pakistanis," he said, "but the least expensive are Indians and Bangladeshis."

It's true. There *are* people from all over the world living in the Aramco camp in Dhahran. It *is* a cosmopolitan, multicultural community. People here all live in the same place, but their lives are separated by occupation, class, language, and culture. An American housewife, who doesn't know that the long white robes Saudi men wear are called *thobe*s, walks along a sidewalk as a Bangladeshi worker sweeps leaf litter from the gutter nearby. Later that afternoon, when the call to prayer sounds, a Saudi man stops jogging and kneels down on the grass by the side of the road to pray. Members of three very different cultures living together, but yet apart.

Steineke Hall serves as a guesthouse for the Saudi Aramco Residential Camp in Dhahran. It's named in honor of Max Steineke, the American geologist whose persistence and determination led to the first major discovery of oil in Saudi Arabia in 1938. Well Number 7, "Prosperity Well," a local landmark, still stands nearby, a powerful symbol of the company's humble origins and its ultimate success. The laundry list for the dry cleaner that serves the guests at Steineke can accommodate clothes worn by people from all over the world: *abaya*s, aprons, bathrobes, *bisht*s (long robes worn by Arab men), blouses, coveralls, dresses, jackets, overcoats, pajamas, safari suites, saris, *sarwalls* (loose trousers from South Asia), scarves, shirts, skirts, slacks, slips, smocks, *thobes*, ties, T-shirts, and wool vests.

The channels available on the new flat-screen televisions in the guest rooms also meet the needs of a very cosmopolitan clientele: CNN, Fox News, and HBO from the United States; ABS-CBN, BRO, and IBC from the Philippines; CNBC Arabiya, Dubai Sports, and KSA 2 (the Saudi English-language channel); the BBC, CCTV from China, PTV from Pakistan, and Yemen TV; not to mention religious channels like Iqraa TV, which advertises itself as a "safe haven" for Muslim families around the world. One evening, a young Saudi waiting in the Steineke lounge was so upset by a romantic scene on an American movie that he went to speak to the Filipino clerks at the registration desk nearby. He warned them to monitor the television more carefully to make sure that nothing inappropriate was being shown.

A few blocks from Steineke Hall is the "commissary," the supermarket that serves camp residents. In addition to several Saudi newspapers in Arabic and English, a stand near the checkout counter has newspapers in many other languages and many different scripts: *Al-Ahram* from Egypt; *Abante*, a Tagalog tabloid from the Philippines; the *Chandikra Daily* and the *Madhyaman Daily*, two Malayalam newspapers from the state of Kerala in India; as well as *USA Today* and the *International Herald Tribune*. The cashier at the checkout counter couldn't tell me much about himself in his limited English—"Philippines . . . twenty-three years . . . budget . . . sacrifice for children"—but the pain and loss his words couldn't fully convey were clear from the expression on his face.

A short walk in the other direction is Kings, the center of camp social life, where the Dhahran Recreation Library is located. Kings also has places to eat out—in public—a Chinese restaurant and an Olive Garden. Unlike like other restaurants in Saudi Arabia, neither provides separate seating areas for "men" and for "families." In addition, Kings has a coffee shop, an ice cream parlor, a bowling alley, a woman's exercise room, and one of Saudi Arabia's only movie theaters, where members of the Aramco community, men and women, can sit together and watch Aramco-approved films. These facilities surround an open area where Aramco's Little League teams used to play baseball, until camp managers made a controversial decision to turn the area into a small park where Saudi families could enjoy picnics on the lush green grass. According to one young Saudi I spoke with, Kings is "a very Saudi place," one of the most "Saudi" places in the whole camp.

Ar-Rabiya is the most exclusive residential area in the Aramco camp. Most Aramcons are provided housing on a rental basis only, but in ar-Rabiya senior executives can buy their own homes. In the past, most senior executives at Aramco were Americans, but this is no longer the case. Almost all the residents of ar-Rabiya now are Saudis. Their large houses are surrounded by beautifully landscaped yards full of flowering shrubs and trees—prices start at 400,000 dollars. Ar-Rabiya also has a fully staffed recreation hall that serves food and provides a space for informal social gatherings.

The Aramco school system is based on the American model and offers education for students through the ninth grade. At that point, Aramco employees receive an education allowance to send their children to high school anywhere in the world. Classes are taught in English, and several different foreign languages are offered. Hardly any American students take Arabic, because when they go off to boarding school, it's more important for them to speak French or Spanish. There are also several internationally accredited private schools located outside the Dhahran camp.

Unlike almost all other American Aramco employees, an African-American woman we met had sent her son to a Saudi school. She wanted him to learn Arabic and really experience Saudi culture. "People at Aramco were really upset with me," she said. "They couldn't understand why I wanted to send my son to a Saudi school. But the world doesn't revolve around the United States any more. I wanted to give him an advantage." Several years later her son converted to Islam.

In the center of the Dhahran camp is the Rolling Hills Golf Club, founded in 1948 when Aramco executives decided to build the first golf course in Saudi Arabia. The original course was constructed by soaking sand with oil to create a surface with the consistency of concrete. Golfers carried small mats of artificial turf from which they played their shots. In the 1990s, Aramco built a luxuriant eighteen-hole grass course, complete with water hazards and rows of shade trees—all made possible by the camp's ample supply of graywater. Nine holes are floodlit for night play.

Two other sports play an important role in life on the Aramco camps—baseball and riding. For many years Dhahran's Little League team represented the Middle East-Africa Region at the Little League World Series. The Dhahran camp also has a world-class equestrian center known as the Hobby Farm; it used to be a real farm where Arab farmers grew food for the American workers. The Chuckwagon, a popular restaurant there, serves chicken nuggets, "good ol' American cheeseburgers," and *kabsa,* a popular

Saudi dish of chicken and rice. Visible from the Hobby Farm, down a road that runs outside the camp fence, is a small restaurant that is said to serve the best camel meat in the area. Aramcons enjoy many other recreational facilities: a gym, a swimming pool, and athletic fields, as well as tennis, squash, and racquetball courts. Less than an hour's drive away on the Gulf Coast is Half Moon Bay, where Aramco employees can go fishing, sailing, and water-skiing.

The camp dining hall is just around the corner from Steineke. It serves three meals a day to camp residents and other Aramco employees who work there. Food is served cafeteria style, and there are several dining areas that provide spaces for mixed-gender seating, as well as separate seating for men, women, and families. On the menu for breakfast are pastries, donuts, hard-boiled eggs, fruit salad, beef sausage, and beef bacon, as well as feta, olives, lentils, fava beans, and strained yoghurt, known as *labna*. Men in informal business attire sit at one table; men in long white *thobe*s and red-and-white checkered *shemagh*s draped over their heads sit at another. Two young women wearing black *abaya*s, *niqab*s covering their faces, and stylish sunglasses are paying for their meals at the cash register, while a man wearing a *thobe* and a baseball cap stands holding his tray looking for a place to sit down.

One morning at breakfast I sat with a man who told me he was from Qatif, one of the oldest and largest cities on the east coast of Saudi Arabia. I knew that most of the people from Qatif are Shia. He described the protests that had taken place there several months earlier. "The people of Qatif just want better lives," he said, but the Saudi police overreacted and several protesters were killed. Then he told me about something that had happened to him when he was a student at Texas A&M: an American attacked him with a baseball bat. "Hatred twists people's brains," he said softly.

Several days later I shared a meal with a group of five or six young Saudi men. One of them, who was of African descent, told me that when he lived in the United States he had experienced more prejudice because he was a Muslim than because he was black. We talked about the meaning of skin color in Saudi Arabia and some of the negative terms used to refer derogatorily to people with dark skin. The worst word was *abd,* which means slave. He told me that discrimination against Shia was a much greater problem than discrimination against people with dark skin.

"The problem with the Shia isn't religious," he said, "it's political. The government's afraid that the Saudi Shia support Iran."

"If you want to know what it's like to be Shia in Saudi, ask Hussein," he added, gesturing to a young man across the table. So I did. Hussein looked a little taken aback.

"Among young people, among my friends, there aren't any problems between Sunni and Shia," Hussein said. "But among the older generation, Shia are definitely discriminated against. A high-level executive would never hire a Shia as his assistant. Some companies actually have directives not to hire Shia for positions in management or security."

"It's good here," said Hussein after a short pause. "We can't criticize the king and the princes, but things are getting better. We have restrictions; we know that. But we're cool. We love our king; he's good to us. We're all the same now. We're all one people; we're all Muslims."

I wasn't convinced and would like to have continued the conversation, but I decided not to. Our conversation moved on to other topics. If there ever were any oil spills in the country, they said, no one would ever know. And they agreed that American Aramco employees *should* earn more than Saudi employees do; they pay taxes in the United States and need to save for retirement. But they shouldn't earn *five times* more.

"Why are some men wearing *thobe*s and not shirts and pants?" I asked.

"Because they're Bedouin," someone said laughing.

Another morning I had breakfast with a heavy-set man from Missouri who had recently been hired by Aramco to teach English. He was eager to tell me about the ministers and the priests that Aramco hires as "special teachers" to conduct Christian services in camp. They keep their Bibles under lock and key in "special classrooms."

As I entered the dining hall one evening, I saw advertisements for various "theme nights." Greek Night featured "menus straight from the taverna kitchens"; Asian Night offered "a taste of the Orient"; and Gulf Night, Mexican Night, and Lebanese Night promised "the best in multicultural dining." On the dinner menu that evening were Arabic Dishes, Asian Dishes, Western Dishes, and Healthy Food. The woman standing behind me in line was an American who taught at the Dhahran elementary school. She described the camp as "the place where the *Stepford Wives* meets the *Truman Show*." In the four years she'd lived in Dhahran, she'd only learned a few words of Arabic. She said she didn't need to learn any more.

After dinner, I joined some of the Bates students I was with and several young Saudis who lived in camp. I was introduced to a young woman who was a member of the Saudi royal family. Unsure about the appropriateness of my question, I asked her how she was related to the king. Her explanation quickly grew complicated, and I couldn't follow it.

"Here's my father," she said, placing a ketchup bottle on the table in front of her. "And here's my father's father," she added, putting a bottle of Tabasco sauce behind it.

But I lost her again, so I took out my notebook and my pen and began to draw a kinship diagram. Never before have I seen students so engaged in the study of kinship. A moment later, all was clear. Her father's father's father's brother was King Abdulaziz ibn Saud, the founder of the Kingdom of Saudi Arabia. King Abdulaziz was also her father's mother's father's father. Her name was Moudi al-Faisal al-Saad Al Saud. She had fifty cousins in Riyadh and many more living all over the world. Moudi lived in the Aramco camp most of the year, but in the summer her family escaped to Jeddah, where it was cooler. She loved to swim in the Red Sea. Moudi felt strongly that Saudi women should be able to work anywhere they want without any restrictions at all.

Then Moudi told us a story about her mother's father, Ali al-Naimi. This was a typical "Aramco story," she said, a story that illustrated what one Saudi called "the American dream, Saudi style." Moudi's grandfather had been born in poverty in a tent in the desert. As a young boy, he herded camels. He had twenty brothers; his father had three wives. Everyone looked down on him, but he built himself up from nothing. He saw Aramco trucks driving through the desert and decided he wanted to go and work for the company. One day in 1947 he hitched a ride to al-Khobar and began looking for a job. He was only eleven, so he had to lie about his age. He started off working as a water boy. He wasn't allowed to drink the cold water; only the Americans could.

Later, when Moudi's grandfather was working as a stock boy, people noticed that he was a hard worker. Since he was completely illiterate, Aramco sent him to school in Dhahran. Then they put him to work in the oil fields. A few years later, they sent him to study at the American University of Beirut, and then at Stanford, where he earned a master's degree in geology. After that, he returned to work for Aramco and was eventually promoted to vice president in charge of oil and gas affairs. In 1983, he became the first Saudi president of Saudi Aramco; in 1995, King Fahd appointed him Minister of Petroleum and Mineral Resources. That is an "Aramco story."

The worldwide headquarters of Saudi Aramco is known locally as the Core Area. It's the center of the company's exploration, drilling, and engineering activities, as well as all its training, financial, and administrative services. This impressive complex of office buildings is located inside the Saudi Aramco compound in Dhahran, but just outside the residential camp itself. On either side of the Core Area, at the edge of the large parking lots that surround it, stand two mosques (see fig. 1).

The newest addition to the Core Area is the Exploration and Petroleum Engineering Center—Advanced Research Center, or EXPEC ARC, a seven-story building of gray stone and glass that houses over 250 scientists engaged in research and development for all "upstream" oil and gas technologies. "Upstream" refers to everything involved in exploration and production; "downstream" to everything involved in processing, refining, and shipping. The scientists here are all devoted to developing new technologies to help the company discover additional oil and gas resources and increase the efficiency with which they're recovered from the ground. Aramco scientists are divided into different teams, each focusing on one specific area of research: geology, reservoir engineering, or computational modeling. EXPEC ARC has the largest geosciences computing center in the world.

Two of the most important projects Saudi Aramco scientists and engineers are working on involve nanotechnology and geosteering. Nanoscale reservoir robots, known as Resbots, are small particles whose diameter is 1/1000 the thickness of a human hair, which are deployed in water that is injected into underground hydrocarbon reservoirs. Resbots contain chemical agents that enable them to measure temperature, pressure, salinity, and other properties of the fluids and rock they encounter. During their journey through the reservoir, the Resbots store this information in their "onboard memory" so it can be retrieved by monitors when they're recovered in the oil produced from the reservoir. By helping Aramco map the flow of oil and gas through rock, Resbots are a crucial tool in the field of reservoir management.

Geosteering, also known as "directional drilling," is another technological development that seems straight from the world of science fiction. Geosteering operations adjust both the angle and the direction of the oil drill, so that after it descends vertically to a certain depth it can turn gradually until it is traveling horizontally. Then the drill can be steered in different directions to reach the specific areas that have the greatest concentrations of oil and gas. With careful monitoring, the drill can travel horizontally for over a kilometer while remaining within a bed of oil-bearing sand or rock that's less than a meter thick. With the latest developments in geosteering technology, Saudi Aramco is able to extract considerably more oil and gas from each of its wells than it could in the past, when it could only drill vertically.

The Oil Supply Planning and Scheduling Department (OSPAS) is the "nerve center" of Saudi Aramco, the heart of its global operations. It's composed of five divisions: Oil; Gas and Natural Gas Liquids; Supply, Planning, and Optimization; Terminals; and Refined Products. The primary responsibility of OSPAS is to manage the company's inventories of oil and gas to ensure that the needs of its customers are met as efficiently and profitably as possible.

The high point of our tour through the Operations Coordination Center of OSPAS was "the Big Wall," a huge curved video screen, sixty-seven meters wide and three meters tall that winds its way through the main control room of the center. Built in 2005, and upgraded several times since, the Wall contains 150 separate screens that monitor in real time the movement of every cubic meter of gas, every drop of oil, and every molecule of hydrocarbon that Saudi Aramco produces. Using digital light processing, these screens are able to project eighteen hundred points of data and update them every fifteen seconds.

By closely tracking the operation of each well, each pipeline, and each tanker, Saudi Aramco is able to plan and coordinate the production, storage, and delivery of all its oil and gas. This Supervisory Control and Data Acquisition system (SCADA) enables supervisors monitoring the Wall to shut down operations in case of drilling accidents, pipeline breaks, or even storms at sea. In this way, Saudi Aramco is able to minimize any disruption of its operations, and to optimize operational processes in order to ensure that all the decisions it makes contribute to the goal of maximizing the Kingdom's profits.

The Exploration Core Laboratory nearby seems many years removed from the high-tech world of the Advanced Research Center with its nanotechnology, geosteering, and computerized monitoring systems. The Core Lab evokes a much earlier, much simpler period in the history of oil exploration. In a big, open work area filled with the smell of dirt and oil, stand rows and rows of tables covered with display racks containing core samples from Saudi

Aramco's twelve thousand wells. Each well costs 100,000 dollars to drill and extends over two thousand meters down to the oil-bearing formations that lie beneath the sands of the Eastern Province. The core samples are thin, cylindrical tubes six meters long—some whole, some cut in half—made of mud, sand, and rock. Sections of many cores are stained black with oil oozing out to the surface.

The Core Lab is the repository for 192,000 meters of core samples. The storage area is filled from floor to ceiling with shelves and shelves of long, thin rectangular yellow boxes stacked in groups of fifty-four, six high and nine wide, on forklift pallets for easy access. The cores are labeled, organized, and stored—"curated" as one geologist working there put it—so carefully and efficiently that a core from any depth, from any well that Saudi Aramco has ever drilled can be retrieved for study and analysis in seven minutes or less.

Core Lab scientists use electron microscopes with the power to magnify up to a million times in order to study the pores of the rocks through which oil and gas are pumped. Aramco scientists also dissolve rock in the cores to analyze the pollen and other microfossils they contain in order to date the layers of sediment where they were found.

"The more data you have, the more control you have, and the easier it is to reduce the risk," a geologist at the Core Lab told us. "We're not guessing; we're scientists. The Core Lab is like our library. Geology is a made up of puzzles, and each puzzle tells a story."

Saudi Aramco manages its human resources in just as innovative and sophisticated a manner as it does its oil and gas. The Upstream Professional Development Center (UPDC), which is housed in a four-story building in the Core Area, was established in 2011 to provide world-class educational and training facilities for Saudi Aramco employees. It is an in-house, corporate university—a Saudi Aramco University.

Every year UPDC offers 250 courses to four thousand employees in fields like petrophysics, reservoir engineering, and upstream computing. The courses taught at UPDC are designed by Saudi Aramco's own "subject matter experts," and are based on a training philosophy that emphasizes experiential, hands-on learning. Lectures and reading make up only a small percentage of the students' workload. In order to emphasize the relevance of their courses, UPDC teachers often make use of case studies and other data from Saudi Aramco's own corporate experience. To ensure the quality of their courses, teachers regularly participate in UPDC's "train-the-trainer program."

Employees enrolled in courses at UPDC study in eighteen high-tech class-rooms. Some are tiered amphitheaters; others have flat floors, mobile seating, and an "instructor island" in the center to maximize interactivity. All the classrooms are equipped with wall-to-wall viewing screens and LCD touch screens, some of which have 3D capability, so that instructors can bring the field—the hydrocarbon reserves and the rock formations containing them—right into the classroom. On the first floor of the UPDC building, is the Upstream Information Center (UIC), a "library" for the teachers and students who work there. Staffed with "hydrocarbon librarians and database engineers," it contains a large print collection of books and journals, as well as all the important electronic databases in all the fields that are relevant to a Saudi Aramco education.

The most impressive facility in the entire training center is the Cave Automatic Virtual Environment—CAVE for short—a small room with four large video screens for walls that offers a virtual-reality display of an oil or gas drill site. Young Saudi trainees sit in "the dog house," the operator's station on a simulated drill platform, where they can experience what it's like to operate a drill rig. They practice using the blowout prevention panel and other well-control equipment in order to gain valuable safety experience. They also learn how to manage virtually the many "down-hole problems"—kicks, stuck pipes, and hole washouts—that can occur. Monitoring these training sessions during our tour was a very experienced, and very real, sixty-year-old Canadian drilling engineer, who after years of working in real oil fields all over North America and the Middle East was now teaching simulation sessions in the CAVE.

As of 2015, UPDC was approaching a particularly challenging period because of what supervisors there refer to as "the Big Crew Change." Since many of its experienced professionals will be retiring over the next decade, UPDC needs to reduce the number of years it takes to train the next generation of skilled workers. As part of its "Hire to Retire" curriculum, UPDC has developed a new "Upstream Professional On-Boarding Program," an intensive eleven-week multidisciplinary course for newly hired employees that makes it possible for young trainees to "capture knowledge from senior staff" in a more efficient manner.

At the graduation ceremony of the Saudi Aramco Professional Development Academy (SAPDA), the corporate culture of Saudi Aramco was on full display. A British public relations officer welcomed us to Saudi Aramco, the "expats' second home." Saudi Aramco's educational programs, he said, have come a long way since 1941, when English, math, and science were taught in a stick hut in the desert. Now the company spends over a billion dollars a year on training and development, operating twenty-three training campuses throughout the country that make it possible for thousands of young Saudis to continue their education at universities all over the world. "This," he said "is the Aramco family."

"The goals of all our educational programs," he continued, "are aligned with the needs of the company and the country. SAPDA operates professional leadership development workshops in the U.S., the U.K., the E.U., Japan, China, Korea, and Australia. We provide international leadership training to support economic growth and social development right here in Saudi. We promote an entrepreneurial ecosystem. SAPDA is a community of commitment; we're dedicated to community service, energy efficiency, conservation, and renewable energy. There are seventy nationalities working at Aramco; so there will obviously be cultural issues if we're not prepared for them. We're a multicultural company; we respect each other's backgrounds. If you can't subscribe to our values, you shouldn't be with the company. We leverage diversity; we invest in human capital. This is a company town. Actually, I think, this is a company country."

In the large reception hall where the SAPDA graduation ceremony was being held, small groups of students were giving presentations on the three *t*'s: technology, talent, and teaming. Each team had a name: Hurricanes, Front Runners, and Synergy. Most of the young graduates were dressed in western clothes, but some wore *thobes* and *shemaghs*. Of the hundred or so young graduates, only four were women. A member of each team gave a short speech about the team's project: "We're up to the challenge. . . . We stand on the shoulders of giants. . . . Be fearless, take chances, and do great things. . . . Aim high, and begin with the end in mind. . . . The best never rest."

THE ARAMCO STORY: BRINGING PROSPERITY
TO THE SAUDI PEOPLE

Given the essential role Saudi Aramco has played in the history of Saudi Arabia, it's not surprising that the corporate history of Aramco has many themes in common with the national history of the Kingdom. Official Aramco history and official Saudi history also have very similar narrative structures of growth, progress, and transformation. Both embody "the American dream, Saudi style."

The "Our History" page on the Saudi Aramco website, the most accessible source for the official version of the company's corporate history, describes the close relationship that has always existed between the company and the Kingdom:

> From the very start, we have been involved in developing the nation in the broadest sense. During the early years of our history, which were also the early years of the young country of Saudi Arabia, our economic and social service programs became woven into the fabric of the country. As time passed, we began supporting or complementing services increasingly led by the government. Once the company became fully Saudi owned, our social responsibility strategy has become focused on . . . being a catalyst, a role model, and a supporter of growth and development in all aspects of society in general, and in the economic sector in particular.[3]

In 1980, Aramco published a lavishly illustrated coffee-table book entitled *Aramco and Its World: Arabia and the Middle East.* Its explicit goal was to promote understanding of what in 1950 had been a mysterious and exotic land and which in the West in 1980 was still a little-known part of the world. In 2005, Saudi Aramco published a new edition of its official corporate history. *A Land Transformed: The Arabian Peninsula, Saudi Arabia, and Saudi Aramco* was a significantly heavier, larger, and longer volume than its predecessor. The book is filled with beautiful color photographs of camels and deserts, malls and skyscrapers, pipelines and refineries, and the Holy Mosque in Mecca, as well as reproductions of black-and-white photographs of King Abdulaziz, the old city of Riyadh, and early meetings between Aramco executives and members of the Saudi royal family. While acknowledging that at the beginning of the twenty-first century people have become much more aware of Islam and the Arab world, the preface of *A Land Transformed* notes—with optimistic understatement typical of most corporate histories—that "the bridges of understanding remain incomplete."[4]

The corporate history of Aramco begins on May 29, 1933, just a year after the founding of Saudi Arabia and the discovery of oil in nearby Bahrain, when Lloyd Hamilton, a lawyer for the Standard Oil Company of California (SOCAL), and Abd Allah al-Sulayman, the finance minister of the new Kingdom, signed a concession agreement in the Khuzam Palace on the outskirts of Jeddah. A month later, King Abdulaziz ibn Saud issued a royal decree granting SOCAL a concession for petroleum exploration according to which the Saudi government would receive an initial payment of 50,000

British pounds, a yearly rent of 5,000 pounds, and a second payment of 50,000 pounds if commercial quantities of oil were discovered. In return, SOCAL obtained exclusive rights to "explore, prospect, drill for, extract, treat, manufacture, deal with, carry away, and export oil and oil products" throughout the country for a period of sixty years.[5] To manage the new concession, SOCAL established a wholly owned subsidiary, the California-Arabian Standard Oil Company (CASOC). Three years later SOCAL sold a 50 percent stake in the company to Texaco. As Wallace Stegner noted in *Discovery! The Search for Arabian Oil,* a 1955 history of Aramco the company hired him to write, agreements like this determine "the future of nations and alter the economic equilibrium of the world."[6]

In September 1933, the first CASOC prospectors set out in small boats from Bahrain and landed near Jubail on the east coast of Saudi Arabia. They were drawn to the area by Jebel Dhahran, a group of low rocky hills later known as the Dammam Dome, a geological formation visible from Bahrain that was virtually identical to the site there where oil had already been found. An exploration party of ten Americans was soon hard at work, supported by "15–20 cargo camels, two trucks and a touring car, a guide, a cook and a cook's helper, a houseboy, a mechanic and a mechanic's helper, an automobile driver, four camel drivers, and an escort of 15–30 armed Bedouin guards."[7] The first "American camp" was a small group of tents set up just outside the small village of Dammam. From there members of the expedition party began their geological reconnaissance survey—exploring, mapping, and searching for oil. They had to transport water in goatskin bags, drive over beaches and sand dunes, and travel eighty kilometers to Jubail to reach the nearest wireless station. The American geologists were in awe of the desert navigation skills of their Bedouin guides.

Over the next few years, conditions improved significantly. The American "pioneers" built a rock pier at al-Khobar to facilitate the delivery of shiploads of material from the United States—toilets, showers, generators, construction material, portable housing, and stills for producing water, not to mention all the equipment needed to drill for oil. Two of the most important pieces of equipment were a single engine plane for conducting aerial surveys (shipped from New York to Alexandria and then flown to Dammam by way of Baghdad), and special photographic film from Kodak that could withstand the extreme heat of the Saudi desert. Eventually CASOC officials received permission from the Saudi government to bring radios, phonographs, and motion picture projectors into the country.

In 1935, a crew of wildcat drillers, rig builders, and pipeline welders, who had worked in CASOC fields in the United States and South America, arrived in Dhahran to begin work. For the next few years they struggled against stuck drill bits, broken casings, and cave-ins, not to mention the heat, humidity, and sand that surrounded them. After a few initial surges of oil, the first ten wells they dug on the Dammam Dome either "went wet" or "went dry." By 1938, CASOC had been working in Saudi Arabia for five years and spent ten million dollars, but had failed to find any significant quantity of oil.

CASOC officials in the United States became discouraged and were considering the possibility of abandoning the Saudi concession. In November 1937, they ordered a halt to all drilling in the Kingdom except at Dammam Well Number 7, the most promising well in the area (see fig. 2). Dammam No. 7 had already reached twice the depth of the "Bahrain Zone," where oil had previously been discovered in commercial quantities in Bahrain. But plagued by accidents and breakdowns, it had still failed to produce any oil. On March 2, 1938, CASOC's board of directors met in San Francisco to make a final decision whether to pull out of Saudi Arabia entirely. They asked Max Steineke, their chief petroleum geologist, what he thought about the prospects for finding oil in Dammam.

"Keep drilling No. 7," he replied.

Two days later the board received a cable from Dhahran announcing that Dammam No. 7 had just struck oil in the "Arab Zone" at a depth of 1,441 meters. Oil was flowing at a rate of 1,585 barrels a day. Commercial production of oil in the Kingdom began several months later, when the first barge of Saudi oil was shipped from al-Khobar to Bahrain. Oil flowed from Dammam No. 7 for forty-four years until it was cemented over in 1982 after producing thirty-two million barrels of oil. At a ceremony in 1999, Crown Prince Abdullah officially named Dammam No. 7 "Prosperity Well."

For the next few years, CASOC's operations in Saudi Arabia expanded tremendously. The infrastructure of the "American camp" was improved with the construction of prefabricated, air-conditioned houses, asphalt roads, a commissary, and a power plant. Soon the first wives and children of American employees began arriving from the United States. CASOC built a small refinery, storage tanks, and terminal facilities at al-Khobar. And in May 1939, King Abdulaziz, with a retinue of five hundred vehicles and two thousand people, traveled from Riyadh to Dhahran, where he spent two days in a city of white tents celebrating the beginning of commercial oil production in the Kingdom. He personally opened the main valve on the new pipe-line from Dammam to al-Khobar to let the first barrels of Saudi oil flow into the tanker that would transport it to the world market. In 1939 alone, two million barrels of oil were shipped from Saudi Arabia. Only five years had passed from the original concession agreement to the beginning of commercial production of oil.

During this period, the original Dammam wells were deepened, more wells were drilled, and additional oil fields were discovered elsewhere in the Eastern Province. CASOC and the king signed a supplementary agreement in which CASOC acquired the rights to explore thousands of additional square miles up and down the Gulf Coast from Kuwait to Qatar. In return, CASOC agreed to pay an annual rent of 20,000 pounds and to provide the government with free kerosene and gasoline. CASOC's workforce soon increased from several hundred to several thousand; over 95 percent of them were Saudis, the majority Shia from the nearby towns of Qatif and Hofuf.

During these early years, CASOC began a tradition of providing additional services to the Saudi government—building roads, schools, water wells, irrigation projects, and port facilities. CASOC also made efforts to improve the diet and health of its Saudi employees by providing them with basic medical facilities to fight diseases like smallpox, malaria, bilharzia, and trachoma, and by offering them a free lunch program, which was called Saudi Noonday Feeding.[8] CASOC quickly assumed the responsibilities of regional water company, port authority, highway commission, and American consulate. It was known as the "Mr. Fixit of the Gulf."[9]

Just as CASOC was poised to become one the major oil producers in the world, the outbreak of World War II brought its operations in Saudi Arabia to an abrupt halt. The company was unable to obtain the manpower, supplies, and equipment it needed to expand or even continue its production. CASOC was forced to close down its wells and reduce its personnel to a skeleton crew. They came to be known in company lore as "the hundred men."

Throughout the war these men received little mail or fresh food; for months at a time they were forced to subsist on canned Brussels sprouts and shredded wheat, supplemented by any fish they caught and any birds or gazelles they could shoot. In time, they began to raise chickens, rabbits, and goats and to grow vegetables in a garden watered by graywater from their sewage treatment plant. The company was even forced to issue food rations to its employees. In one of the most heroic episodes of the company's wartime history, a Bedouin herdsman made three successful cattle drives a thousand miles across the Arabian Peninsula from Yemen to Dhahran to supply company employees with beef. In the fall of 1940, an Italian bombing mission sent to destroy the British refinery on Bahrain accidently bombed Dhahran. Mussolini promptly apologized to King Abdulaziz for the mistake.

The conclusion of World War II brought an end to the "frontier period" in company history and marked the beginning of a time of tremendous growth for both the company and the Kingdom. In 1944, CASOC changed its name to the Arabian American Oil Company, Aramco. Then in 1948, in an effort to gain access to additional investment capital to finance its anticipated expansion, the company, which had previously been joined by Texaco, brought in Standard Oil of New Jersey (Exxon) and Standard Oil of New York (Mobil). The new Aramco was now jointly owned by all four major American oil companies.

In the 1950s, Aramco employed over twenty thousand people, a third of them Saudis. To house them all, Aramco built three new cities: Dhahran, where company headquarters were established; Ras Tanura, near the company's refinery and port facilities; and Abqaiq, where major production facilities were located. Aramco continued its efforts to expand its infrastructure in order to support its growing oil operations. In the process, it demonstrated its commitment to finding oil *and* to building the Saudi state. In other words, Aramco proved it could simultaneously serve the interests of both its American shareholders and the Saudi government.

During this period, Aramco built an international airport, a 50-million-dollar oil refinery, three new marine terminals, its own telephone and radio systems, three hundred kilometers of paved roads, and an eleven-hundred-kilometer pipeline network. It also maintained a fleet of three thousand cars and trucks, forty-seven boats and barges, and its own private airline of seventeen planes, the most famous of which was a DC-4 known as "the Flying Camel." In the early 1950s, Aramco flew three hundred thousand pounds of fresh vegetables from Beirut to Dhahran every month in two converted British bombers. Aramco's payments of 10 million dollars a year to local Saudi contractors supported a thriving local economy.

To improve its ability to meet the growing energy needs of Europe and North America, in 1950 Aramco built the Trans-Arabian Pipeline, known as the Tapline, which was able to transport half a million barrels of oil a day over a thousand miles from Abqaiq on the Persian Gulf to the Lebanese city of Sidon on the Mediterranean. Over the next few years, the Gawar and Safaniya oil fields proved to be the world's largest on-shore and off-shore oil fields, respectively. During the 1960s, Aramco diversified its operations by expanding into the production of natural gas liquids (NGL) with the construction of several gas-oil separation plants (GOSPS). In the following decades, the company discovered additional oil fields south of Riyadh and at Shaybah in the Rub al-Khali Desert, the Empty Quarter. Aramco also expanded into shipping by acquiring its own fleet of Very Large Crude Carriers (VLCCs) to transport a significant portion of its own exports. By the mid-1990s, Aramco had attained a crude oil production capacity of ten million barrels per day.

During the postwar period, Aramco continued to contribute heavily to the economic development of the Kingdom. At the request of the Saudi government, Aramco built roads and schools all over the country; it also constructed desalinization plants, industrial complexes, and entire planned cities. The company was instrumental in strengthening and diversifying the Saudi economy by single-handedly building steel mills, aluminum smelters, and petrochemical plants. During the first decade of the twenty-first century, Aramco took on other major projects for the government as well. Among its most impressive accomplishments were the construction in 2009 of King Abdullah University of Science and Technology, a world-class research university on the Red Sea coast north of Jeddah, and the creation of the King Abdulaziz Center for World Culture, a futuristic museum complex in Dhahran designed to promote creativity and cross-cultural understanding throughout Saudi Arabia.

In one article of the original 1933 concession agreement, SOCAL had promised to "employ Saudi nationals as far as practicable" and employ other nationals only if it could not find suitable Saudi employees.[10] In an effort to fulfill its commitment to "Saudization," Aramco has always operated a variety of educational programs for its Saudi employees. Beginning with basic language and vocational skills, Aramco gradually developed more sophisticated professional training centers. In the 1950s, the first Saudis were hired to fill senior staff positions. In 1951, Aramco initiated a home-ownership program through which Saudi employees could purchase their own homes with the help of long-term company-subsidized loans. And in 1959, the first two Saudis were elected to the company's board of directors. By the 1980s, over 45 percent of the company's managers and supervisors were Saudis; many of them had studied abroad at company expense. Aramco, by then the Eastern Province's largest employer, had thirty-eight thousand employees from forty-five different countries; twenty-two thousand of them were Saudis and thirty-four hundred of them from the United States.

In a portrait of life in Dhahran in the 1980s, *Aramco and Its World* describes Saudi and American cultures "flowing together" and meeting "in mutual respect" as Saudis and Americans learned "to enjoy each other's cooking and exchange friendly greetings in each other's language."[11] This official history of the world's largest oil company concludes by asserting confidently that in Saudi Arabia "tradition and modernity can live honorably side by side," that "women will be able to take a more active part in society . . . within the context of Islam," and that "even in the rush of twentieth-century commerce and industry" men can take the time to "pull a truck to the side of the road at sunset, kneel in the vastness of the desert, and offer thanks to God for what He has given."[12]

In another article of the 1933 concession agreement, SOCAL agreed that it had "no right to interfere with the internal political or religious affairs of Saudi Arabia." According to *Aramco and Its World,* the fact that the company had always adhered strictly to this agreement is one of the main reasons why it has always enjoyed a close relationship with the Saudi government. While disagreements between Aramco and the Saudi government have occasionally arisen, they "have always been resolved through negotiation and agreement rather than through confrontation and crises."[13]

In 1950, for example, Aramco signed what has come to be known as the "50–50 agreement," in which the company promised to pay the Saudi government 50 percent of all its profits. It also agreed to begin paying Saudi income tax for the first time. During the 1960s, in a process known as "participation," the Saudi government began to share in the management of company operations; in the next phase of the process it gradually acquired complete ownership of the company. By 1973, the Saudi government had gained a 25 percent interest in Aramco, and in 1980 it acquired a 100 percent interest by purchasing almost all the company's assets. Then, in 1984, Ali al-Naimi became the first Saudi president of Aramco. The transfer of ownership of the company from its American shareholders to the Saudi government was officially marked in 1988 with the founding of the Saudi Arabian Oil Company, Saudi Aramco.

Company histories emphasize that Aramco was not *nationalized,* as most other oil companies were, but was *purchased* by the Saudi government at fair market value. According to *Aramco and Its World,* this process confirmed the "amicable . . . relationship between Saudi Arabia as a sovereign state exercising its rights over its oil resources and the American shareholders as partners in the Aramco enterprise."[14] This new arrangement not only benefited both

Aramco and Saudi Arabia; it served important strategic interests of the United States. It helped maintain the "special relationship" between Saudi Arabia and the United States, but more importantly it guaranteed the United States, an oil-importing country, easy access to seemingly limitless quantities of Saudi oil far into the future.

Since 1933, oil has transformed Saudi Arabia from a poor, isolated land into one of the twenty-five wealthiest countries in the world. It is now the world's largest oil exporter; it also has approximately one-quarter of the world's oil reserves, which have the potential to last at least seventy years. Saudi Arabia supplies 60 percent of the world's energy needs, and earns 90 percent of its gross national income from its exports of oil and gas. Saudi Aramco has the ability to produce oil at a sustainable maximum rate of twelve million barrels per day through its twenty thousand kilometers of pipeline and the nine thousand tankers that dock each year at its Sea Island Terminal at Ras Tanura (see fig. 3). It employs a workforce of fifty-three thousand people, 87 percent of whom are Saudis; the rest are expatriates from fifty countries around the world.

The last chapter of *A Land Transformed* offers a portrait of Saudi Aramco at the beginning of the twenty-first century. The former president and CEO of Saudi Aramco, Abdallah S. Jumah, who grew up in a home of palm-thatched walls in al-Khobar, contrasts Saudi Aramco with other major oil companies around the world. "An international company," he says, "would deplete [its] reserves for a quick economic return. We look at our oil and gas reserves as our children. We nurture and protect them." *A Land Transformed* concludes with the assertion that Saudi Aramco is committed to using "the resources of human ingenuity, energy, adaptability, and creativity" in order to convert "the resources bestowed upon the country by God into prosperity for the Saudi people and fuel for an energy-hungry world."[15]

THE GOSPEL ACCORDING TO ARAMCO

Corporations, like nations, write their own histories, and corporate histories, like their national counterparts, present heavily sanitized accounts of the past, in which founding heroes are celebrated and challenges overcome, while failures are forgotten and mistakes ignored. Corporate histories are often superficial exercises in public relations and self-promotion written by authors who are paid for their work by the companies whose histories they are hired to write. The corporate history of Aramco, "the Aramco story," is a self-serving account of exceptionalism, in which the company portrays itself as unique among international oil companies because of its deep commitment to serving the interests of its host country. That is why Aramco has always enjoyed a "special relationship" with the Saudi government.

Aramco's corporate history has made use of several ideologically motivated myths to characterize this "special relationship." In these mythical accounts, Aramco is cast in many roles: benevolent colonial power, caring friend, dedicated missionary, and agent of economic development. According to the "Aramco story," the company has always treated Saudis honorably. In an interview for an Aramco-sponsored oral-history project, Frank Jungers, a former company president, described Aramco's policies toward Saudis as based on "cooperation and mutual respect," rather than the "adversarial, exploitive, or even colonialist" attitudes that characterized relations between other oil companies and the citizens of the countries where they were drilling for oil.[16]

In *Big Oil Man From Arabia,* a book whose very title undermines the "Aramco story" he is trying to tell, Michael Cheney, Aramco's first director of public relations, offers a romanticized description of the world of early Aramco officials in the 1950s: "Set against the popular picture of the big bad oil industry, our little band of altruistic executives clinging to their shining doctrine amid the Stygian night of Middle Eastern politics suggested a troop of boy scouts set adrift in a brothel."[17] Cheney also notes that during their orientation program, Aramco employees who had just arrived in Dhahran from the United States were told that "the first principle of this operation" was "the Arab is always right."

"Always remember," Cheney said, "it's their country. It's up to us to make allowances, to give way, to adjust to them, not the other way around. . . . Aramco didn't come here in the old style, with gunboats and a garrison. . . . It came by invitation."[18]

In Aramco-authorized accounts of its dealings with the Kingdom, the company never assumes the role of evil imperialist interested in domination and rule, motivated exclusively by self-interest and greed. It takes on the role of benevolent colonial power, whose paternalistic goals have always been to "civilize the natives" and "uplift the race." Old black-and-white photographs in Aramco publications show white Americans teaching darker-skinned Saudi employees how to read and write English, how to play basketball and baseball, and how to drive trucks and operate complex drilling machines.

Aramco corporate history suggests that the relationships of friendship that existed between individual Americans and Saudis replicated at a personal level the economic and political relationships that existed between the governments of the United States and Saudi Arabia. According to a 1984 public-relations document entitled *What It Means to Work for Aramco,* early American employees of the company felt "great affection" for Saudis and "loved" the Saudi people. Aramcons "shared the hardships" of the Saudis they worked with, learned their language, and even adopted some of their customs and dress. Aramcons were motivated by altruism, generosity, and good will, and they left behind them a "legacy of love and labor on behalf of the Saudis that gave rise to a 'partnership in progress.'"[19]

Describing this version of the company's history as "the gospel according to Aramco" is to invoke another role the company has often cast itself in, the role of devoted missionary attending faithfully to the needs of non-Christian "natives" in some remote corner of the world. The use of such religious language is surprising given the Saudi government's ban against both proselytism and the practice of Christianity within the Kingdom. Stegner describes the work of early Aramcons as a "missionary effort" to build "something new in the history of the world: not an empire made for plundering by the intruding power, but a modern nation in which American and Arab could . . . profit mutually by their association."[20]

William Eddy, the son of actual American missionaries living in Syria, served as a U.S. intelligence officer in Jeddah, helped establish the CIA, and then worked for much of the 1950s as a consultant for Aramco. In an essay incongruously entitled "The American Invasion of the Near East," Eddy describes early Aramcons as "pioneer missionaries" like his parents, dedicated to establishing "programs of education, health, imparting skills for vocations, and extending goodwill for the U.S.A."[21] In this way official Aramco historiography portrays the company as the savior of the Kingdom of Saudi Arabia.

The primary role that Aramco plays in its own corporate history is that of loyal business partner committed to the transformation of Saudi Arabia from a poor, undeveloped, and isolated desert land into a modern industrialized state. Aramco, in its own words, has acted as an agent of economic development and positive social change; it has been almost entirely responsible for the wealth and stability that the people of Saudi Arabia now enjoy. This impressive feat of social engineering was accomplished through a "partnership in oil and progress" that has made Saudi Arabia one of the richest and most powerful countries in the world. By teaching Saudis what one of its early executives called "the gospel of free enterprise and American business practices,"[22] Aramco provided Saudi Arabia with a private corporate Marshall Plan that brought it unimagined prosperity. According to Michael Cheney, the self-styled "big oil man from Arabia," Aramco's history proves that it's possible to "develop the resources of an 'underdeveloped' Eastern country, with equal profit to company and county, and without abridging the host nation's sovereignty or the rights and interests of its people."[23]

From a critical perspective, Aramco-sponsored accounts of the first fifty years of its history are little more than thinly disguised propaganda whose goal is to present the company in the most favorable light possible. In addition to promoting its own positive account of the past, Aramco has also made substantial efforts to suppress all negative accounts. As Robert Vitalis, one of Aramco's most articulate critics, bluntly puts it, "All the lying, censorship, buying of journalists, burying of histories, and the rest was driven by a desire to ward off the company's critics and keep the huge profits flowing."[24]

The most egregious example of Aramco's efforts to control its image and suppress critical accounts of its past involves Wallace Stegner's *Discovery! The Search for Arabian Oil,* a book whose complicated and troubled path to publication illustrates the problems that arise when a corporation commissions an independent author to write its history. In 1955, Aramco hired Stegner, the Pulitzer Prize–winning author best known for his work on the opening of the American West, to write an account of the company's early years. But when Stegner completed his manuscript, Thomas Barger, Aramco's president, refused to publish it on the grounds that its "glorification of the early American oilmen tended to put our Saudi friends in a bad light."[25] In fact, *Discovery!* was suppressed because it contained uncomplimentary and embarrassing accounts of Aramco's own policies and practices.

Much to Stegner's dismay, Aramco published an expurgated version of his book in Beirut in 1967 to give as a gift to all its new employees. Three years later, this "Aramco version" of Stegner's book was serialized in *Aramco World,* the magazine the company distributes free of charge to interested readers around the world. In 2007, without the permission of Stegner's estate, Thomas Barger's son Tim published what Stegner's agent has called another "bowdlerized version" of the book that omitted any material even mildly critical of the company. In its present expurgated form, *Discovery!* offers a romantic account of brave "oil pioneers" struggling in the midst of "the Saudi wilderness" until after World War II, when "the frontier era" gave way to a much less exotic period of corporate growth and expansion.[26]

A DIFFERENT HISTORY: FROM SAND NIGGERS
TO MASTERS OF THEIR OWN COMMODITY

Fortunately there are excellent alternatives to Aramco-authorized versions of the company's history. The most valuable of these are critical accounts of the history of Aramco and the oil industry in Saudi Arabia written by serious scholars interested in labor relations, government regulatory practices, and economic history. Among the best of these are *America's Kingdom: Mythmaking on the Saudi Oil Frontier,* by Robert Vitalis; and *Oil, God, and Gold: The Story of Aramco and the Saudi Kings,* by Anthony Brown. The personal memoires of former Aramco employees also contain material that casts the company in a rather unflattering light. The most revealing of these are Michael Cheney's *Big Oil Man from Arabia* and Philip McConnell's *The Hundred Men.* Together these accounts provide ample material for a more honest and more accurate history of Aramco's complicated relationship with the Saudi government and with its employees—both Saudi and American.

From this more critical perspective, the concession agreement signed by representatives of SOCAL and King Abdulaziz ibn Saud in 1933 marks the beginning of what could be called "a special deal," rather than "a special relationship," a deal that can be compared to another legendary deal, the purchase of Manhattan from Native Americans by the Dutch in 1626 for 24 dollars. The motive driving Lloyd Hamilton, SOCAL's chief negotiator, was profit, not the desire to help the people of Saudi Arabia. As many Aramco employees admit, "We're not do-gooders; we're here to get oil out of the ground."[27] In the original manuscript of *Discovery!* Stegner described the negotiations that led to the signing of the concession as a "high-stakes poker game," but Thomas Barger told Stegner to remove the passage because it implied that SOCAL was more interested in maximizing its profits than improving the standard of living of poor Saudis.[28]

The agreement between SOCAL and the Saudi government was negotiated in the midst of an intense struggle between British and American companies for access to the oil resources in countries around the Persian Gulf. In his correspondence, Hamilton makes it clear that SOCAL's primary goal was to acquire monopoly control of all Saudi oil. All the while, the British were trying to prevent their American competition from gaining a foothold in the Persian Gulf.

A key player in all the backroom maneuvering that preceded the signing of this agreement was H. St. John Philby, a figure of intrigue and adventure very much in the tradition of Lawrence of Arabia. At the time, Philby was serving as an officer in the British Foreign Service and was reportedly helping the Anglo-Iranian Oil Company and the British government gain access to Saudi oil. Philby, however, double-crossed his British contact in Jeddah by meeting secretly with SOCAL lawyers in London and agreeing to intercede on their behalf with King Abdulaziz, whose full trust and confidence he had gained as a result of his recent conversion to Islam.

After signing the concession agreement, SOCAL hired Philby as an advisor and paid him a substantial bonus, which he kept secret from everyone except his wife. King Abdulaziz, who had also hired Philby to represent his interests, rewarded Philby handsomely by granting him a long-term monopoly on the importation of motor vehicles to the Kingdom. Philby's son Kim, who like his father became an officer in the British intelligence service, gained notoriety when he became a double agent for the Soviet Union during the Cold War.

From the days of the first explorers in the 1930s right up through the 1960s, when Aramco employed over five thousand Americans, fifteen thousand Saudis, and five thousand workers of other nationalities, racism pervaded life in the three Aramco camps in the Eastern Province. Some of the terms Americans used to refer to Saudis were "blacks," "coolies," "junglies," "dirty Ayrabs," and "sand niggers." The transformation that Aramco brought about in the standard of living of its Saudi employees was often described in derogatory, but nicely alliterative phrases: from "camels to Cadillacs," "Bedouin to bourgeoisie," and "rag heads to riches." Some Americans openly expressed their cultural superiority with condescending comments like these: "the [Saudi] government couldn't scratch their butts without Aramco's help," and "if it weren't for us, these poor ignorant Arabs would still be in the Stone Age."[29]

In *Big Oil Man from Arabia,* Michael Cheney notes that while Americans addressed Saudis by their first names, Saudis addressed Americans with the title "Mr." or "Sahib" ("Master"). Cheney describes the *niqab* that many Saudi women wear over their faces as "hideous," and compares Arabic script to "the tracks of a drunken chicken." Upon his arrival in Dammam, an American colleague looked at the Saudi airport security guards and said to Cheney: "If some of these boys is Ayrabs, we sure got a lot of Ayrabs back in

Mississippi." A more culturally sensitive American Aramco employee encouraged Cheney to "see the Saudi side," adding that most Americans just see "a bunch of characters with rags on their heads, picking their noses and crapping around the sand dunes. . . . They don't bother to sympathize with tribal elders faced with working out a whole new social system for a new nation."[30]

During this period, the Aramco compounds operated under the Jim Crow laws that governed race relations in the United States until the 1960s. This system of racial discrimination and segregation dominated all aspects of Aramco life. The fundamental principle governing Aramco's housing policies was that no Arab, regardless of his skill level or seniority, should be allowed to live in the "American camps." Such an undesirable development was to be avoided at all costs.

In the 1950s, the American camps were eerily reminiscent of small suburbs of Phoenix or Los Angeles; they were "more American than America." Life inside these white-only enclaves was completely isolated from Saudi culture; they were "as encapsulated from the native world around them as if they had been established on the dark side of the moon."[31] Hanging from a barbed-wire fence by the guardhouse at the main entrance to each camp, the withered hands of Saudi thieves, cut off in accordance with the Saudi government's strict interpretation of Sharia law, were intended to serve as a deterrent to other Saudis. To most Americans, however, they simply demonstrated the barbarity of Saudi culture.

In her memoir *You Can Go Home Again,* the American writer Nora Johnson describes the sense of isolation she felt during the two years she lived in Dhahran in the late 1950s. Aramcons, she observes, thought of themselves as "enlightened colonials, in the first stage beyond pith helmets." While "the intellectuals of Dhahran" cherish Muslim culture, "the less inspired . . . consider the Arabs repulsive." And the only Americans who even considered living outside the American compound in al-Khobar were "cross-cultural freaks . . . crazy enough to want to get away from Aramco and mingle with the rag heads." It was as if American housewives in Dhahran wanted to "seal out Arabia, scrub it out, pretend it wasn't there." Johnson painfully acknowledges the "impossible gulf" that separated her from the few Saudis she had the chance to interact with, as well as the sensitivity surrounding the rare points of contact that did exist between the two groups. One day Johnson found her old Saudi gardener asleep on her living room floor. She reached out slowly and touched his hand. "I had touched him," she writes, "[I] felt his human flesh, the closest I would ever get to his people."[32]

Just outside the American camps were the "coolie camps" where Saudi workers lived. Sometimes referred to as "the slums of Aramco," they consisted of long rows of cinder-block buildings—dormitories or barracks with small rooms, communal kitchens, and shared bathrooms. Americans called them "sheep sheds" or *barasti*s, the small floorless huts made of palm fronds that Saudis lived in before Aramco provided them with four-person tents set on wooden platforms. Unlike the American camps, the Saudi camps had no electricity, no sewers, and no running water. While Americans drank distilled "American water," Saudis drank "raw water."

Aramco's Saudi employees were not allowed to live with their families as the Americans were, so on weekends the Saudis were transported back and forth to their homes in Qatif and Hofuf on open trailers. In keeping with the color line that separated Americans from Saudis, drinking fountains and toilets in Aramco facilities were "for Americans only," as was the Aramco movie theater. The schools and medical clinics that Aramco provided for its Saudi employees were not up to American standards. Over time the wives and families of Saudi employees and subcontractors settled in squatter camps around the American compounds, where they lived with their sheep, goats, and camels in huts made of scrap lumber and flattened oil drums. Aramco officials eventually bulldozed them because they had become eyesores.

In the early 1960s, Aramco made efforts to mask the racist hierarchy that governed life in the compounds. Company executives changed the official terminology used to designate the camps. Racial categories were replaced with employment categories based on skill levels, but since there were no Saudis among the "senior staff," it didn't really make any difference. The "American Camps" became "Senior Staff Camps," the "Saudi Camps" became "General Camps," and a third term, "Intermediate Camps," was introduced to designate the areas assigned to the semiskilled, nonsupervisory staff who were mostly Italian, Lebanese, Palestinian, Pakistani, and Indian. The maids, cooks, housekeepers, and gardeners lived in "Domestic Camps."

Throughout the company's history, there have been significant points of tension in the relationship between Aramco and the Saudi government. These conflicts, particularly acute during the first few decades of the company's existence, were caused by the unwillingness of Aramco's American employees to respect the conservative Islamic traditions that pervade Saudi culture. During the negotiations that led to the concession agreement of 1933, Aramco executives obtained assurances from the Saudi government that its American employees would be allowed access to American radio, television, and movies. Conservative Saudi religious authorities strongly objected to these provisions, and there were periods in the 1940s and 1950s when American media were banned at the insistence of Saudi clerics.

Because the Saudi government forbids the practice of any religion other than Islam, the religious activities of Aramco's American employees have always been a sensitive issue. While Saudi officials actively discouraged the hiring of Jews, they generally tolerated the practice of Christianity on Aramco compounds. In the early years, Christian services were held quite openly, but on Fridays rather than Sundays. In later years, services were held more discreetly in recreation rooms, community centers, and private houses.

In the 1970s, Saudi authorities put an end to nativity scenes and parties celebrating Santa Claus's arrival in camp on an Aramco helicopter. With the imposition of increasingly restrictive measures like these, Americans began objecting to the "killjoy" attitude of Saudi officials; they complained that all the fun was being taken out of their lives. The Christian cemetery at the Aramco compound in Dhahran is the only one of its kind in the Kingdom. The graves are lined with concrete, since it is against Saudi law for the bodies of Christians to pollute "Muslim earth."[33]

Surprisingly perhaps, the presence of pork on Aramco compounds has not been a major problem. In the early 1970s, the Aramco commissary in Dhahran had a separate "pork store." In order to enter, employees had to show an ID card to prove that they weren't Muslims. According to the account of one long-time Aramcon, every morning a chef at the dining hall in the Dhahran camp would cook several pounds of bacon, crumble it up, and sprinkle it on all the food to keep the Saudi staff from stealing it. Eventually pork products were forbidden from all Aramco facilities.[34]

Alcohol proved to be a much more contentious issue. During the early years of Aramco's operations, alcohol was permitted in the American camps, and by the 1940s it was openly sold at camp liquor stores. As a result of frequent abuses, however—drinking in public, providing Saudis with alcohol, and several high-profile drunk-driving accidents—alcohol was officially forbidden in the mid-1950s, but this prohibition did little to limit the consumption of liquor by expatriate Aramcons. Some of them smuggled alcohol into the country from Bahrain; many more produced it themselves in significant quantities.

With condensers, temperature gauges, a good supply of wood chips, and a sixty-gallon water heater for a still, Aramcons could produce an impressive variety of homemade alcoholic beverages—beer, red and white wine, sherry, whisky, gin, cognac, and even champagne. Blueprints for the houses of senior American staff had a "work room" or "trunk room" specifically designed for the production of alcoholic beverages. One enterprising American Aramcon even produced a guidebook, *The Blue Flame,* to provide new employees with enough information to build a still and operate it safely.

A photograph of a party held at the home of an American Aramco employee shows couples drinking around a well-stocked bar, which is decorated with images of scantily clad and erotically posed women. Behind the bar hangs a big Saudi flag. According to one Aramcon, it seemed that by the late 1950s the Saudi government had "closed its eyes to the thousands of stills in Aramco towns—reasoning that, without booze, there would be no Americans, and without Americans, the oil would remain in the ground." But there were limits. American employees who were caught selling large quantities of alcohol were immediately escorted to the Dhahran airport, put on a plane, and sent back to the United States.[35]

In 1955, at the invitation of Aramco's training department, Solon Kimball, an anthropologist at Columbia University's Teachers College, traveled to Dhahran to conduct a series of seminars for Aramco's elementary school teachers. The following year he published a revealing account of life on the Aramco compounds straightforwardly entitled: "American Culture in Saudi Arabia." Kimball noted serious "manifestations of discontent, anxiety, and frustration" on this "tiny outpost of American civilization." Many of Aramco's American employees resented the restrictions they had to endure as a result of the Saudi government's imposition of conservative Muslim values on their "American community." While some Americans told Kimball, "We've never had it so good," others said: "It isn't like home," and, "I'm here for the same reason as everyone else—the money."[36]

Kimball was struck by the hierarchical nature of the Aramco community. He realized that the bureaucratic structure of American corporate life had been imposed on the social life of the camps. Because Americans had superior technological and managerial training, the corporate hierarchy of skilled and unskilled employees perfectly replicated the racial hierarchy of American and Saudi employees. Kimball was impressed with the "magnificence of American technical competence and the related ability to create and operate a complicated organizational structure." He was much less enthusiastic about Aramco's ability "to comprehend or . . . deal adequately with problems of human relationships and emotions."[37] Aramco, in other words, was doing a much better job finding oil than they were creating open, egalitarian communities in which people were able to live meaningful lives. Kimball responded to this paradox with "mixed feelings of admiration and disquiet" and concluded his report with two vexing questions: "Is it desirable or necessary that community life be a mirror image of bureaucratic structure?" and, "Is it possible for viable human groupings to survive if individuals are subordinate to the requirements and direction of an organization serving technical ends?"[38]

The racist policies that pervaded Aramco in the years after World War II had two critical effects on company operations. First, in spite of repeated promises that Saudi employees would be offered meaningful educational and training programs, all Aramco's skilled engineering and managerial positions were held by Americans. Second, housing in all three Aramco compounds was strictly segregated. The early challenges to this Jim Crow system took place in the 1950s, but they were strenuously resisted by Aramco officials. It was not until the 1960s that the company began to make significant progress toward integrating both its senior management and its residential communities.

Aramco has a well-kept secret: a little-known history of labor unrest—demonstrations, protests, strikes, riots, and the violence required to suppress them—that seriously undermines the official corporate narrative of concern and respect for its Saudi employees. Aramco's "special relationship" with Saudi Arabia, was not, in fact, very special at all. The first strike against Aramco by its Saudi employees took place in 1945. Workers protested the racist Jim Crow system that Aramco forced them to live under. More specifically, their complaints focused on bad food, inferior housing, inadequate health care, lack of training programs, poor working conditions, and unequal pay. Labor problems grew worse over the next few years, and other more serious strikes followed.

During this difficult time, Michael Cheney reports some painful conversations he had with a few of his Arab colleagues. A Saudi employee shared with Cheney his frustration, his sense of being trapped, of having nowhere to go. "The government is for princes," he said, "and the company is for Americans." A Lebanese journalist visiting Dhahran told Cheney, "You have built many fine things, and you are trying very hard to help the people, but I do not think you understand very much what is happening. . . . It is very sad."[39]

In 1954, leaflets were scattered all over the streets of al-Khobar. Underneath a hammer and sickle, they read in Arabic:

O Workers!
Get rid of the American pigs and seize the profitable [exploiting] oil company.
O Arabs!
Unite because the Arab Peninsula is for the Arabs.[40]

A year later, in 1955—the same year Rosa Parks was arrested in Montgomery, Alabama—Saudi workers boycotted the Aramco bus system, demanding the same quality buses that served American employees. The following year, striking Saudi employees presented a list of demands to Aramco officials, who passed them on to the Saudi government. When King Saud visited Aramco headquarters in Dhahran, he was shocked to be greeted with banners reading: "Down with American Imperialism!" and "We Want an Elected Trade Union."[41]

Saudi officials quickly realized that ensuring the stability of Aramco's oil operations served their interests better than protecting the rights of Aramco's Saudi employees, especially since so many of them were members of the country's Shia minority. This was why the Saudi government saw the political mobilization of Aramco's Saudi employees as such a threat. Aramco officials refused to negotiate directly with the striking workers. Instead, they worked closely with Saudi intelligence and military personnel to bring the strike to an end. Saudi labor leaders were condemned as rabble-rousers, communists, and antigovernment agents; they were arrested, imprisoned, and tortured by Saudi police; then they were deported or sent into exile.

In response to this labor unrest, King Saud issued a royal decree banning all strikes and demonstrations throughout the Kingdom. At the same time, he directed Aramco to increase the pay of its Saudi employees and improve both their working and their living conditions. Over the next decade, the Jim Crow system that had dominated life in the Aramco camps was gradually dismantled, more progressive labor policies were implemented, and the standard of living of the company's Saudi employees was raised. By far the most difficult challenge facing Aramco officials during this process was the integration of the company's residential compounds.

Aramco had long offered generous housing allowances to its American employees. In response to pressure to provide this expensive benefit to its Saudi employees as well, the company decided to change its policy, end the allowance program, and require all employees to pay for their own housing. In this way, the quality of employee housing became dependent on the employees' income, rather than their nationality.

The first people to integrate the "American camps" were Saudis and other Arabs who had been educated abroad, often at Aramco's expense. There are many poignant stories about this sensitive period in the company's history. Before moving into the Dhahran compound, a Palestinian physician and his wife were invited to an American home for dinner in a test to make sure they could eat properly with a knife and fork, to make sure that they were "civilized" enough to fit in with their future neighbors. In the mid-1950s, the first Saudi family moved into the American camp at Ras Tanura. They celebrated the festival of Eid al-Fitra, marking the end of Ramadan, by slaughtering a lamb in their bathtub and roasting it over a fire they built on their living-room floor. When smoke began pouring out of the windows, the Aramco fire department was called. A short time later the family quietly left the compound.

One of the first Saudis to move into the "American camp" in Dhahran was Abdullah Tariki, a Saudi geologist with an advanced degree from the United States and, perhaps more significantly, an American wife. He was challenged whenever he tried to swim in the camp pool or watch a movie at the Aramco theater. Years later Tariki told a reporter, "I was the first Arab to penetrate into the tight Aramco compound, and I never saw such narrow people." [42] Tariki, later known as the "Red Sheikh," went on to become one of the cofounders of the Organization of Petroleum Exporting Countries (OPEC). In that capacity, he was one of the earliest and most vocal critics of Aramco, calling persistently for the appropriation by the Saudi government of Aramco's vast assets and the nationalization of Arab oil.

In 1962, King Faisal removed Tariki from his position as minister of oil and petroleum resources and sent him into exile. It is ironic that by making possible the emergence of the first generation of Saudi engineers and administrators, Aramco was simultaneously facilitating the emergence of the first generation of Saudi dissidents and government critics. Aramco-sponsored histories celebrate the former; not surprisingly they are silent about the latter.

Another aspect of its postwar history that is missing from official company-sponsored accounts is the close relationship Aramco enjoyed with the U.S. government's newly created Central Intelligence Agency. During the 1950s, several CIA agents, including William Eddy, served undercover while working at Aramco headquarters in Dhahran. Aramco's Government Relations Organization, established in 1946 to manage the company's dealings with the Saudi government, was modeled on the Office of Strategic

Services, the precursor of the CIA. It operated like a private diplomatic and intelligence service working for "the sovereign state of Aramco."[43] Several of its early employees had previous experience working in U.S. intelligence in the Middle East. The U.S. embassy in Riyadh, as well as the Consulate General and the air force base in Dhahran, worked closely with Aramco's government-relations specialists, who often had more experience and better funding than their American government counterparts.

One of the most difficult jobs facing Aramco executives was to balance their conflicting obligations to the government of the United States and the government of Saudi Arabia. The United States' unwavering support for Israel posed the greatest challenge in this regard. During the 1948 Arab-Israeli War, the Saudi government, which regularly used Aramco planes to transport King Abdulaziz on his official travels, commandeered whatever Aramco equipment it needed for the use of its troops fighting against Israel. And when the Arab-Israeli War of 1967 broke out, Aramco tried to persuade the United States to downplay its support for Israel and distanced itself as much as possible from the U.S. government and its foreign policy in the region. At the Ras Tanura docks, Aramco's Saudi employees shouting "Stop the oil!" tried unsuccessfully to prevent Aramco from loading oil onto U.S. navy ships. Increasingly violent demonstrations soon forced the company to shut down operations entirely.

On June 7, 1967, which came to be known as "Rock Wednesday," protesters attacked the U.S. consulate in Dhahran, taking down the American flag and raising the Saudi flag in its place. One Aramco official called this a "native uprising."[44] On the Aramco compound, protesters burned the cars of American employees and threw rocks through the windows of their homes. The Saudi national guard and the Saudi police were notified, but they didn't intervene until several days later. After seeking temporary refuge in the compound school, many Americans were quickly evacuated from the country. Aramco, it seems, had not yet been able to shed its image as an American company.

From the late 1950s until the 1980s, Aramco succeeded in transforming itself from an American company into a Saudi company. While Aramco authorized histories present this transition as a smooth and inevitable process, it was neither. The firsts steps were referred to formally as "participation" and less formally as "the greening of Aramco," in reference to the traditional color of Islam and the color of the Saudi flag. This process involved providing Saudi employees with higher pay and better conditions in which to live and work. Over time, an increasing number of Saudis were integrated into the upper levels of management and administration. Many American employees, faced with the prospect of losing their jobs, resented being replaced by Saudis they considered unprepared for their new positions.

In 1958, as a result of the Saudi government's insistence on playing a greater role in the management of the company, Aramco officials agreed to appoint two Saudis to the company's powerful and secretive Executive Committee. Aramco officials, however, did not fully trust the Saudi government; they were afraid that its ultimate goals might include nationalizing the company and appropriating all its assets. Therefore, Aramco officials immediately established another committee, the Committee on Agreements and Negotiations, which had no Saudi members and which from that point on assumed responsibility for making all important company decisions.

Of the many points of conflict between Aramco's American board of directors and the Saudi government that surfaced during this time, the most controversial were the rate at which Aramco was producing oil and the rate at which Saudi reserves were being depleted. On one side of the issue stood senior Aramco executives who staunchly opposed the policy of "participation." Because they had the short-term profits of Aramco shareholders at heart, they advocated a "smash and grab" approach, in which oil production was maximized and the company's contributions to Saudi society minimized.[45]

In the early 1970s, these American Aramco officials "systematically overproduced the major Saudi oilfields" because they were afraid the Saudi government was about to nationalize the oil industry and because they wanted to extract as much oil from the fields as quickly as possible. According to a more blunt account that emerged in a secret 1974 U.S. Senate hearing, Aramco's American owners made a conscious decision to "milk these fields for every salable drop of oil and put back as little investment as possible." They made this decision in the face of substantial evidence that the long-term productivity of oil fields that experience this type of overproduction can be seriously harmed.[46]

On the other side of the issue stood representatives of the Saudi government like Abdullah Tariki and Sheikh Ahmed Yamani, his successor as Saudi minister of oil and petroleum resources, who both advocated a much more conservative approach that placed highest priority on the long-term productivity of Saudi reserves. Saudi authorities also accused Aramco of having exploited the Saudi government in the initial concession agreement, of not fulfilling its obligation to train Saudi employees to replace their American supervisors, and of cheating the Saudi government by concealing the actual profit it earned from the sale of Saudi oil. These Saudi officials demanded an immediate increase in Saudi "participation" in Aramco affairs and sought the "dispossession of Aramco" and the assumption of full control by the Saudi government of all the country's natural resources.[47]

With the establishment of OPEC in 1960, the balance of power in the struggle between Aramco and the Saudi government for the control of Saudi oil shifted dramatically. Aramco bitterly opposed the formation of OPEC and for several years refused to recognize its existence. During this period, Aramco fears that the Saudi government would nationalize the company were at their height. Sheikh Yamani, who as minister of OPEC played an important role in determining the price of oil during the 1973 oil embargo, was the leading proponent of a policy giving the Saudi government complete control of Aramco and all its energy reserves.

In 1962 under Yamani's guidance, the General Petroleum and Mineral Organization (Petromin) was founded with the assumption that it would eventually become the Saudi national oil company. A year later the College of Petroleum and Minerals was established in Dhahran in order to educate and train Saudis to "participate" more fully as engineers, scientists, and executives in Aramco, as control over Saudi oil gradually shifted from the Americans to the Saudis themselves.

During the 1970s, the Saudi government began buying out Aramco in stages; by 1983 it had acquired 51 percent ownership of the company. During the early years of this process, when control of all oil operations remained in the hands of Aramco's American board of directors, "participation" amounted to little more than tokenism. By 1973, however, with the outbreak of the Yom Kippur War and the OPEC oil embargo it provoked, all decisions involving the management of Saudi oil were fully in Saudi hands. This was when, in a popular metaphor of the time, King Faisal "unsheathed" and proceeded to "wield" his "oil sword" by announcing a 10 percent cut in oil production and a complete ban on petroleum shipments to the United States in retaliation for its continued support of Israel. As a result of these decisions, the price of oil quadrupled, and Sheikh Yamani was able to say: "This is a moment for which I have been waiting for a long time.... We are masters of our own commodity."[48]

As the Saudi government steadily gained control of Aramco, it exerted greater effort to ensure that Saudi customs were respected and Saudi laws obeyed on all the Aramco compounds. Rules forbidding the consumption of pork and alcohol were tightened, and the ability of Christian employees to conduct religious services was restricted. Crucifixes, holy water, and church bulletins were no longer permitted at the celebration of Roman Catholic masses.[49]

From the perspective of many American residents, when the Aramco compounds began to lose the almost extraterritorial status they had previously enjoyed—when their activities became increasingly subject to Saudi law—their lives became less secure, less carefree, and ultimately less American. In the words of one Aramco executive, "Generally things became more and more unpleasant. The pressure was on, and the feel of total freedom just vanished."[50] An ever-increasing number of Americans were replaced by Saudis, lost their jobs, and retired. And on November 8, 1988, when King Fahd issued a royal decree establishing a new company—the Saudi Arabia Oil Company, Saudi Aramco—the era of American control of Saudi oil came to an end.

GROWING UP IN MAYBERRY: A HAPPY ENDING?

Children of American Aramco employees who grew up on one of the Aramco compounds refer to themselves affectionately as "Aramco Brats." Some people think "second generation Aramcons" or "children of Aramcons" would be a more dignified way of referring to them. Today there are over five thousand Aramco Brats living scattered around the world; the great majority of them are Americans. They form a community of expatriates who share the experience of having spent their childhood growing up on an Aramco compound.

According to the "About Us" section of its website, AramcoBrats, Inc. was founded in 1996 "to promote continued contact and fellowship among Aramco Brats through biennial reunions, newsletter publications, and maintenance of Aramco Brat contact information." Reunions are held on Memorial Day weekend in cities like San Diego, Tucson, and Houston. On their website, Aramco Brats share personal news, childhood memories, and recipes for their favorite Saudi foods: *shawarma,* samosas, and *kabsa.* They also collect "administrative baksheesh" (membership dues) and provide information on how to obtain birth certificates and find lost classmates.

In another section of the website—the *Suq,* or market—Brats can purchase baseball caps, tennis visors, and iPhone covers all made from the red-and-white checkered cloth used to make Saudi *shemaghs*. They can also buy DVDs of the 1975 Dhahran Nativity Pageant complete with the Three Wise Men arriving on real camels. On Bratchat, they reminisce about the good old days in "Camel-lot," sharing childhood stories of sunburns and jellyfish, Girl Scout campouts, dances at the Teen Canteen, and the square hamburgers they used to eat at the Chuckwagon. And finally, at the Black Camel, they post the obituaries of Aramco Brats who have died.

Todd Nims, one of the directors of the documentary film *Home: The Aramco Brats' Story*, spoke with me in Dhahran in May 2012. Nims was born in Saudi Arabia and was ten years old in 1990 when the First Gulf War broke out. He remembers hearing air-raid sirens, putting on gas masks, and doing duck-and-cover drills. People were afraid that one of Saddam Hussein's scud missiles loaded with nerve gas might land in Dhahran. Nims and his family were evacuated back to the United States, but they returned to Dhahran a few months later. During the war, many Aramco families invited American soldiers stationed in the area to their homes on weekends for barbeques. Nims told me that after the war, he found some pieces of a Scud missile that had fallen harmlessly in the desert outside camp.

According to the Aramco Brats' Story website, Nim's interest in world cultures "prompted him to live with one of the last traditional Australian Aboriginal mobs, mix with the African Maasai in Kenya, and learn ancient traditions from the Kahunas of Kauai, Hawaii." After working in the film and music industries in Hollywood for a few years, Nims returned to Saudi Arabia. Since then he's been active in what he calls "the creative community" there. He organizes comedy shows and directs short YouTube videos. Nims is also chairman of Aramco Brat Media, the organization he founded to offer accurate representations of "American-Saudi relations by documenting and revealing the true-to-life cross-cultural relationships existing between Saudis and Americans that go unreported by the media."

Against a backdrop of beautiful red sand dunes, the website advertising Nim's documentary, *Home: The Aramco Brats' Story*, introduces the country of Saudi Arabia: "Once upon a time in a land far, far away there lived a King and his peoples that agreed to work with several Americans to find oil. After much searching in the desert along side one another, they found not only oil but new bonds of friendship and together they happily labored to make the Kingdom into the largest supplier of petroleum the world had ever seen. They would come to call their partnership ARAMCO."[51] And in a trailer posted on the same website, one of the film's producers tells us: "Most of the world only hears the negative press about Saudi Arabia. But in our film you'll see a beautiful country filled with gentle, peaceful people that misguided fanatics disgrace, Hollywood consistently misrepresents, and the media until now seems to have overlooked." *Home: The Aramco Brats' Story* consists of newsreel footage of historic moments in the history of Saudi Arabia and Aramco, home movies in color and black and white depicting everyday life on the Aramco camps between the 1940s and the 1990s, and interviews with Aramco Brats of all ages conducted at their 2005 reunion in Houston. During these interviews, Aramco Brats describe their experiences as children growing up Abqaiq, Ras Tanura, and Dhahran.

Early in the film, the narrator emphasizes that some knowledge of Saudi history is essential to understanding the "Aramco Brat experience." In the brief summary that follows, King Abdulaziz ibn Saud is described as a "brilliant visionary" who succeeded in unifying the tribes of Arabia with "the divine inspiration of Allah." Then in order to develop his country into a great nation, he formed "a beautiful partnership" with Aramco, in which "Saudis and Americans worked together for the common good of their countries and the world."

Later middle-aged Brats discuss the value of having been exposed to different cultures, while the screen is filled with images of American and Saudi flags flying side by side, an American boy wearing a T-shirt and shorts playing with a Saudi friend in a white *thobe* and red-and-white *shemagh*, and American families on vacation standing with Bedouins in front of black-and-white striped tents. A group of young Brats tell stories about ATV rides through the desert, Boy Scout meetings, and fishing, sailing, and shopping for new dresses at JC Penny's at the Dhahran mall. Then a white-haired former Aramco elementary school teacher reminisces fondly about "natural kids leading natural lives," as photographs of swimming pools, Little League games, and middle school dances fill the screen.

Aramco Brats seem to have only positive memories of their experiences with Saudis. They describe the Saudis as "great people" who were always "very nice" to them. Although Aramco Brats couldn't speak Arabic, they remember bonding with Saudis using gestures and facial expressions whenever they were invited to "goat grabs." They loved sitting cross-legged on beautiful carpets and eating with their bare right hands. A mother remembers when her son, dressed up in his John Wayne cowboy outfit, sat on the lap of King Abdulaziz during his visit to the Dhahran camp. Her son was a little confused though; he thought he had just met Jesus.

Tim Barger, the son of Thomas Barger, a former CEO of Aramco, describes traveling through the desert with his father and meeting "real Bedouin," who "except for gunpowder and raw sugar were living like Moses." His father "knew who the Saudis were. They weren't foreign people; they were real people. He knew them heart to heart." Later in the film, Nims jokingly reenacts what must have been another frequent encounter between Saudis and young Aramco Brats. "Give to me your ID!" he says in the strongly accented English of an angry Saudi police officer, before adding with a laugh, "That's something you never heard in camp."

During the final interview of the documentary, Nim's codirector articulates his goals for the film. His "personal mission" is to show "how great Saudi culture is" and "how great Arabia and America are getting along."

"If you like happy endings," he says, "I've got one for you: 'And they lived happily ever after.' That's what I want to pass on to future generations. And I'm an Aramco Brat."

The film's credits roll to the accompaniment of a song from the producer's CD, *Tunes from the Dunes*.

> Some people don't like the custom,
> But for some reason I love 'em.
> In S.A. In S.A.
> I love chicken *kabsa,* cheese bread, and honey *labna*.
> In S.A. In S.A.

The credits end with an expression of thanks to the Saudi royal family: "Our humble appreciation to you for the virtues you instilled through the kindness you and your people showed us and for having shared with us your home."

As its title suggests, the central theme of this film is "home." Many of the Aramco Brats interviewed for the film speak with affection and nostalgia about the childhood years they spent on Aramco compounds in Saudi Arabia. "That was my home," says one. "I still think of it as home," says another.

Comments like these hide a fundamental ambiguity. Just what precisely is the "home" Aramco Brats are referring to—Saudi Arabia or an Aramco compound? When I asked Todd Nims this very question, he acknowledged the ambiguity.

"For me," he said, "it's a little bit of both. In some ways I feel more at home in Saudi than in America. I feel very at home among Saudis, but leaving the expats out of it would be missing something for sure. The expats need to be a part of it. Home is where you can feel yourself. And when Brats get together they feel comfortable; they feel at home."

Nims told me he had two reasons for making the film. The first was to explore the experience of growing up on one of the Aramco compounds, to convey what it meant to be an Aramco Brat, a third culture kid. The second was to fight against what he called "the 9/11 backlash," to challenge the media images and popular stereotypes of Saudi Arabia as a land of terrorists.

On the first count, I think, the film succeeds. On the second, unfortunately, it fails. To accomplish this second goal—to challenge the widespread negative images of Saudi Arabia—the film would actually have to be about Saudi Arabia. But it's not. The film is not about Saudis or Saudi Arabia; it's about Aramco Brats and the Aramco compounds. And except in the most literal geographic sense, Aramco compounds are not "*in* Saudi Arabia." The two places could not be further apart. *Home* contains no serious information about the religion, politics, or culture of contemporary Saudi Arabia. Nowhere in the film is there any mention of sectarian conflict, restrictions on women's lives, or the lack of democracy, religious freedom, and human rights, which are all fundamental aspects of life in Saudi Arabia.

Failure to articulate more explicitly this crucial distinction between the Aramco compounds and Saudi Arabia explains the contradictory descriptions Aramco Brats offer of their childhood home. On the one hand, they describe somewhat naively, but with great sincerity, the value of having had the opportunity to experience different cultures and meet people who speak different languages. On the other hand, they describe the joy of having grown up "in small-town U.S.A. . . . in an American suburb in the desert." As one Aramco Brat put it, growing up on an Aramco compound "was like growing up in Mayberry," the small, fictional North Carolina town of the *Andy Griffith Show*. And Mayberry, as we know, was certainly not a hotbed of cultural and linguistic diversity.

The Aramco Brats' nostalgic accounts of their happy childhoods on Aramco compounds in Saudi Arabia are reminiscent of the stories Americans tell about their luxury vacations at gated resort communities somewhere in the third world. After claiming to know what "real Saudis are like," one Aramco Brat interviewed in the film says: "They are a warm, wonderful group of people." But the experiences Aramco Brats had with Saudis outside the Aramco compounds were usually limited to superficial tourist encounters. For many Aramco Brats, then, Saudi culture is reduced to the crudest of stereotypes—camels, sand dunes, exotic foods, and "real Bedouins."

The goal of challenging the negative stereotypes of Saudi Arabia perpetuated by the American media is an admirable one. The producers of *Home: The Aramco Brats' Story* promote the film as "an amazing depiction of Saudi Arabia, Arabs, and Islam." The cover of the DVD announces in capital letters "If you want too know more about Saudi Arabia, you MUST SEE THIS FILM."

But in the final analysis, *Home* is *not* a story about Saudi Arabia; it's a story about Aramco Brats. It is *not* a Saudi story; it's an American story. And these are two very different stories.

After a private showing of the film in Saudi Arabia, a Saudi man approached Todd Nims. He was angry.

"You should have done better than that," he told Nims. "You didn't show Saudi Arabia. That isn't life in Saudi Arabia. You showed a piece of the United States that just landed on Saudi Arabia."

TWO

Driving While Female

PROTESTING THE BAN ON WOMEN DRIVING

There are wolves in the street, and they'll rape you if you drive.[1]

M.I.A., THE CONTROVERSIAL ENGLISH SINGER of Sri Lankan Tamil descent, released the song *Bad Girls* in early 2012. The accompanying video, which received worldwide acclaim and attracted millions of viewers on YouTube, opens with shots of an empty desert road and a town of square cinder-block buildings. Women dressed in leopard-skin-patterned gold-lamé caftans—only their eyes visible from behind their veils—dance provocatively around an old car in a dusty alley. From nearby rooftops, rows of Saudi men dressed in long white *thobe*s, their heads covered in red-and-white *shemagh*s, stand watching.

> Live fast, die young,
> Bad girls do it well.

M.I.A. sits in the driver's seat of a car stroking the steering wheel sensually. Two women race down the street, leaning out the windows, clenched fists raised in defiance. Their cars begin "drifting." They weave dangerously through traffic, twisting, skidding sideways, spinning in circles, and doing violent U-turns, as plumes of smoke pour from the wheel wells.

> My chain hits my chest
> When I'm banging on the dashboard.

Now their cars are "skiing," balanced precariously on two wheels tilted at a perfect forty-five degree angle. M.I.A. sits on the roof of a white sedan above the passenger's side window, her legs draped over the front windshield, calmly filing her nails (see fig. 4).

When I get to where I'm going, gonna have you trembling.
But if I go to bed, baby, can I take you?[2]

An Orientalist fantasy set in an imaginary Saudi Arabia, M.I.A.'s *Bad Girls* raises provocative questions about the relationships among sex, gender, cars, and power in Saudi culture. Many people know that women are not allowed to drive in Saudi Arabia. Less well known is the Saudi practice of drifting, in which unemployed young men go joyriding in poor neighborhoods on the outskirts of large Saudi cities. Bored and alienated, these young Saudi men, often of Bedouin origin, inhabit an underworld of car theft, petty crime, and the illegal use of tobacco, alcohol, and other drugs. Drifting became popular in Saudi Arabia in the late 1970s as an expression of resistance to mainstream Saudi culture, a form of protest against the strict social order maintained by Saudi authorities.[3] As M.I.A. herself joked in an interview, she filmed the video in Morocco, not Saudi Arabia, because she didn't want to go to jail.[4]

Thousands of YouTube viewers have commented enthusiastically on the "Bad Girls" video. Many have interpreted it as a feminist statement supporting Saudi women's right to drive, praising it as an expression of solidarity with oppressed Saudi women. One blogger called it "a great big middle finger to Saudi Arabia's inhumane laws about women."[5]

Other viewers have been less positive. Some thought M.I.A. was exploiting offensive Orientalist stereotypes by exoticizing and eroticizing Muslim Arabs of the Middle East. Romain Gavras, who directed the video, seemed to confirm this interpretation when he said that the sequel would "have to be shot on the moon with hookers."[6] Other critics labeled the video "crass," "commercial," and "politically vacant," insisting that it had absolutely nothing to do with the serious subject of women's rights in Saudi Arabia. A reviewer for *Rolling Stone* dismissed it an "anthem to recklessly empowered car sex."[7]

WOMEN IN SAUDI SOCIETY

Saudi Arabia is widely known for its repressive policies toward women.[8] In 2009, The World Economic Forum's Global Gender Gap Report ranked Saudi Arabia as 130th out of 134 countries in its comparison of the gender-based inequality that exists in societies around the world. Saudi Arabia was the only country to score zero in the category that measured the political empowerment of women.[9] In its 2010 *Country Reports on Human Rights Practices,* the U.S. Department of State noted that Saudi government discrimination against women is "a significant problem" and that Saudi women have few political rights as a result of these discriminatory policies. Human Rights Watch, in a report on the position of women in Saudi Arabia entitled *Perpetual Minors,* concluded forcefully that "the Saudi government sacrifices basic human rights to maintain male control over women." This discrimination persists in spite of the fact that the Saudi government is a signatory to the Convention on the Elimination of All Forms of Discrimination against Women, which the UN General Assembly adopted in 1979. When it did sign the convention, however, the Saudi government stipulated that none of its articles could override Islamic law, while paradoxically insisting that there were no contradictions or conflicts between the convention and Islam.

While it is clear that discrimination against women pervades all aspects of Saudi society, the position of Saudi women has varied both geographically and historically. Women in Riyadh and the conservative central desert region of Najd experience many more restrictions than women in Jeddah and the more cosmopolitan Red Sea coast region of Hijaz. And after 1979, with the Islamic Revolution in Iran and the seizure of the Holy Mosque in Mecca, Saudi women throughout the country lost significant ground in their struggle to gain social, political, and legal equality with Saudi men and to become full citizens of the Kingdom of Saudi Arabia.

Many efforts to understand the position of women in Saudi Arabia begin by asking whether it can be attributed to Saudi religion or Saudi culture—to Islam or to the patriarchal nature of the traditional Bedouin way of life. This dichotomy is misleading because it fails to acknowledge that Saudi culture, like all cultures, is a complex whole comprised of what Clifford Geertz has called "cultural systems"—a religious system, a kinship system, a legal system, a political system—all of which interact with each other in an intricate network of dialectical relationships that can never be reduced to simple relationships of cause and effect.[10] Islam is no more inherently patriarchal than Christianity, and like Christianity, Islam can take different forms in different historical and cultural contexts.

Saudi women face significant discrimination as a result of both tradition and law. Their rights are most severely limited by the system of male guardianship, according to which every Saudi woman has a *mahram,* a male guardian. The term *mahram* means "taboo," in the sense of both "sacred" and "forbidden." It is derived from the same *h-r-m* Arabic root as the words *haram,* which means "taboo," in the sense of "sacred" or "holy," and the word *haraam,* which also means "taboo," but in the sense of "forbidden" or "impure." If a woman is married, her *mahram* is her husband, the man with whom intercourse is sacred. If she is not married, her *mahram* is one of her male relatives, men she cannot marry and with whom intercourse is forbidden—her father, an uncle, a brother, or even a son.

A Saudi woman must have the permission of her *mahram* to engage in virtually any economic, political, or legal activity. She must have his permission to marry or divorce, to take a job or open a bank account, to start a business or obtain health care, to register at a hotel or rent an apartment, and to attend a university or travel abroad. Saudi women, in other words, are not legal adults; they do not enjoy even the limited rights of Saudi men. Saudi women remain legal minors all their lives. Although they are legally entitled to own property and receive financial support from their guardians, many Saudi women are not well informed of their legal rights, and they are often unable to take advantage of them because of informal cultural practices.

The position of women in Saudi society is most visibly marked by their dress. All Saudi women are expected to "cover" whenever they appear in public or in the presence of men who are not *mahram,* according to widely shared cultural norms that are strictly enforced by the religious police, the *mutawwa.* For a Saudi woman, "covering" means wearing a loose fitting, black, ankle-length *abaya,* as well as a black *hijab,* that covers her hair. Many Saudi women also cover their face (except for their eyes) with a *niqab.*

The prohibition against "gender mixing," *ikhtilat,* which many Saudis believe is required by sharia law and ultimately the Quran, is strictly enforced throughout the Kingdom. Men and women are not permitted to interact socially in public spaces. This system of strict gender segregation is maintained in restaurants, malls, parks, schools, and businesses, which generally have separate hours or separate areas for men and women. Restaurants, for example, either have a separate "women's dining area," where women can sit apart from men, or a separate "family dining area," where family members can sit together apart from groups of unrelated men. Women also run the risk of being stopped by the *mutawwa* for riding in a private car driven by a male who is not a hired driver or a *mahram.*

The segregation of men and women throughout Saudi society has particularly dramatic effects in education and employment. Almost all schools, including universities, are strictly segregated by gender. One of the rare exceptions is the new King Abdullah University of Science and Technology, a graduate-level research university founded in 2009, where women are allowed to attend class without covering, work together with men, and drive cars on campus. In spite of the gender discrimination and segregation that exist in the Saudi educational system, the women's literacy rate of 81 percent is close to that of men, and more than 58 percent of Saudi university students are women. Saudi Arabia is home to Princess Nora bint Abdulrahman University, the world's largest women's university, which has over fifty thousand students and is located in Riyadh.

In spite of impressive progress in the field of education, Saudi women continue to suffer severe discrimination in employment as a direct result of the widespread Saudi prohibition against gender mixing. According to a 2010 estimate, in a total labor force that numbers over nine million, only thirty-six thousand Saudi women work in the public sector and only forty-eight thousand in the private sector. The vast majority of the 1.4 million women working in the country are foreign workers who experience even greater discrimination than Saudi women.

With some exceptions, including hospitals, some newspapers and advertising agencies, and international corporations such as Saudi Aramco, where men and women are allowed to work together on private compounds, most Saudi companies adhere to policies that require the separation of their male and female employees. Women are banned from working in some professions and must telework from home in others. The Ministry of Labor does encourage the employment of women in specific sectors of the economy, such as medicine and energy, but women who want to start their own businesses still need the permission of their *mahram*. In 2011, the ministry announced a widely publicized and controversial decision to require that all stores selling women's cosmetics and underwear must be staffed exclusively by women.

Saudi women also face serious discrimination when confronting the Saudi legal system. In court, the testimony of one man equals that of two women. All judges are male, and only in 2010 were women allowed to serve as lawyers representing other women in court. Family law is biased against women. Daughters only receive half the inheritance of sons, and a woman must have the permission of her *mahram* in order to marry. To obtain a divorce, a woman needs her husband's permission, or else she must present legal justification, such as proof of harm. A man, however, can divorce his wife without any legal grounds at all. Courts generally grant custody of children to their father in the case of divorce and to their father's family in the case of his death.

In cases of rape, the fate of Saudi women is particularly dire. According to the 2012 U.S. Department of State's report on human rights practices in Saudi Arabia, while rape is a criminal offense under sharia law, a female victim can be convicted for illegal "mixing of genders" whether or not the perpetrator is convicted. In addition, according to sharia law, spousal rape is not considered a crime. There have even been cases where court authorities have returned abused women directly to their legal guardians, who were the very men who had abused them.

Since King Abdullah assumed the throne in 2005, the position of Saudi women has gradually improved. Women have begun to play a more active role in some of the organizations that make up Saudi civil society; they have also increased their participation in charitable foundations, community groups, voluntary and professional associations, and other nongovernmental organizations. In 2008, the election of two women to the board of the Jeddah Chamber of Commerce and Industry drew a great deal of attention, and in 2009 a woman was named as deputy minister for education, the highest position ever held by a woman in the Saudi government.

In another significant development, in 2013 King Abdullah appointed thirty women to serve for the first time on his 150-member advisory board, the Consultative Assembly. And although women campaigned unsuccessfully for the right to vote in 2011 municipal elections, King Abdullah announced that they would be eligible to vote and run for office in the country's 2015 municipal elections.[11] In the field of family law, women have also made progress. In 2005, forced marriage was banned, and in 2013 the King Abdulaziz Center for National Dialogue organized a campaign entitled "No More Abuse" to combat domestic violence.

In spite of these signs of progress, Saudi women continue to face significant challenges in their quest to achieve all the rights—limited though they may be—that are their due as Saudi citizens. Fawzia al-Bakr, a well-known sociologist who teaches at King Saud University in Riyadh and who has been active in the struggle for women's rights, has issued this persuasive call for the equal treatment of women in the Kingdom:

> I wish any man could experience these restrictions just for a while so that he can understand what it means to be enslaved by another man who dominates him and controls his destiny, his study, his work, his children, his subsistence, and his documents. . . . Women's destiny is dependent on the man's goodness and generosity: if he is good and decent, she is . . . protected, but if he is morally sick or of unsound mind, then she has no consolation.[12]

Saudi Arabia is infamous for being the only country in the world where it is illegal for women to drive.[13] This blanket statement is not, however, completely true. As is often the case with claims about Saudi Arabia, it is an overgeneralization. While it *is* true that women are not allowed to drive in Saudi cities, Bedouin women in rural areas have driven for decades. Driving is part of their everyday life; they drive pick-up trucks transporting water tanks, camels, and other goods from one settlement to another, sometimes carrying a handgun for safety.[14] In the Province of Hail, an important agricultural region in the north of the country, women often drive out of economic necessity. The Saudi religious police, the *mutawwa,* recently asked provincial officials in Hail to arrest fifteen women for driving, but they simply ignored the *mutawwa's* request. Arresting these women would have posed a serious threat to their families' livelihood.[15]

Some Saudis claim that the ban on driving is just a symbolic issue, a lightning rod that only diverts attention from the more serious problems women face, such as the guardianship system and the laws governing inheritance, divorce, and travel. Others disagree, arguing that the ban on women driving creates serious economic problems at both the national and the household level. Since there is virtually no public transportation in Saudi cities, driving is the only viable means of travel.

Because women are not allowed to drive, they must hire drivers, most of whom are non-Saudis. According to some estimates, there are eight hundred thousand foreign drivers in the country, each earning several hundred dollars a month, in addition to room and board.[16] A single woman may spend half her salary paying her driver to take her back and forth to work. The inability to drive, therefore, is a major obstacle to women's full participation in the workforce. If a woman can't afford to hire a driver, she has to depend on a close male relative for all her transportation needs. This inconvenience is a staple of conversation for both men and women. Some Saudi women go so far as to leave the country to work in one of the other Gulf States, where such drastic restrictions on their mobility and their right to work do not exist.

The issue of women driving, long a taboo subject in the Kingdom, suddenly broke into public consciousness in November 1990, when a group of professional women from respected Saudi families engaged in a controversial act of civil disobedience—"driving while female" through the streets of Riyadh. These women were both angered and inspired by the sight of female

American military personnel driving jeeps, trucks, and even tanks freely through Saudi cities during the First Gulf War. This protest provoked an immediate response. Leaders of the group were arrested by the *mutawwa,* but they were quickly released by Prince Salman, the governor of Riyadh. After the Saudi religious establishment published their names and phone numbers, the protesters were subject to a campaign of vilification, in which they were viciously denounced and accused of trying to destroy Saudi society. As a result, many of these women lost their jobs and were denied permission to travel abroad.

One of the participants in the 1990 protest was Dr. Aisha al-Mana. After receiving a Ph.D. in sociology from the University of Colorado in 1980, al-Mana returned to Saudi Arabia, where she established a company that helped women find jobs in the field of scientific research and technology. When we spoke with her in Dhahran in May 2012, al-Mana was the director of the Mohammed al-Mana College of Health Sciences in al-Khobar.

"Our main obstacle was mobility," she said. "The lack of mobility hindered women from working. One night two women came to my office. We had coffee and talked about women's rights. This was November 1990, during the Kuwait War. I had recently been traveling from Bahrain to Dhahran, and I passed a convoy of American troops. I saw American women driving trucks. And I can't even drive my car?

"I said to myself, 'I'm going to drive and tell the Americans to go back home.' Americans here are doing whatever they want. They talk about democracy. It's democratic for them, but not for us. So I just drove from Dhahran to Riyadh. Then I called the minister of the interior. I said, 'If anyone reported that they saw me driving, I was.'

"The next day forty-five women—young women in their twenties and thirties, students, wives, employees—got together. 'We want our rights. There need to be changes for women. Now is the time for driving.'

"We met again and wrote a letter to the governor of Riyadh: 'We want permits to drive.'

"One week later on Tuesday, November 6, we went out into the streets. We had to be conservative and wear our *abaya*s. We picked a supermarket parking lot, a Safeway parking lot. We started driving at prayer time, in the afternoon when the *mutawwa* were all praying in the mosques. When they began the call to prayer, when they said 'Allahu Akbar,' we started driving. Fourteen cars, forty-five women, and three children.

"One woman's husband told her she couldn't protest, so she just said she was going shopping. She took her children, went to the supermarket, and joined the protest."

Madeha al-Arjoush, the daughter of a Saudi diplomat, was also involved in the 1990 protest. Growing up in New York City, she had witnessed firsthand the power of the women's movement and the civil rights movement in the United States. When she returned to Saudi Arabia with her husband, a professor of mathematics at King Saud University in Riyadh, she attempted to establish a career as a professional photographer, but as a woman she had difficulty opening her own studio and growing professionally.

"So I became an advocate of women's rights," al-Arjoush told me, when we spoke at her home in Riyadh.

"There were many women's issues in the Kingdom, but the king refused to meet with us. He just ignored us. We chose driving; it was a perfect symbol— to be out in the streets and be protected by a car. It was dangerous at the time. The religious people were at the height of their power.

"We met at a local supermarket. All the men got out of the cars. All the women got in the driver's seat. At 4:30 on November 6, 1990, after the *asr* prayer, we started driving.

"The police stopped me.

"'Where are you going?' they asked.

"'I've been waiting for you to catch me,' I said.

"'You must have an emergency.' He was making excuses for me; he couldn't comprehend the idea of a peaceful protest.

"'I'm waiting for you to arrest me.'

"Then someone reported us to the *mutawwa;* they were there in seconds. The police were confused. We closed the windows. The *mutawwa* were pounding on our cars and shouting, 'Evil women! How dare you!'

"We didn't know what would happen to us. Our husbands were watching; they were afraid a fight would break out. There were negotiations about how to get us to the police station. What would they do with forty-five women at the police station? We couldn't all fit.

"The Gulf War journalists were here in Saudi Arabia. Reuters and the international press wrote about us. That was our savior."

In Dhahran, Aisha al-Mana had told me what happened next.

"They interrogated us: 'Who was behind you? Why did you do it?'

"'It's simple,' we said. 'It's a right we want. No one's listening to us. We need it, and we did it.'

"The interrogation lasted all night. The whole country was up in arms. For women to demonstrate was a little too much. Fourteen Ph.D.s, university professors, doctors, teachers—all mature women; there were a few young ladies. We were very demanding. Finally they let us go.

"The next day the religious fundamentalists started a campaign against us. They sent out faxes saying we should be killed. We were ostracized; we were prohibited from working, from traveling. All our businesses were closed; they took our passports away. They stopped me from traveling for a year. Two years later we got back the right to work. The women who drove twenty years ago still haven't been promoted to positions they deserve. Most of them are still suffering. We celebrate every year on the anniversary of the protest by having dinner together."

Madeha al-Arjoush explained how much she herself had suffered professionally.

"I was stopped from working for several years. They burned all my photographs and negatives. I lost my studio; that was my main source of income. I was ready for flogging, for prison, but you can't kill a photographer if he still has eyes.

"They talked about us in the mosques: 'They're evil women. They're not Muslims.' Every horrible thing. They attacked our honor. They tried to take away the power of the act."

Fawzia al-Bakr, another sociologist, joined us at the home of Madeha al-Arjoush. She had also participated in the protest.

"In the time of Muhammad," al-Bakr said, "women drove camels. Women can drive wearing the *niqab*. Driving means you're mobile. You have access to education and employment; you're independent. Segregation of the sexes destroys the relationship between men and women; there's no understanding between them. Men will either protect you or eat you. Men can't challenge the government—they have no power in public—so they go home and behave like kings toward their women.

"Saudi women are minors until they die," she continued. "You can't marry or work or travel. If your husband gets angry, you could be out in the street. If you're under the care of your father or brother, you're oppressed as much as a woman in the street. If you're divorced, you lose everything. As an individual I don't have the authority to be myself. I had to transfer land to my husband's name in order to get a loan from the bank.

"This is not Islam," insisted Madeha al-Arjoush. "What feminists are trying to do is show real believers that the main concept of Islam is equality. Throughout history, it's men who've been interpreting the Quran. Now women are going through and reinterpreting the Quran and the hadith to see what's possible. If we do it from within Islam, we'll be more successful. If we don't, then we'll be rejected. We can't take over unless we empower women to interpret the Quran themselves."

"NO MORE VIRGINS!"

The Saudi government made significant efforts to suppress all knowledge of the protest. Saleh al-Azzaz, a well-known Saudi photographer and journalist, was present at the Safeway parking lot to document the protest. Later that day, he took his notes and photographs to the Intercontinental Hotel in Riyadh, where he had arranged to meet Thomas Friedman of the New York Times. At the reception desk, a man approached him and asked him to step outside into the street. Then he put al-Azzaz in a car and drove him away. Later that day, the secret police searched his house and confiscated all his photographs and cameras. Al-Azzaz was released from prison several months later.

The response of the Saudi *ulama*, the country's leading religious council, was immediate, forceful, and negative. Abd al-Aziz ibn Baz, the grand mufti of Saudi Arabia and the country's highest religious authority, issued the most famous and controversial fatwa of his career. He ruled that the ban against women driving was supported by the Quran and should remain in force. Ibn Baz declared that people who advocated lifting the ban were "evil mongers," and that allowing women to drive would provoke the "wrath of Allah." According to Ibn Baz, if women were allowed to drive, they would be tempted to remove their veils, mix with men, commit adultery, and engage in other forbidden acts.

In his fatwa, Ibn Baz supported his ruling by citing two specific hadith, statements attributed to the Prophet Muhammad that have been gathered into collections by Islamic scholars over the centuries: "Allah (glorified and exalted be he) commanded the wives of the Prophet (peace be upon him) and all believing women to remain in their homes"; and "The Prophet (peace be upon him) also said: 'No man sits alone with a woman except that Satan is the third party.'" The unambiguous conclusions of Ibn Baz's fatwa were that "Allah's sacred sharia prohibits all things that lead to vice," and that "allowing women to drive contributes to the downfall of the society."[17] Other members of the Saudi *ulama* agreed, declaring that ending the ban on women driving would "provoke a surge in prostitution, pornography, homosexuality, and divorce." They warned that within ten years of lifting the ban there would be "no more virgins" in the Kingdom.[18]

In April 1991, Crown Prince Nayef, the conservative and widely feared minister of interior, issued a statement in support of Ibn Baz's fatwa, declaring that it was "inadmissible for women to drive cars," and that it was necessary "to punish those who do drive cars in order to restrain signs of evil." The fatwa, Nayef said, cited "legitimate religious evidence that requires banning that which might expose women to temptation." In this "clarification," Nayef confirmed that "all women are strictly prohibited from driving in the Kingdom of Saudi Arabia," and stressed that all "violations of this prohibition will receive deterrent punishment."[19]

Some Saudi religious leaders disagreed with Ibn Baz's ruling. The head of the Committee for the Promotion of Virtue and the Prevention of Vice in Mecca declared that "clerics have studied the issue, and no one has come up with a verse [of the Quran] that would forbid female driving. I do not consider it to be forbidden."[20] In fact, Ibn Baz's own son, Sheikh Ahmed ibn Baz, an Islamic affairs researcher and important cleric in his own right, has stated that in his opinion it was not religiously forbidden for women to drive. He said that a fatwa was not the appropriate way to deal with the issue, and that women in Saudi Arabia should have the right to drive.[21]

In a televised interview with Barbara Walters of ABC News, which took place on October 14, 2005, King Abdullah himself seemed to offer some support, however tentative, for the right of Saudi women to drive. "I believe strongly in the rights of women," the King told Walters. "My mother is a woman, my sister is a woman, my daughter is a woman, my wife is a woman. I believe the day will come when women drive. The issue will require patience. In time, I believe it will be possible."[22]

Like the views of Saudi religious and political authorities, public opinion is sharply divided on the subject of women driving. Conservatives who support the ban generally do so on moral or religious grounds. Lifting the ban, they argue, will lead to increased mixing of the sexes, flirting, dating, and general moral decay. If a woman driving alone has a breakdown or an accident, she will be at the mercy of strange men.

A young Saudi male explained to a BBC interviewer why he thought women should not be allowed to drive: "If you start now to let women drive, if you let them go wherever they want, then Saudi Arabia will be like New York. It's about Islam. We've got a generation who were raised watching *Gossip Girl.* They only want to be like that, dress like that, drive like that. It's not about need. Now it's driving. In five years it will be taking off the *abaya;* in ten years they will ask to be allowed to wear short skirts."[23]

One conservative female Saudi activist, Rawdah al-Yousif, has enraged opponents of the ban by arguing that Saudi society was "not ready yet to accept the idea of women driving cars." As she put it in one public statement, "I hope there will be no decision to allow women to drive at this stage because we have first to respect the wish of the people and the society."[24] In 2008, al-Yousif organized a campaign to maintain the Saudi guardianship system entitled "My Guardian Knows What's Best for Me." In two years it gathered over five thousand signatures.[25]

Saudis who support women's right to drive dismiss out of hand the argument that it is a religious issue. With an admirable sense of humor, they point out that in the time of the Prophet women were allowed to ride donkeys and that now in the twenty-first century they are allowed to fly planes. Both these activities, they note, take considerably more skill than driving a car. Supporters also mock the hypocrisy of people whose efforts to protect women from harassment and prevent mixing of the sexes lead to situations in which women must be driven by unrelated, non-Saudi men, because they are not allowed to drive themselves.

Many Saudi women understand perfectly well why women are not allowed to drive. They realize it has nothing to do with religion; it's simply an attempt by the government to control women's lives. As Farzaneh Milani, an Iranian American translator, poet, and literary critic, put it: "The driving ban stems from universal anxiety over women's unrestrained mobility.... Gender apartheid is not about piety. It is about dominating, excluding and subordinating women. It is about barring them from political activities, preventing their active participation in the public sector, and making it difficult for them to fully exercise the rights Islam grants them to own and manage their own property. It is about denying women the basic human right to move about freely."[26]

#WOMEN2DRIVE

Manal al-Sharif, who has come to be known as the "Rosa Parks of Saudi Arabia," does not have what King Abdullah would consider the requisite patience. She spoke with me about her work on behalf of women's rights when she visited Bates College at my invitation in September 2013.

Al-Sharif is a member of a tribe believed to be descended from the Prophet Muhammad. She was born in 1979 to conservative religious parents in a working-class neighborhood in Mecca. Her mother was from Libya; her father was a truck driver. The family home had two entrances, one for men and one for women. As a child, al-Sharif dreamed about being the first female minister in the Saudi government. Her friends jokingly called her "your excellency." When she was ten years old she decided to cover herself by wearing both a *hijab* and a *niqab*.

Al-Sharif graduated from King Abdulaziz University in Jeddah in 2002 with a degree in computer science. She was the first Saudi woman to be named a "certified ethical hacker." When she took courses taught by male professors, she watched their lectures on closed circuit television from a remote classroom. After her graduation, she decided to stop wearing the *niqab,* but she still avoided speaking to men in public. When al-Sharif started working as an information technology systems analyst and security consultant for Saudi Aramco, she wore a brightly colored *hijab;* all the other women in her office wore black *hijab*s. In 2004, al-Sharif married a fellow Aramco employee. He asked her to cover herself again, completely, and she did.

"When I started wearing the *niqab* at Aramco," she said, "the men I worked with thanked me. They were relieved that I was wearing it because it made them feel more comfortable. But my face is my identity. I couldn't communicate how I was feeling with my mouth. So during meetings I drew a little smiley face on one side of my pencil eraser and a little frowny face on the other. I would hold up the pencil one way or the other to show them how I was feeling."

Three years later, when she and her husband were divorced, al-Sharif was angry. She stopped wearing her *hijab* at work, and stopped wearing the *niqab* entirely.

"In 2009, I went to the United States, to New Hampshire, on an Aramco-funded internship. Every year on my birthday, I do crazy things. So that year I got my driver's license and went skydiving. With the right to drive I was an adult; I could live a normal life. I didn't have to ask my father every time I wanted to do something. The United States opened my life. I had problems going back to Saudi the next year; I was less mobile there."

In early 2011, al-Sharif launched #Women2Drive, a social media campaign urging Saudi women to drive on Friday, June 17, 2011. With the slogan "Teach me how to drive so I can protect myself" and bumper stickers proclaiming that "Real Women Drive Cars," the #Women2Drive campaign drew tens of thousands of followers on Facebook and Twitter.

"We're not alone," al-Sharif told me. "The Internet changed everything; it's our window to the world. Social media has created a global support system for us. We used it to start a revolution. Twitter is our parliament; it lets citizens act as journalists in states where the government controls the media."

A short YouTube video promoting the #Women2Drive campaign opens with a close-up of a woman's hand holding a set of keys in front of the door of a shiny red sports car.[27] Al-Sharif then describes what she hopes her followers will do on the appointed day. Insisting that her campaign is not intended to provoke any kind of public protest or demonstration, she invites women who have a valid international driver's license to go about their daily routine—with one significant difference. She asks them to drive themselves, instead of having their driver or a male relative drive them. She suggests they dress modestly, wear a seatbelt, and drive safely. Finally, she encourages them to record themselves and upload the video to YouTube.[28]

On May 19, 2011, almost a month before the scheduled protest, al-Sharif decided to take action herself. She wanted to see how the police would react when they caught a woman driving. She also wanted to prove that men were not wolves.

"I'm going to do something crazy," she told her brother.

"What?" he asked.

"I'm going to go out and drive," she replied.

"I'll come videotape you," he said.

But when her brother overslept, al-Sharif asked Wajeha al-Huwaider, a cofounder of the Association for the Protection and Defense of Women's Rights in Saudi Arabia, who like al-Sharif lived in the Aramco compound in Dhahran, to join her and record the event.

"You know when you have a bird and it's been in a cage all its life?" al-Sharif told a reporter later. "When you open the cage door, it doesn't want to leave. It was *that* moment."

For over an hour, al-Sharif drove her Cadillac SUV through the streets of al-Khobar while al-Huwaider videotaped the trip with her iPhone. In her purse, al-Sharif had a valid New Hampshire driver's license. As soon as a traffic policeman stopped her, he was joined by a group of *mutawwa* who surrounded her car.

"Girl!" they screamed. "Get out! We don't allow women to drive!"

Al-Sharif was arrested and detained for six hours. Then she was released. No charges were filed against her.

"Sir, what law did I break?" she kept asking the policemen.

"You didn't break any law," they said. "You violated *urf*—custom."[29]

The next day the #Women2Drive team uploaded al-Huwaider's video to YouTube. With seven hundred thousand views in twenty-four hours, it was the most-viewed video in the world that day. Al-Sharif couldn't believe it.

"I started receiving phone calls, death threats. I had four hundred emails, hateful emails. Someone at Aramco must have put my business email out there. I received phone calls from Riyadh: 'You are digging your grave.' It was very annoying.

"A colleague at Aramco came running into my office: 'Oh my God, I saw your video.' And it was trending. I didn't know it would cause all this hate. It was just a woman driving. It's not *haraam,* there isn't any law against it.

"My boss at Aramco called me into his office. 'Manal,' he said, 'do you realize what you're doing? You're going to put yourself in so much trouble.' I'm like, 'I can take the trouble, but I don't want to loose my job.' And he said 'Are you sure about what you doing? Just don't bring in the Aramco name.'

"I told him, 'This is the year the whole world is changing, and we're part of that change.'"

Two days later, on May 21, al-Sharif decided to drive again. She wanted to check the response of the police and the government. She didn't want June 17 to come and have women be sent to jail.

"It was me and my brother and my whole family; we went out for lunch. My brother drove. When we arrived at the parking lot at the mall, I said 'Can I drive? Can I take the wheel?' He said, 'Of course.' We'd talked about it before.

"My son, my sister-in-law, and my nephew were all sitting in the back seat; my brother was in the passenger seat. I was driving. We drove around for maybe half an hour. It was amazing. No one shouted at me; no one. People just gave me these looks when I stopped in traffic. That was it. A lot of people saw me driving, but no one followed me.

"A police officer stopped me on the Corniche road. He didn't know what to do, so we knew he didn't have orders from the government. He just said 'Are you aware that in Saudi Arabia women are not allowed to drive?' And I'm like: 'Sir, are you aware there is no law? I have a driver's license, and I'm not breaking any law.' He smiled; he didn't know what to do. He told me he'd give me a ticket and let me go. That's what they usually do. They make you and your guardian sign a pledge promising not to drive again.

"And then another car stopped. The guy said 'Who's that driving?' 'Her name is Manal al-Sharif.' He'd seen the video, so right away he called the *mutawwa*. It wasn't the traffic police that called, it was a citizen.

"The *mutawwa* came in ten minutes. They were shouting, dragging us out of the car, and making a big scene. My brother said, 'Please don't make a scene in the street, take us to the police station.' So they drove our car to the police station. They interrogated me for six hours. I told them I just wanted to drive. They gave me a pledge to sign. I'm like, 'I'm not going to sign this.' I was laughing at them.

"We were in the police station from four to eleven. Then they let us go. I didn't know the whole country was talking about it. I had an interview that night on TV. Saudis were so mad. The girls on my team started a page called 'Free Manal,' and a thousand people joined in just a few hours. It was unbelievable.

"I was in detention with my brother; I had no clue what was happening outside. After two hours this police guy said, 'Do you want to go home and spend the night with your son, or do you want to spend the night alone here with us? You need to sign this.' So I signed it. I said, 'I'm going to sign it, but I don't believe it. I'm going to drive again; I'm just signing it to leave.'

"The police were so nice and kind: 'We're sorry to delay you. These are formalities we have to go through.' So we left; we went home. Apparently Prince Muhammad bin Fahd, the Prince of ash-Sharqiyah, the Eastern Province, was really mad when he heard the news. He gave the order to arrest me and send me to jail right away.

"We got home at midnight. At two A.M. the religious police with Aramco security knocked on the door.

"'Is this the house of Manal al-Sharif?'

"'Yes.'

"My brother was with me and his wife and four kids.

"'We need her to come with us.'

"'Who are you?'

"'We just we need her to make a statement and sign some more papers. She can return in the morning.'

"I panicked, but I had to go with them. They sent me to jail without a single word. I found myself completely naked being searched. They didn't even have enough cells. They cram everyone into this old jail—drug dealers, hookers, thieves—and then this woman who didn't commit any crime, me. I was really shocked; I didn't know I'd go to jail. In Saudi Arabia if you're put in jail, you could stay forever, because there are no trials. Once you're locked up, your life is over.

"I felt shock and anger. They didn't give me a blanket or a place to sleep. I couldn't sleep for two days; I was so tired and confused. Most of the women in jail didn't speak Arabic. Only a few of them were Saudi. One was a drug dealer, one helped her son kill her husband, one was raped by her father. A Saudi woman came and calmed me down. She brought me water and started asking about my story. That helped.

"'You're the girl on YouTube,' she said.

"I was like 'Wow! Even in the most closed places in the country they know about the woman who drove.'

"I kept my *abaya* on the whole time. They kept telling me to take it off. But I was so sure I was leaving. I wasn't a criminal.

"Right away my father went to the prince—apologizing, apologizing, apologizing. For nine days he didn't do anything else. They wanted an apology to the king from our clan to get me out of jail. My family called and said, 'We'll do whatever you want to release our daughter.' I think that support was huge. I come from a big tribe, a very honorable tribe. I had no clue they would stand by me; I thought they'd just like let me rot. But they stood up for me. Even today a lot of people from the Sharif tribe contact me online and say, 'We're proud of you, cousin.' In Saudi Arabia you need a tribe.

"Dad begged the people in ash-Sharqiyah for a week, but nothing happened. People from the Human Rights Association came to interview me. After that, they started to treat me better. They let me use the phone; they let me see my family. I told my Mom not to come. I'm like, 'She's not going to see me here in jail behind bars.' Manour, my sister-in-law, came, and I passed her a small piece of paper. It said 'Dad should see the king; if he doesn't, I'll be here forever.' I'm like 'Don't read this now. Hide it.' She had to put the piece of paper in her bra. It was so funny.

"Right away they booked Dad on a flight to Jeddah, and he went to the king's palace. The guards knew who he was.

"They said, 'You're Manal al-Sharif's father.'

"He said, 'Yes. I came to talk to the king.'

"'The king can't see you now. He can only see you on Friday.'

"That was the response. So my father wrote a letter to the king. Then he went to see him on Monday; Friday was far away. But on Monday, the king gave the order to release me even before my father went to see him, just based on his letter. On Friday, my whole family went to see the king.

"I asked Dad 'What did the king tell you when you went to see him?'

"The king said one word: 'Advise her. Advise her. Advise her.'

"The prince—we have a prince of our family, not a royal prince, a tribal prince—and the sheikhs of the family met the king on Friday. The king gave Dad a check; he gave him money—ten thousand dollars—because he knew that Dad was a truck driver and that he wasn't working. We were so taken by his generosity and his kindness. He took action right away. He was unhappy that I was in jail. This is what I heard from his daughter's assistant. I was like 'Wow. He let me out.'

"While I was in jail, the whole world went into a frenzy. 'How could this horrible country jail this woman?' Wahhabi Islam is an ideology of hate. Wahhabi officials take weak hadith and use them to justify their views repressing women. It's interesting; I had my picture on my Facebook page. Usually Saudi women cover their face and don't use their real name or their picture in public. 'But this woman has a picture; she has a face.' That's what created the sympathy for me."

Amnesty International declared al-Sharif a prisoner of conscience and demanded her immediate and unconditional release. A letter from the Saudi Women for Driving Coalition referred to Saudi Arabia as "the world's largest women's prison."[30] Then Secretary of State Hillary Clinton stated that she was moved by the protest and that she supported Saudi women in their effort to gain the right to drive. "I want to underscore the fact," she said, "that this is not coming from outside of their country. This is the women themselves, seeking to be recognized." Finally, Clinton said, she and other U.S. officials had raised the matter with officials "at the highest level of the Saudi government."[31]

Al-Sharif was released from prison on May 30. She had been charged with multiple offenses: driving a car within the city of al-Khobar, allowing a journalist to interview her while driving, disseminating a video of the event to the media, disturbing the public order, and inciting public opposition to government regulations by encouraging Saudi women to drive.[32] Within days, her Facebook campaign was taken down, and her YouTube video, which had become the most popular video in Saudi Arabia and was trending around the world, became unavailable at its original location. It has since been reposted many times and is now easily accessible. The #Women2Drive movement estimated that in the weeks following her release over a million people around the world changed their Facebook picture to al-Sharif's portrait in a gesture of support. Some people began referring to her as "the female Che Guevara."[33]

Hackers altered al-Sharif's Twitter account to suggest that she had called off the campaign and admitted that "foreign forces" had incited her to act against the best interests of her country. Then someone pretending to be al-Sharif announced that she had repented because she realized that #Women2Drive was "an atheist conspiracy that would lead to moral decadence," but the deception was quickly exposed.[34] Al-Sharif responded publicly that she had started her campaign because she loved her country and believed that her society would not be free unless its women were free.

"When I was released from jail," al-Sharif told me, "I started calling everyone. I wanted June 17 to happen. I didn't want it to stop because girls were so terrified that they'd get sent to jail. The police told me this while they were interrogating me: 'The use of YouTube, that's what got you in trouble.' Their harsh response shows how insecure they are and how afraid they are of people using social media. We found out what a treasure social media is; we found out that it really scares them."

In a CNN interview al-Sharif said, "We're not doing anything that is breaking the law. We have a saying, 'The rain starts with a single drop.' This is a really symbolic thing for us women, driving. It is a very basic thing."[35]

During the year after her arrest, al-Sharif's relationship with her employer, Saudi Aramco, grew increasingly strained.

"After my release from jail, a manager at Aramco shook my hand and said, 'Shall I buy a car for my daughter now?' He thanked me; he supported our efforts, but only privately. My boss said, 'Manal, when you were in jail, I couldn't sleep. Every morning I went to places I don't usually go online just to follow your news. And when you were released, I could breathe again.'

"I was really touched when he told me that. He's an Aramcon. Later he had to be harsh with me; he had to fire me because the government didn't want me to work there.

"People at Aramco warned me not to do interviews, not to speak at conferences, not to do anything. They refused my requests for time off because they were afraid I'd speak out. It was a constant struggle. My job was my only source of income. They kept pressuring me to shut up, but I couldn't. You can't shut up. You've been sent to jail; you've been smeared all over the local media. The imams have been saying horrible things about you every Friday in the mosques.

"The people at Aramco said, 'We don't want your name to be associated with us.'

"I'm like, 'I don't talk about Aramco.'

"They said, 'Whether you like it or not, your name is associated with us.'

"Aramco is like the government. They don't want to hear anything about themselves in the news. I was a very successful engineer with Aramco, but they marginalized me. They removed me from the information security department and put me in archiving. It has nothing to do with my degree. They pressure you. They pressure you until you just . . .

"I have two hundred thousand followers on social media now. You have to look at the lives you touch positively. You're a villain to some people and a hero to others. The people who see you as a hero are afraid of the people who attack you. They'll tell you they're proud of you in private, but they won't say anything in public. They come up and shake your hand with tears in their eyes, and they tell you what you're doing is brave and inspiring. So you have to live with these two vastly different images of yourself."

The video of al-Sharif driving her car through the streets of al-Khobar would be remarkable for its banality, if it weren't illegal for women to drive in Saudi Arabia. Wearing a black *abaya* and *hijab* and large, stylish dark glasses, al-Sharif turns the steering wheel back and forth and checks her rearview mirror, occasionally adjusting her *hijab* and repositioning her glasses. Everyday street scenes flash by out the driver's side window. Al-Sharif and al-Huwaider discuss the frustrations of not being able to drive and complain good naturedly about the expense of hiring a driver, the inconvenience of trying to find a taxi during rush hour, and the indignity of being so completely dependent on male relatives.

"We're ignorant and illiterate women when it comes to driving," al-Sharif tells al-Huwaider in the video. "You'll find a woman with a Ph.D., a professor at a university, and she doesn't know how to drive. During an emergency what's she going to do? God forbid her husband's with her, and he has a heart attack. I went to take my car to renew the registration. It was about to expire, and I had to beg somebody to take it in for an inspection. This is my car, and it's under my name. Oh, my heart! Never mind! Things will change. *Inshallah,* God willing."

While al-Sharif's campaign generated a huge outpouring of support on the Internet, the actual turnout on June 17 was less impressive. The *Arab News,* an English language daily published in Jeddah, characterized the protest as a "nonevent."[36] According to various reports, between twenty-five and a hundred women drove with relative impunity. The streets were full of both traffic police and *mutawwa,* but there were few confrontations. Half a dozen women were stopped, escorted home, and told not to drive again, but none of them were arrested. One woman, unafraid and well prepared, had brought a change of clothes and a prayer rug with her, just in case she was detained by the police overnight.[37]

While the #Women2Drive campaign did receive some support from human rights organizations and women's groups in Saudi Arabia, public reaction within the country was strong and largely negative. A political cartoon depicted a set of car keys in a woman's hand linked to a grenade. Al-Sharif herself was called a traitor, a slut, a Shia, a Zionist, and a "Westernized woman seeking to Westernize the country." She received more threatening phone calls and email messages. The worst one read: "Your grave is waiting."[38]

Conservative religious figures accused her of "besmirching the Kingdom's reputation," "betraying her country and her culture," and called for her to be flogged or beheaded. One cleric told her, "You've just opened the gates of Hell on yourself." Another said, "God willing these women will die."[39] An Internet campaign called for men to punish any woman they found driving by beating her with their *agal,* the black cords Saudi men wear to hold their *shemagh* in place. Other critics engaged in a campaign of fear, warning women of the terrible fate that awaited them should they attempt to drive by themselves. "There are wolves in the street," they said, "and they'll rape you if you drive." In response to all these threats, al-Sharif said: "There needed to be one person who could break that wall, to make the others understand that it's OK, you can drive in the street. No one will rape you."[40]

In late September 2011, as the controversy over the right of Saudi women to drive continued to attract public attention within the country and embarrass the Kingdom internationally, King Abdullah made a surprising announcement. "Because we refuse to marginalize women," he declared, "we have decided to involve women in the Shura Council as members, starting from the next term." King Abdullah also announced that women would be allowed to run as candidates in the 2015 municipal election and that they would even have the right to vote.[41]

Since the Shura Council, like the municipal councils, has little real power, some observers considered the king's announcement nothing more than a superficial gesture; others thought it was an important step toward granting Saudi women full civil rights. Still others thought that Abdullah's decision was part of a skillful balancing act in which he promised women increased civil rights at some point in the indefinite future, while ignoring the more significant issues of women driving and male guardianship. In this way, the king hoped to placate demands for increased liberalization without angering conservative religious leaders.

The next step in al-Sharif's campaign was to encourage women to apply for driver's licenses.

"Because there's no law against it," she told me, "I went and applied for a Saudi driver's license. They rejected my application, but I kept the papers. We were hoping to get at least ten women from each major city to apply. I published a video with all the documentation on how to do it; I even offered them legal consultation. Only three other women applied, but when the time came to take their papers to the court, all three backed out. I went to court alone. I filed my lawsuit in November 2011.

"It's fear that stops women from taking action. We need to break that fear. People are always saying, 'No. No. No. We're waiting until they *let* us drive.'

"I'm like, 'They'll never *let* you drive.' You need to create pressure. If you don't create pressure, you won't get anything. No one will give you your rights on a silver plate.

"I didn't know how influential I was, until I saw the reactions to my tweets and my articles. One guy sent me an email. He said, 'You ruined my life. After my girlfriend read your article, she dumped me.'

"I was like, 'Yes. She's a strong woman. Maybe you deserved it.'

"When I was married, they kept telling me, 'You're a woman. You have to obey the man in your life.'

"But he's insulting me; he's disrespectful to me; he doesn't help me at all. Why should I have to obey him and get nothing in return? They say, 'No. No. No. You're a woman; you can't talk back. You can't say anything. His wishes are your orders.'

"So you go through all this brainwashing, and you feel guilty the whole time. But something inside you says, 'No, *I'm* not doing anything wrong. *He's* doing something wrong. *This society* is doing something wrong.'

"Women just need someone to tell them, 'It's your right to ask for custody of your child; it's your right to go to court and ask for child support; it's your right to pursue your education and get a job.'"

In February 2012, al-Sharif sued the Saudi government for refusing to issue her a driver's license and not allowing her to drive a car. She filed a lawsuit with the Board of Grievances of the Eastern Province against the General Directorate of Traffic, which is under the jurisdiction of the Ministry of the Interior. Several other Saudi women joined her in the case; it was the first of its kind to be heard in a Saudi court.[42]

Although he agreed to take her case, the head of the Board of Grievances indicated he would ultimately have to reject her plea. In response to her lawyer's argument that there was no law in Saudi Arabia against issuing driver's licenses to women, the judge said that his court remained controlled by social norms and that Saudi society was not ready yet to accept women driving. He added that even if Saudi society *were* ready to accept such a change, final approval would be needed from the king himself.[43]

By now al-Sharif had begun to receive considerable international acclaim. In 2011, *Forbes* named her one of "The 10 Women Who Rocked the World." Just two months later *Foreign Policy* named her one of "The Top 100 Global Thinkers." The following year she was chosen one of "The 100 Most Influential People in the World" by *Time*. The same year the Oslo Freedom Forum awarded her its first annual Vaclav Havel Prize for Creative Dissent.[44]

In May 2012, al-Sharif went to Oslo to receive the Havel Prize. To do so she needed the written permission of her father, who had become her guardian again after her divorce. Her acceptance speech was entitled "The Drive for Freedom." By June the video of her speech, available on YouTube, had been seen by almost four hundred thousand people.[45] Wearing a dark blue *hijab,* a white jacket over a long print shirt, dark blue pants, and high heels, al-Sharif described growing up in a conservative religious environment in the shadow of the siege of the Holy Mosque in Mecca in 1979, the year she was born.

For these extremists, al-Sharif said, women are *awrah*—imperfect, defective, sinful—and must be covered.

"For them, I was *awrah.* My face was *awrah;* my voice was *awrah;* even my name was *awrah.* So we were faceless; we were voiceless; we were nameless. We were just invisible.

"Do you remember the first time you listened to music?" al-Sharif asked her audience. That was the first turning point in her life. The plaintive sound of electric guitars and young male voices filled the large auditorium in Oslo where she was speaking.

"Do you remember the first song you ever listened to? I remember. I was twenty-one years old. It was the first time in my life I allowed myself to listen to music. I remember the song; it was 'Show Me the Meaning of Being Lonely' by the Back Street Boys."

Al-Sharif smiled, as laughter rippled through the audience.

"I used to burn my brother's music cassettes in the oven. Sorry, brother. I was that extreme. They had been telling us music is Satan's flute, a path to adultery. But this song sounded so pure, so beautiful, so angelic. That day I realized how lonely I was in the world I isolated myself in."

The second turning point in al-Sharif's life occurred on September 11, 2001. Displayed on a huge screen behind her was a horrifying photograph of a man falling head first to his death from one of the Twin Towers of the World Trade Center. Al-Sharif described the traumatic moment when she realized that Osama bin Laden and the other men she'd thought were her heroes, were in fact "nothing but bloody terrorists."

At that point in her talk, she skipped ahead ten years to describe her "Driving for Freedom" campaign.

"I used my face, my voice, and my real name," she said. "I used to be ashamed of who I am—a woman. But not any more. The child cannot be free if his mother is not free. The husband cannot be free if his wife is not free. Society is nothing if women are nothing.

"Here, I am free," al-Sharif concluded, her voice filled with dignity and passion. "But when I go back home to Saudi Arabia, the struggle has just begun. I don't know how long it will last, and I don't know when it will end. But for me the struggle is not about driving a car. It's about being in the driver's seat of our destiny."

After her speech at the Oslo Freedom Forum, campaigns were mounted on Twitter both for and against her. A campaign attacking her, #OsloTraitor, received 9,380 tweets, while a campaign supporting her, #OsloHero, received only 120. In another Internet poll, 90 percent of the thirteen thousand participants thought she had betrayed her country in Oslo; only 4 percent of them were proud of her speech there.

Al-Sharif's work on behalf of Saudi women's right to drive has not been without serious personal cost to both her and her family. In the year between her arrest and her appearance at the Oslo Freedom Forum, al-Sharif received several invitations to appear at international conferences. Each time her employer, Saudi Aramco, denied her request for time off. When she asked for permission to travel to Oslo to accept the Havel Prize, her request was again denied.

The executive director of her division told al-Sharif, "We don't want your name to be associated with us." Her manager was more blunt: "What the hell are you doing?" She left him a message on her office blackboard: "2011. Mark this year! It will change every single rule that you know."[46] While Saudi Aramco did not actually fire her, al-Sharif says she was "increasingly marginalized at the company for her activism." So she resigned.

"It wasn't about Manal," she told me. "It was about all the women who call for their rights, so they'll be afraid because they saw what happened to me. I don't want to tell my son in twenty years that I chickened. I couldn't. I had to make the hard decision. It was either my work at Aramco or what I was doing. I'd saved enough for about ten years, so I was brave, and I submitted my resignation so I could go and give my Oslo Freedom speech."

When al-Sharif left Saudi Aramco, she lost the one-bedroom, company-owned apartment in the Dhahran compound where she lived with her young son, Abdullah.[47] He too had been having a difficult time. One day he came home from elementary school with bruises on his face. Two of his classmates had seen pictures of his mother on Facebook. They beat him up because he was the son of the woman who had driven a car. They told him his mother should be in jail.[48]

Al-Sharif now lives in Dubai, in the United Arab Emirates, with her second husband, a computer security expert from Brazil whom she met when they both worked for Aramco. Even though he converted to Islam, al-Sharif had to request special permission from the Saudi Minister of the Interior to marry him because he was not a Saudi citizen. Her request was denied. Now she has to return to Dhahran from Dubai every weekend in order to see her son because her first husband refuses to allow him to travel outside the Kingdom with her.

With the support of other Saudi women involved in her #Right2Dignity movement, al-Sharif signed an appeal to King Abdullah in June 2012, asking him to take a stand in support of women's right to drive. The appeal was based on the argument that denying women the right to drive is "based on customs and traditions that do not come from God."[49] Four times the #Right2Dignity movement submitted a similar petition with over three thousand signatures to the Shura Council, which serves as the formal advisory body to the king, but it was rejected each time. On the fifth try it was finally accepted.

Later the same year, al-Sharif traveled to California to address the San Francisco Freedom Forum. Her presentation was entitled "The Saudi Women's Spring."

"My name is Manal al-Sharif," she began. "I come from the Kingdom of Saudi men."

She explained to her audience why lifting the ban on women driving would have such significant social, political, and economic consequences in her country, and she stressed the pivotal role that YouTube and Twitter have played in her #Right2Dignity movement. Since Saudi citizens have no other means to express their political views publicly, she said, "social media have become a democratic sandbox, our personal bully pulpit, and, yes, our comfort blanket and shield."[50]

Al-Sharif told the audience how moved she's been by all the support she's received from artists all over the world. She cited one artist and one work in particular, "the beautiful pop star from England M.I.A. and her song 'Bad Girls.'"

"All we want," she concluded, "is a Saudi Arabia that respects the humanity of women. Because I'm proud to be a Saudi woman and because I love my country, I will not wait. Women's rights are not a special interest or a privilege. Women rights, or the lack of them, affect the whole society! And societies that keep women in the back seat will always be on the wrong side of history."

As she left the stage to enthusiastic applause, familiar images of women dressed in gold-lamé caftans dancing provocatively around an old car in a dusty alley appeared on the large screen behind the podium where al-Sharif had just finished speaking. And M.I.A. sitting in the driver's seat of a car stroking the steering wheel sensually began to sing:

> Live fast, die young,
> Bad girls do it well.

In September 2013, the prospects that Saudi women might be allowed to drive at some point seemed to improve when the new head of the Committee for the Promotion of Virtue and the Prevention of Vice stated that sharia law contained no text forbidding women from driving. He also noted somewhat paradoxically that while he did not have the authority to change the Kingdom's policies on women driving, no women had been stopped for driving since King Abdullah had appointed him to office a year earlier.[51] Perhaps in reaction to this small, but significant, shift in government policy, Sheikh Saleh al-Loheidan, a leading Saudi cleric, forcefully condemned women driving. "Medical studies," he said, "show that [driving] would affect a woman's ovaries and that it pushes the pelvis upward. We find that for women who continuously drive cars, their children are born with varying degrees of clinical problems."[52]

At about this time, a new campaign began, which invited Saudi women to participate in another "day of defiance" against the ban on women driving. A petition entitled "October 26th, Driving for Women" appeared online encouraging women to drive and post videos of themselves in the act. The first woman to announce her commitment to join the protest was Madeha al-Ajroush, when she tweeted, "Yes, I will drive again on October 26." Within two days over eight thousand women had signed the petition.[53]

Several ominous developments took place in the days leading up to this most recent protest. The Saudi Ministry of the Interior reaffirmed its determination to uphold the prohibition against women driving. This announcement and the scare tactics the Saudi government used to enforce the ban—harassing phone calls, travel restrictions, and arbitrary detentions—were widely criticized by international human rights organizations. In addition, several well-known women's rights activists reportedly received phone calls from someone claiming to be associated with the Ministry of the Interior who warned them explicitly not to participate in the protest. And finally, the day before the protest, hackers took down the oct26driving.org website and replaced it with the message "Drop the leadership of Saudi women ... Accident."[54]

Accurate information about what actually happened on October 26, 2013, is hard to come by. Organizers of the protest reported that over sixty women from across the country had driven that day. They also reported that the police had not set up any roadblocks or checkpoints and that no one had been stopped, ticketed, or fined. According to other reports, more than sixteen women were arrested and forced to sign statements promising not to drive again. A spokesman from the Ministry of the Interior said that October 26, 2013, was a "normal day, just like every Saturday."[55]

The day after the protest, a video of a song entitled "No Woman, No Drive" appeared on the oct26driving.org website featuring Hisham Fageeh, a young Saudi comedian and social activist who is well known for his satirical YouTube videos. Within five days, seven million people had watched Fageeh offer a devastating critique of the Saudi ban on women driving with his parody of Bob Marley's famous reggae anthem "No Woman, No Cry."[56]

In the original 1975 version of the song, Marley offers comfort to women living in desperate poverty in the projects of Kingston, Jamaica. Shaking his thick dreadlocks angrily, Marley closes his eyes and points to the sky as if in a trance. With a voice full of pain and agony, he sings:

> No woman, no cry.
> Say, say, say,

I remember when we used to sit
In a government yard in Trenchtown,
Oba-obaserving the hypocrites
As they mingled with the good people we meet.
Good friends we had, and good friends we've lost along the way.
In this great future, you can't forget your past,
So dry your tears.
Hey, little sister, don't shed no tears.
No woman, no cry.

In his 2013 parody, Hisham Fageeh, with an air of smug satisfaction, patiently explains to Saudi women why it's not a good idea for them to drive. Wearing a white *thobe,* a red-and-white checkered *shemagh,* and large glasses, Fageeh sings an upbeat acappella version of Marley's song. Whistling, smiling, and snapping his fingers, Fageeh is a Saudi hipster, a Wahhabi Whiffenpoof.

No woman, no drive.
Say, say, say,
I remember when you used to sit
In the family car, but backseat.
Ova-ovaries all safe and well
So you can make lots and lots of babies.
Good friends we had, and good friends we've lost on the highway.
In this bright future, you can't forget your past,
So put your car key away.
Hey, little sister, don't touch that wheel.
No woman, no drive.

When asked about the song in an interview, Fageeh said simply "We do entertainment. We don't have a specific political agenda." Fageeh just wants to show the world that Saudis have a sense of humor too.[57]

MOCKING YOUR OPPRESSOR

In her "Bad Girls" video, M.I.A. sings provocatively about having sex in a car while "drifting" wildly down an exotic—and imaginary—Saudi street. In her #Women2Drive video, Manal al-Sharif speaks with frustration about the restrictions she faces every day as a Saudi woman while driving carefully down a mundane—and very real—Saudi street. In her speech at the 2012

Oslo Freedom Forum, al-Sharif speaks movingly about her courageous act of civil disobedience while standing on an international stage addressing a worldwide audience. And in "No Woman, No Cry," Hisham Fageeh parodies Bob Marley's powerful protest against social injustice in order to express his support for Saudi women's right to drive.

Each of these four acts is transgressive; each threatens to subvert the Saudi social order, but in very different ways. M.I.A.'s defiant sexuality is a perverse fulfillment of Saudi clerics' worst nightmare; it's a fantasy of exactly what they are afraid will happen if Saudi women are allowed to drive. In any other country in the world, al-Sharif's #Women2Drive video, with her modest dress, safe driving, and everyday conversation, would be unremarkable. In the Saudi context, however, it too is profoundly transgressive. Al-Sharif is not violating Saudi traffic rules; she is violating Saudi gender norms. She is guilty of "driving while female." In her Oslo speech, al-Sharif expresses her opposition to the Saudi ban on women driving with straightforward, even blunt language. Fageeh uses the complexity and indirectness of humor to test the limits of the Saudi government's efforts at censorship and social control.

To many western observers, the veil is the quintessential sign of women's oppression in the Muslim, Arab world. The issue of "covering," however, is much more complex. Veiling occurs in many different contexts and has many different meanings. But in Saudi Arabia, driving is a very different and much simpler matter. For Saudi women, the ban on driving, like the restrictions imposed on them by the guardianship system, imposes a serious infringement on their personal freedom. In the Kingdom of Saudi Arabia, both the government and the religious establishment on which its legitimacy depends continue to uphold the ban against women driving. In this way they continue to deny Saudi women freedom of movement and full participation in Saudi society.

"In Saudi Arabia," al-Sharif told me, "women are treated like cars. They have to be registered to someone. The guardianship system is the umbrella of all evil. But nothing is more powerful than mocking your oppressor."

FIGURE 1. Saudi Aramco's Core Area in Dhahran. Photograph courtesy of Saudi Aramco / Hussain A. Ramadan.

FIGURE 2. (left) A 1936 photograph of an American drill chief and his Saudi crew at Dammam No. 7, also known as "Prosperity Well," the first Aramco well to strike oil. Photograph courtesy of Saudi Aramco / Lester Hilyard.

FIGURE 3. (above) Saudi Aramco's refinery at Ras Tanura, which produces 550,000 barrels a day. Photograph courtesy of Saudi Aramco / Abdulla Y. al-Dobais.

FIGURE 4. M.I.A. perched on a "skiing" car in a screen shot from the music video for her song "Bad Girls."

FIGURE 5. *The Choice* (2005–7), by Manal al-Dowayan. Photograph courtesy of Manal al-Dowayan.

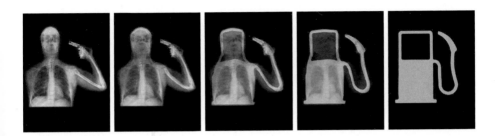

FIGURE 6. (left) *Magnetism 1* (2012), by Ahmed Mater. Photograph courtesy of Edge of Arabia Projects and The Artist.

FIGURE 7. (above) *Evolution of Man* (2010), by Ahmed Mater. Photograph courtesy of Edge of Arabia Projects and The Artist.

FIGURE 8. (below) *The Path / Siraat* (2009), by Abdulnasser Gharem. Photograph courtesy of Edge of Arabia Projects and The Artist.

FIGURE 9. (right) A page from Harun Yahya (pseudonym of Adnan Oktar), *Atlas of Creation*, claiming to refute the validity of the process of biological evolution by showing that shrimp have survived unchanged for millions of years. Photograph courtesy of Harun Yahya.

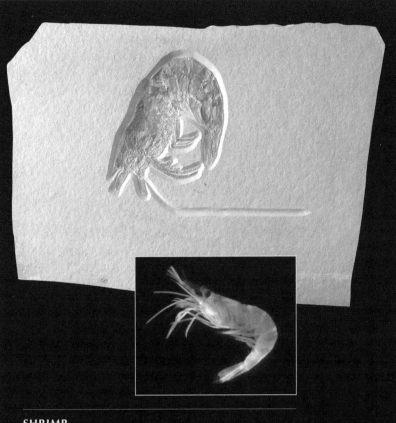

SHRIMP

Age: 208 to 146 million years old

Size: 19.5 centimeters (7.7 in) from tip to tail

Location: Solnhofen Limestone, Eichsatt, West Germany

Period: Jurassic

Shrimp, having survived unchanged for millions of years, show us that they did not evolve but were created. If a living thing has the same features now as it did millions of years ago, then this creature cannot have developed by way of evolution. The fossil record is proof that evolutionists' claims are untrue.

FIGURE 10. The cover of *A Brief Illustrated Guide to Understanding Islam,* a booklet presenting what it claims to be scientific evidence for the truth of Islam. Photograph courtesy of Phyllis Graber Jensen / Bates College.

FIGURE 11. Qasr al-Farid, "the castle that stands alone," one of the most spectacular tombs in the necropolis of the ancient Nabataean city of Hegra, which is now known as al-Hijra or Madain Saleh, in northwestern Saudi Arabia. Photograph courtesy of Eric Lafforgue.

FIGURE 12. An anthropomorphic sandstone stele from the fourth millenium B.C.E. that stood at the entrance to the Roads of Arabia exhibition in Washington, DC. Photograph courtesy of Album / Art Resource.

FIGURE 13. A basalt tombstone of the late ninth or early tenth century, from the al-Mala Cemetery in Mecca, that was included in the Roads of Arabia exhibition. Photograph courtesy of Album / Art Resource.

FIGURE 14. (left) Ottoman houses in al-Balad, the old city of Jeddah, many of which now provide shelter for Somalis, Yemenis, and other immigrants who have been "washed ashore" by the Red Sea. Photograph courtesy of Eric Lafforgue.

FIGURE 15. (above) *Road to Makkah* (2011). A work of art by Abdulnasser Gharem depicting the actual road sign that directs non-Muslims not to enter the city of Mecca. Photograph courtesy of Edge of Arabia Projects and The Artist.

FIGURE 16. *Golden Hour* (2011), from the *Desert of Pharan* series, by Ahmed Mater. A powerful image of the area around the Holy Mosque in Mecca as one huge construction site. Photograph courtesy of Edge of Arabia Projects and The Artist.

THREE

Saudi Modern

ART ON THE EDGE

Art can't be broken.[1]

THE NEW HOME OF DESERT Designs is near the busy intersection of King Abdullah and Prince Hamood Streets in al-Khobar, across the street from KFC and Pizza Hut. The first-floor showroom is crowded with expensive art and antiques from Saudi Arabia and other parts of the Arab world—furniture, carpets, camel saddles, incense burners, water pipes, and *dallah*, the shiny brass coffee pots used for serving Arabic coffee in the traditional Saudi ritual of hospitality. On its website, Desert Designs advertises its "ethnic collections" and promises to provide customers with a unique shopping experience by bringing Bedouin art from the desert to their homes. It offers products that are "guaranteed to be heirlooms of the future." In 2010, Desert Designs won the Prince Muhammad bin Fahd Trophy for Best Establishment in Tourism and Antiquity in Saudi Arabia.

The second floor of Desert Designs is a very different place. Most of the space is devoted to a gallery of contemporary art, where young Saudi artists have a rare opportunity to display their work in their own country. Off the gallery is a small coffee shop, one of the few places in al-Khobar where men and women can sit together and talk with little chance of attracting unwanted attention from the *mutawwa*. The second floor also contains offices, a small gift shop, and artists' studios.

Farid Bukhari, a successful businessman, and his wife, Qamar Ahmed, an artist, founded Desert Designs in 1990 with the hope of filling a niche in the market for high-end gifts, souvenirs, and home furnishings. They thought they could attract a wide range of customers to their store: American GIs stationed in the area during the First Gulf War; members of the expatriate community, especially employees of Saudi Aramco living in the nearby compound in Dhahran; as well as wealthy Saudis who were just then beginning to appreciate the value of traditional Arab arts and crafts. Bukhari and Ahmed built their collection by traveling to markets—souks all over Saudi Arabia. As they became more successful, they began selling custom-made furniture and offering their services as interior designers.

When we visited Desert Designs in May 2012, Ahmed spoke with me about her goals as an artist and a businesswoman.

"We wanted to do something firmly Saudi," she said. "The rich always bought stuff abroad. The oil money came in, and people went to Europe for luxuries. They weren't buying Saudi things. We forgot our own heritage. I wish we'd stop buying plastic and go back to our traditions. I said 'I'm going to bring things from the souks in Qatif and al-Hasa to al-Khobar.' I realized there was a market. I was alone at home at the time and had nothing to do, so I started a small store. Then my husband left his family business and joined me. I couldn't sell things, so my husband did. He was the front man; I worked behind the scenes."

As we walked around the downstairs show room, Ahmed pointed out some camel bags and talked about the Bedouin.

"This was their Samsonite," she said. "That's all camel equipment, so if you have a camel, you're all set."

I asked her about the lives of contemporary Bedouin in Saudi Arabia.

"Most Bedouin *want* to live in poverty," she replied. "There's no excuse for being poor in this country now with the Saudization program. God helps those who help themselves. The Bedouin don't want to modernize. They've failed; they've lost their culture."

When we went upstairs, I asked Ahmed whether she had any problems managing a contemporary art gallery in the face of the conservative values of Saudi society in general and the strict Wahhabi prohibition against depictions of the human form in particular.

"I'm not here to paint a rosy picture for you," she said. "You can get that from the interior minister."

Then she described a visit she received once from the *mutawwa*.

"We had busts made of clay to display our jewelry—earrings and necklaces. The *mutawwa* came in and said, 'You have idols in the store! Take them down! Maybe in a hundred years you'll be worshiping them.'

"My husband just dropped one of them on the floor and broke it. I told the *mutawwa* that my faith in God was stronger than any idol: 'We don't believe in idols anymore.'"

All Ahmed's employees know the code word: "hot potatoes." They use it whenever the *mutawwa* are coming. Ahmed has lookouts. Before the *mutawwa* can come upstairs to inspect the gallery, she and her staff quickly hang any potentially controversial paintings upside down or sideways, so the *mutawwa* won't realize what they're looking at. When the *mutawwa* leave, they hang the paintings right side up again.

"I censor myself," she said. "I know the limits; I know what will get us in trouble. I act like the *mutawwa* myself, to protect the artists; I watch over them. The *mutawwa* know I'm a responsible person."

ART IN THE MIDDLE EAST

The distinction between Islamic and Arab art is difficult, if not impossible, to draw. Art historians often define Islamic art with a fairly unhelpful tautology: art produced by people living in Islamic cultures.[2] Well-known for its calligraphy, painting, architecture, and ceramics—Kufic script, Persian miniatures, the Dome of the Rock, and tiles from Isnik—Islamic art has widely avoided the depiction of both human and animal forms. By the end of the nineteenth century, Islamic art had entered a period of stagnation and decline, as it became increasingly subject to western influence as a result of European colonialism.

This is the point at which many art historians identify the emergence of Arab, as opposed to Islamic, art. This is also the period when many Arab artists adopted western styles, including ironically the style of Orientalist painters, who were producing stereotypically exoticized representations of the Middle East. Among the first countries in the Arab world to experience the influence of western aesthetics were Egypt and Lebanon, with the establishment there in the early twentieth century of art schools where modern European art was taught. Arab artists of the period began traveling more frequently to European capitals to study. Many of them abandoned traditional Islamic themes in an effort to imitate western models, a process that continued with the founding of academies and institutes of fine arts in other parts of the Arab world.

After World War II, a new generation of Arab artists came of age who were committed to reestablishing a relationship with their own artistic heritage. This revival involved the assertion of both Arab and Muslim identities and the integration of indigenous subject matter with western styles. The resulting synthesis of western and Arab (or Islamic) art marks the beginning of what has been called Arab modernism.

Early developments in this movement, which were closely associated with other important cultural and political changes taking place at the time, occurred in North Africa and the eastern Mediterranean. The First Cairo International Exhibition of Art was held in 1947, and the American University of Beirut opened its Department of Fine Arts in 1955. By the 1960s, Beirut had become the cultural center of Arab world, with a lively international art scene drawing on the richness of Arab cultures while simultaneously participating fully in new developments in European art. The First Congress of Arab Artists was held in Damascus in 1971, the First Arab Art Biennale took place in Baghdad in 1974, and the Jordan National Gallery of Fine Art was established in Amman in 1980.

Over the next two decades, the center of gravity of the world of contemporary Arab art shifted from the Levant to the Gulf States. Funded by the seemingly limitless growth of oil revenues in the region, interest in contemporary Arab art exploded. New arts NGOs were established, national art museums were founded, and closer ties developed between artists in the Gulf and the West. European museums, galleries, and auction houses began paying attention to the flourishing art scene in the Gulf States, where patronage, scholarships, and prizes fostered the creation of a new artistic community.

In 2006, Abu Dhabi in the United Arab Emirates announced plans to build a Louvre Abu Dhabi *and* a Guggenheim Abu Dhabi. The same year Christie's held its first auction of modern and contemporary Arab art in Dubai. In 2007, the first annual Art Dubai fair was held; and in 2010, the Arab Museum of Modern Art opened in Doha, Qatar. The growing interest in modern Arab art was also marked by the publication of new scholarly monographs, some offering broad surveys of the field, others presenting the work of individual artists. An online magazine entitled *Contemporary Art from the Islamic World* was founded in 2003, and the next year *Bidoun,* a quarterly print magazine dedicated to the art and culture of the Middle East, appeared.

A number of important themes have featured prominently in contemporary Arab art. Perhaps *the* central question for many young Arab artists is how to define and assert their identity as Arabs. What does it mean to be an Arab artist? What is the relationship between Arab cultural traditions and heritage—*turath*—on the one hand, and Arab modernity, on the other?

What does authenticity—*asala*—mean in an Arab world flooded with western fashion, media, and consumer goods? Is the desert the only place left for camels?

The processes of globalization, homogenization, and hybridization that have generated these dilemmas of authenticity—processes that Arjun Appadurai has referred to as "global cultural flows"—are themselves a focus of many contemporary Arab artists.[3] Opposing these trends of cross-cultural exchange, are the significant political and cultural restrictions that citizens of many Arab states confront every day. It is not at all surprising, then, that much contemporary Arab art deals directly or indirectly with the subjects of government surveillance, repression, and censorship. Another prominent theme in this work is the social control of women: the restrictions placed on women's dress, freedom of movement, and educational and professional opportunities. Also inescapable is the impact sectarian violence, revolution, and war have had on the art of the Arab world.

A defining feature of much contemporary Arab art is the pervasive presence of Arabic script. Because figural representation has often been discouraged, calligraphy—the art of handwriting—has always occupied a central place in the world of Islamic art. Contemporary Arab artists have tried to assert their identity as Arabs and express important aspects of their religion and culture by bringing Arabic letters, words, and texts directly into their work. This practice, known as *hurufiyya,* involves experimentation with the use of Arabic script in art. It bridges the gap between traditional Islamic and contemporary Arabic art in creative and intriguing ways by blurring the distinction between calligraphy per se and painting.

Wijdan Ali, founder of the Jordan National Gallery, has coined the delightful term *calligraffiti* to refer to recent developments in the exploration of the role of writing in Arab art. She defines calligraffiti as "personal handwriting" that is "inspired by calligraphy," but that "strips letters of their classical restrictions" and creates "personalized images of them" instead.[4] Calligraffiti exploits the tension between reading a text and viewing an image. Calligraphy evokes all that is formal, traditional, and sacred; graffiti, on the other hand, is associated with the informal, the modern, and the secular. Calligraffiti, then, is a hybrid cultural form wonderfully appropriate for a variety of experimental, installation, and performance works. Artists who use writing in their work by placing a caption or title *in* the composition itself, rather than on a label on a wall nearby, are setting their art firmly in a meaningful religious, literary, and artistic tradition.

As I walked through the upstairs gallery at Desert Designs, a brightly colored digital painting immediately caught my eye. Against a clear blue sky, a red and black Eiffel Tower rises from rolling dunes of yellow sand. In the foreground stand three women dressed entirely in black carrying Louis Vitton handbags whose garish pink, green, and purple colors bleed down onto the trains of their long flowing black *abaya*s. In Arabic script right on the horizon is the title of the painting: *Au Revoir*.

It was clear to me that the artist, Mona al-Qahtani, was commenting playfully on the ironies of a globalized world where Paris meets the desert, where immediately recognizable and immensely desirable artifacts of high fashion meet the "backward" dress of "oppressed" Muslim women. But there were some aspects of the painting I didn't understand. Were the three Saudi women bidding farewell to Paris on their way back to Saudi Arabia? Or were they saying goodbye to their traditional desert way of life on their way to the fashion capitals of Europe?

Au Revoir is one in a series of three paintings by al-Qahtani entitled *Bedouins: The Trendsetters.* Another painting in the series, entitled *Shame on U,* was also on display at Desert Designs: a gray male camel flirts with a bright pink female camel kneeling next to him; he is whispering something in her ear, much to her amusement. In the third painting of the series, *Speedy the Camel,* an orange camel kneels on the sand with a huge, purple Louis Vitton bag for a saddle. *Khaleejesque,* a lifestyle and culture magazine published in Kuwait City, describes al-Qahtani's work enthusiastically as "Andy Warhol meets Bedouins."[5]

Mona al-Qahtani is from the industrial city of Jubail on the east coast of Saudi Arabia, 110 kilometers north of al-Khobar. She is interested in fashion, graphic design, and digital art, and has a deep commitment to promoting art education for children. When I contacted her to inquire about her "Bedouin" paintings, al-Qahtani tried to explain the relationships she felt between the traditional culture she grew up in and the western world of the twenty-first century, where she feels equally at home.

"I'm a Bedouin girl from a Bedouin family," she said. "We don't live in the desert anymore; we're originally from a town in the desert south of Riyadh, where only members of my family live. My grandmother still lives there; she makes money for her cattle by selling dates.

"Camels mean a lot to us; they're icons of patience, adaptation, generosity, and survival. The Louis Vitton bags are part of the fashion craze that's possessed the minds of young Saudis. It saddens me that Saudi woman are thought of as oppressed—always covering up with meters of dull black material. The reality is absolutely the opposite! People think we're poor and that we never get to explore the world. They think we don't have a sense of style because they only see us wearing our *abaya*s and *niqab*s. But we love fashion. A Bedouin wedding is like the red carpet! We love to be up to date and look our best.

"What I'm trying to capture in these paintings is that we can combine modern fashion and culturally authentic fashion. We have the right to create our own heritage, to act freely without being accused of abandoning our values."

Painted directly on the gallery wall around the corner from al-Qahtani's *Au Revoir,* was a work by Hussein al-Mohasen. In the center of a dark blue rectangle, al-Mohasen had spray painted in white a stenciled image of a tank. Lines of white acrylic paint dripped down from the treads of the tank. Across the tank, spray painted in yellow-green Arabic letters was the word *boudha*— "ice cream." Al-Mohasen, who was at Desert Designs that afternoon, offered us his own interpretation of the painting.

"A tank is a scary thing for us in the Middle East. I wanted to change the tank, to transform it into an ice-cream tank, like an ice-cream truck. We need ice cream, not tanks. We don't need to kill people to overthrow regimes. We don't need protests and war and violence. Art is the best form of expression. Art can't be broken."

Al-Mohasen is from Qatif, just north of al-Khobar on the eastern coast of Saudi Arabia. He studied art in Boston and often goes back there to visit museums. He's had solo exhibitions in Jordan, Lebanon, Saudi Arabia, and several of the Gulf States. Al-Mohasen described his work as bridging the gap between fine art and graffiti. He's thought about doing some work on the streets of Qatif, but he's afraid he'd be arrested. He may eventually spray paint some of his new work on walls in Boston or New York. According to the catalog of one of his exhibitions, al-Mohasen is "well known throughout the Middle East for his colorful, expressionist style, referencing Arabic popular culture through his use of calligraphy. He explores these themes through the use of spray paint and stencils, creating calligraphic graffiti."

While al-Mohasen said that Saudi officials had never censored any of his work, he admitted that some of his new paintings were controversial. As we crowded tightly around him, he showed us photographs of some of his most recent work on his iPhone. This was the only way he could show them to us, since they'd never been exhibited in Saudi Arabia.

Against backgrounds of blue, red, and gray, we could make out small, black, stenciled images of the famous photograph of President George W. Bush being informed of the attack on the World Trade Center as he sat reading a children's book to students at an elementary school in Sarasota, Florida on September 11, 2001. Al-Mohasen had produced several versions of this work, which is entitled *I Love Music*. Each one has a different caption in which al-Mohasen imagines President Bush receiving a very different message from the one he actually received on that terrible day. One reads, "I Love Music, Poetry, and my Small Garden"; another reads "Toi Qui Sait," a reference, al-Mohasen explained, to a calm, flowing piece for oud, piano, and accordion, by Anouar Brahem, a Tunisian composer. In this work al-Mohasen pointedly substitutes lighthearted messages of happiness and joy for the painful messages of tragedy and horror that are all too often associated with recent events in the Middle East.

As we looked at small images of his work on al-Mohasen's iPhone, the actual paintings were on display at a solo exhibition at the XVA Gallery in the Dubai International Finance Center. Al-Mohasen told us that if his exhibition in Dubai goes well, he would try to show it in Saudi Arabia. He's testing the water gradually to see whether it's well received or whether it's attacked by the *mutawwa*.

ART IN SAUDI ARABIA

Throughout the eighteenth and nineteenth centuries most of the Arabian Peninsula remained relatively isolated from the artistic and cultural developments taking place in western Europe, the Mediterranean, and other parts of the Middle East. With the exception of the Hijaz on the Red Sea coast, which includes Jeddah and the two holy cities of Mecca and Medina, the Ottoman Empire exerted very little influence over the peninsula. During the early decades of the twentieth century, Abdulaziz ibn Saud expanded his rule over much of the region and in 1932 founded the Kingdom of Saudi Arabia with the support of the conservative Wahhabi religious authorities. The discovery of oil in the 1930s transformed the country tremendously, but it remained in many ways a very closed and traditional society. With the oil boom that followed, cars and cement came to dominate the Saudi landscape.

The introduction of a western educational system in the 1950s brought with it art teachers from Egypt, Lebanon, and Palestine. By the 1970s, the first organizations devoted to supporting the fine arts were established. Then in the 1980s, as a result of the Iranian Revolution and the siege of the Holy Mosque in Mecca by Islamist extremists, the Kingdom entered an extremely conservative period in its history. Religiously based restrictions on the mixing of men and women; on photography and the depiction of the human form; and on women's freedom of dress, movement, and employment were strictly enforced.

It was difficult for the few Saudi artists working in the country to obtain the materials they needed. They had to purchase paint and canvas from abroad; they even found it difficult to buy art books, since depictions of the human figure were forbidden. Female artists couldn't attend the openings of exhibitions of their own work. At the beginning of the twenty-first century, there was still virtually no contemporary art scene in Saudi Arabia. There was no infrastructure to support the development of the arts—no schools, no journals, no galleries. Even films couldn't be shown in public, since—with a few exceptions—there were no movie theaters in the country.

By 2012, the contemporary art scene in Saudi Arabia had come alive. As the director of one art gallery told me, "Modern art is booming here." Young artists doing comic book art, conceptual art, digital art, installation art, performance art, pop art, street art, and video art were forming networks and collaboratives all around the country. Several new art galleries had even opened in Riyadh, one of the most conservative cities in the Kingdom.

The Lam Gallery opened in an upscale mall in Riyadh in 2005. Originally established as a gallery for female artists from the Gulf, it has since broadened its focus to include a broad range of paintings, photographs, and sculptures from the all over Middle East. Lamya al-Rashed, Lam's founder and director, said that when she opened the gallery her male guardian had to sign the official paperwork. She admitted that she'd experienced some difficulties with the religious police. The *mutawwa* had confiscated all her favorite art books, because they contained photographs of ancient Greek statues of nude men and women. They even removed some works of sculpture that were on exhibit in the gallery. A male visitor had been offended and called the *mutawwa*.

"Some people in Saudi still don't understand art," she said. "But Saudi artists enjoy much more freedom of expression now then they ever did before."

Edge of Arabia is a new, nonprofit arts initiative dedicated to promoting the contemporary art of Saudi Arabia and the entire Arab world. It has rapidly become one of the most important institutions in the Saudi contemporary art scene. On its website, Edge of Arabia describes itself as "Saudi Arabia's first independent platform for contemporary art." From its base in London, Edge of Arabia is bringing the work of new Saudi artists to the attention of international audiences by sponsoring seminars, publications, and exhibitions. It works closely with some twenty-five artists in Saudi Arabia and an equal number from elsewhere in the Arab world and the diaspora. Much of its funding comes from Abdul Latif Jameel Community Initiatives, the corporate social responsibility wing of the ALJ Company, a Saudi-based multinational conglomerate with investments in hotels, electronics, automobiles, and financial services.

Edge of Arabia was founded by two young Saudi artists, Ahmed Mater and Abdulnasser Gharem, and a British artist, Stephen Stapleton, when they met in 2003 at the al-Meftaha Arts Village, a local arts community that had recently been established in the city of Abha under the sponsorship of the governor of Asir, a poor region in the mountains of southwestern Saudi Arabia near the border with Yemen.[6] The first major exhibition sponsored by Edge of Arabia was held in the Brunei Gallery at the School for Oriental and African Studies at the University of London in 2008. The exhibition generated an overwhelmingly positive response. Three years later, at the Fifty-fourth Venice Biennale, Edge of Arabia produced the first Pan-Arab exhibition of contemporary art. It has also provided valuable international exposure to Saudi artists with exhibitions in Berlin, Istanbul, and Dubai.

The most exciting show Edge of Arabia has organized was its first public exhibition inside Saudi Arabia, which opened to much acclaim in January 2012. This "homecoming" of sorts was the first, and by far the most significant, exhibition of contemporary art to have ever taken place in the Kingdom. The exhibition, entitled We Need to Talk, was held in an unfinished wing of the al-Furisiya Marina and Mall in Jeddah. As Stephen Stapleton told a reporter from the *New York Times* at the opening, modern art is hardly the first thing people associate with Saudi Arabia.[7]

The curators of "We Need to Talk" recognized the need to make the show accessible to local Saudi audiences, many of whom were completely unfamiliar with contemporary art. Mater, Gharem, and Stapleton were determined to be "gently provocative." Officials from the Saudi Ministry of Culture and Information inspected the exhibition and removed one work. Eight representatives of Christie's and four from Sotheby's attended the opening. The exhibition included forty works by twenty-two Saudi artists, half of whom were women.

The title of the exhibition suggests the emphasis the organizers placed on the need for open conversation—genuine dialogue—about the place of art in contemporary Saudi society. It also acknowledged the many controversial issues that were raised by the art itself—the position of women, freedom of speech, human rights, and the role of Islam in Saudi society. After all, King Abdullah was known as the "King of Dialogue" because of his repeated calls for national dialogue among the various segments of Saudi society.

The success of Edge of Arabia has been impressive. The contemporary Saudi art it has presented to international audiences powerfully demonstrates the creativity and vitality of Saudi culture. This success is testament to the dramatic changes that have transformed Saudi society—the rise of individualism and consumerism, the growth of new technologies and social media—but it also confirms the continued relevance of traditional Islamic beliefs and tribal practices. In this way, Edge of Arabia opens an instructive window Europeans are rarely privileged to look through, a window onto the complexity and richness of Saudi culture in the second decade of the twenty-first century. Here contemporary Saudi artists are testing the limits of what is possible in their very conservative culture. They are working right at the edge of Arabia.

MANAL AL-DOWAYAN: "EACH PHOTOGRAPH I TAKE IS PART OF MY SOUL"

The work of Manal al-Dowayan has featured prominently in exhibitions sponsored by Edge of Arabia. Born in 1973, al-Dowayan grew up in what she calls the "semi-cocooned camp" of the Aramco compound in Dhahran.[8] Of the sixty young women in her high school class, she was the only one who refused to sign a petition denouncing the women who participated in the 1990 protest against the ban on women driving. Al-Dowayan's work can be found in the permanent collections of the British Museum and the Jordan National Gallery of Fine Art; she is now represented by the Cuadro Fine Art Gallery in Dubai. For many years, al-Dowayan has been employed as a computer information systems analyst for Saudi Aramco. The company, she says, has always been supportive of her work as an artist.

Al-Dowayan is committed to documenting the struggle of Saudi women against the many restrictions that limit the roles they're allowed to play in Saudi society. *My Name* is an installation project that consists of seven huge strings of Muslim prayer beads hanging down from the ceiling, their long tassels suspended just above the floor. Each string consists of about thirty soccer-ball-sized beads on which a Saudi woman has written her name in bold, black Arabic script. To create *My Name,* al-Dowayan invited several hundred women from all over the Kingdom to attend a workshop in December 2011. During the workshop, each woman wrote her name on one of the large prayer beads. Then al-Dowayan strung them together to form one collaborative piece. She was delighted at the sense of community and warmth that developed among the women who participated in the project.

The power of this particular work stems from the close relationship between a woman's name and her identity, and from the taboo associated with the public use of women's names in Saudi culture. Many Saudis, both men and women, consider it inappropriate and disrespectful to use a woman's name in public. With *My Name,* al-Dowayan seems to be suggesting that traditions like this, which are often justified as demonstrating respect for women, can at the same time serve to deprive them of their individuality and their identity. Al-Dowayan hopes that *My Name* will empower not only the Saudi women who participated in making it, but also the Saudi women who see it. In this way, she says, "we will not allow Saudi woman's names to be erased, replaced, or become a source of shame."[9]

In another installation that has been displayed in several Edge of Arabia exhibitions, al-Dowayan confronts a striking limitation imposed by the Saudi state on the freedom of movement of its female citizens. *Suspended Together* consists of some two hundred white laminated fiberglass doves, each about a foot long from head to tail with a wingspread of three feet. Some of the doves stand perched on the gallery floor looking around nervously or pecking on the ground for food, but most of them seem to fly freely, swirling around each other in a tight flock. But of course these doves aren't really free; they can't fly at all. They just hang there, frozen in midair, completely immobile, suspended by thin wires from a metal frame that hangs down from the gallery ceiling.

A closer look reveals that on the shiny white surface of each dove al-Dowayan has carefully reproduced the official document that every Saudi woman must have in order to travel outside the Kingdom, her *muwafaqa,* complete with a blue stamp, the small yellow and green Saudi state seal, and the signature of the woman's *mahram,* her male guardian, giving her permission to travel abroad. To create this piece, al-Dowayan collected the travel documents of many Saudi women—scientists and engineers, young girls and old women—in order to demonstrate that "regardless of age and achievement, when it comes to travel, all these women are treated like a flock of suspended doves."[10] In the catalog of a 2009 exhibition in Dubai, the doves were naked; the reproductions of the women's travel documents had been removed from their bodies with no explanation. A short time later, al-Dowayan was surprised to see photographs of her doves wearing their travel documents again in the in-flight magazine of Saudia, the Saudi national airline.

"Saudi artists," al-Dowayan observed, "are constantly negotiating self-imposed censorship and layers of self-appointed censors."

Black-and-white photography is another important component of al-Dowayan's work. She has produced several series of stark photographs depicting the challenges facing contemporary Saudi women. In *I Am,* al-Dowayan presents portraits of successful Saudi career women trapped between the traditional Saudi jewelry that partially covers their faces and the objects they work with in their traditionally male professions. With this series al-Dowayan raises many unsettling questions. "What job suits my nature as a woman?" she asks. "Where can women work? And what can they do? Is my nature as a woman another limitation on my potential that I need to overcome or accept?"[11]

In *I am a Computer Scientist,* a white keyboard covers the right half of a woman's face. In *I Am a Petroleum Engineer,* a woman wears a white plastic safety helmet and a worker's uniform with a patch stressing "Safety First," while her entire face except for her eyes is covered in a heavy veil made of braided metal work, filigree, chains, and old coins. And in *I Am an Educator,* a woman wears a thick metal headband over her forehead and elaborate metal bracelets that suggest handcuffs. She holds up a blackboard that covers the lower half of her face. Written over and over again on the blackboard in neat Arabic script is the short sentence, "Ignorance is Darkness. Ignorance is Darkness. Ignorance is Darkness." The mouths of the women in al-Dowayan's photographs are often covered, but through her work their voices can be clearly heard.

In another series of photographs entitled *The Choice,* al-Dowayan offers dramatic images that capture the tension of the present moment when Saudi women confront a future full of difficult options. *The Choice VI* is a tight, closely cropped photograph of a woman voting. Her hand, beautifully deco-rated with floral patterns of henna and dark fingernail polish, inserts a white paper ballot into the top of a black ballot box, which is locked shut with a large, slightly out-of-focus padlock. In *The Choice,* the image the series is named after, a woman holds a car steering wheel over her face so that her nose, mouth, and chin are completely covered by the hub of the wheel. She grips the brightly lit steering wheel in her right hand, which is decorated with henna. Encircling her head and shoulders, the steering wheel forms a huge halo—or is it a peace sign? Her eyes look out at the viewer through the upper opening of the steering wheel; her hair is just visible through a diaphanous black *hijab.* Is she asking for something? Demanding something? (see fig. 5).

"Each photograph I take," says al-Dowayan, "is part of my soul."[12]

AHMED MATER: THE SON OF THIS STRANGE AND SCARY OIL CIVILIZATION

Ahmed Mater, one of the cofounders of Edge of Arabia, is a pioneering figure in contemporary Saudi art. Prince Khalid al-Faisal, the governor of Mecca, said that Mater "woke up a slumbering corner of the world with a brush and a camera."[13] Born in 1979 in a small village in the Asir region, Mater was introduced to art at an early age by his mother, a painter and calligrapher. When his family moved to Abha, the provincial capital, Mater was exposed to a very different world.

"The new, globalized culture made me question the values established by my conservative upbringing," Mater told an interviewer. "I had assimilated all these ideas in my childhood; then I tried to destroy them. A dilemma arose from this turmoil, and I began to explore my obedience, my religion—everything that surrounded me. All of this influenced what I call 'the change' and gave birth to new experiments in my art."[14]

As a young man of nineteen, Mater entered the Abha College of Medicine. The following year he joined the al-Meftaha Arts Village. Some of his early work—religious symbols and texts painted on x-rays of human beings—stirred controversy when they were first exhibited in the Kingdom in 2004, but they also attracted the attention of European critics and curators. In 2005, one of Mater's "x-ray paintings" was purchased by the British Museum, and his work received the endorsement of King Abdullah. Since then he has had solo exhibitions in Dubai, Beirut, and London.

Mater continues to live in Abha, where he pursues his two careers. As a physician he treats Saudi soldiers who have been wounded in fighting on the border with Yemen; as an artist he explores new visual languages to express his identities as a Saudi, an Arab, and a Muslim. In a trailer for *Detour,* a documentary film about contemporary Saudi art produced by Edge of Arabia, Mater says "An artist is an agent of change or a revolutionary in a beautiful way, in a humane way."[15]

Like much of Mater's best work, *Magnetism* epitomizes the creative synthesis of religious tradition and scientific experiment. It is both an installation piece and a work of photography. Mater has placed a magnet, a small black cube, on a bright white surface; he has hidden another magnet out of sight under the white surface. When he spreads a thin layer of thousands of black iron filings around the magnet, something miraculous, but entirely predictable and natural, occurs. Energized by the magnetic field, the iron filings stand vertically on end. As Mater twists the magnet, thousands of tiny particles of iron begin whirling slowly around it in concentric circles (see fig. 6).

To someone immersed in the world of science, Mater's work may evoke electrons spinning around the nucleus of an atom, miniature planetary rings revolving around a tiny black Saturn, or huge galaxies rotating eternally in deep space. But to someone immersed in the world of Islam, these are *not* the images that Mater's work evokes. To a Muslim, *Magnetism* immediately suggests the *tawaf,* the counterclockwise, seven-fold circumambulation of the Kaba in the Holy Mosque of Mecca, which is the high point of the Hajj, the pilgrimage that every Muslim should perform at least once.

The magnet is the Kaba, the small building that stands at the center of the Holy Mosque draped in a black silk curtain embroidered with quotations from the Quran in gold. According to Islamic tradition, the Kaba was built by Abraham; it was the first building in which humans worshiped Allah; it is the navel of the earth. The iron filings are the human beings who worship Allah as they circle the Kaba. In Mater's piece, the iron filings are energized by the magnetic field that engulfs them. What power attracts millions of pilgrims to Mecca every year? What force prevents non-Muslims from entering the sacred zone around Mecca, where only Muslims are allowed to go?[16] According to Mater, *Magnetism* had its origin in a simple childhood game he used to play.

All our parents and ancestors thought about the Hajj. They used to say there was a magical attraction, something irresistible drawing you to this spiritual state of mind. One day I remembered a game we used to play. We used iron filings and a magnet. We put the magnet in the middle, and the filings would create this circular shape like a procession. There was such an attraction that the filings erected, as if turning, in a procession, in adoration. A beautiful attraction.[17]

The *Yellow Cow* is an even more playful piece of conceptual art, and it too is influenced by the pervasive role of Islam in contemporary Saudi culture. One day during a visit to his family's farm in the mountains of Asir, Mater was thinking about a story in the Quran, the story of the yellow cow, a story that all Muslim children learn. Mater imagined "living the experience" of the yellow cow, which had influenced him so much when he was a boy. Mater decided to paint one of his family's cows yellow. He mixed saffron powder with water, took a big sponge, and proceeded to paint a cow a beautiful bright saffron yellow. The other cows in the herd were afraid of it and refused to come near, but it pleased everyone who saw it. People had never seen anything like it.

Mater documented the project with still photographs and a short film. He wondered what else he could do with his yellow cow. What would happen if he transformed this ancient religious story, this fond childhood memory, into something more contemporary, more useful, more profitable? What would happen if he introduced the yellow cow of the Quran into the secular world of twenty-first-century capitalism? Should he kill it and sell its meat? No. But what about "mass producing" a whole line of Yellow Cow brand products—Yellow Cow milk, Yellow Cow yoghurt, and Yellow Cow cheese?

That's when Mater started selling his new line of "ideologically free" Yellow Cow products at art shows and exhibitions around the world. At the 2007 Sharjah Biennial in the United Arab Emirates, Mater—sporting a Yellow Cow baseball cap—stood in front of a wall of shelves well stocked with bright yellow and blue packages of Yellow Cow dairy products, each bearing the Yellow Cow logo—the smiling face of the Yellow Cow herself, complete with red lipstick, a white flower on one horn, and a cow bell hanging from her right ear.[18]

In the second sura, or chapter, of the Quran, *al-Baqarah* (The Cow), Moses tells the ancient Israelites that God has instructed them to sacrifice a cow. Instead of just complying with God's straightforward request, the children of Israel insist on knowing what kind of cow—how old a cow, what color cow—they should sacrifice. "Behold," replies Moses. "He says it is to be a yellow cow, bright of hue and pleasing to the beholder." Finally the children of Israel obey God's instructions. They sacrifice the cow, although, as the Quran explicitly puts it, they "almost left it undone" (2:69).

What are we to make of the original story of the yellow cow? And what are we to make of Mater's Yellow Cow brand dairy products? From the perspective of many Muslims, the moral of the story is perfectly clear. Don't complicate things! Don't ask too many questions! Some scholars, however, have suggested that the ancient Israelites were trying to circumvent their obligation to God by making His command virtually impossible to fulfill.[19] Mater seems to be suggesting that mass production and consumption run the risk of destroying traditional cultural forms and the values they embody. What happens when all those Yellow Cow products are thrown away?

With *Evolution of Man,* Mater's playful sense of humor turns bitterly caustic. Five jet-black rectangular light boxes hang next to one another on a gallery wall. Each displays a slightly different x-ray illuminated from behind by a bright blue light. The x-rays morph from a sharply outlined gasoline pump, at one end, to the skeletal image of a man holding a pistol to his head, at the other. In the middle three images, the nozzle of the gas pump gradually turns into a human hand holding a pistol, while the body of the gas pump grows progressively more irregular and curved, until it becomes the x-ray of a human head and torso (see fig. 7).

One of the first questions viewers face, when confronted by this work, is literally how to read it. From left to right, as texts in European languages are read? Or from right to left, as texts in Arabic are read? On Mater's website, in several books, and in an exhibition in Jeddah, the sequence from left to right is from the gasoline pump to the act of suicide. In exhibitions in Cairo, Dubai, and London, however, the sequence is reversed. Does it matter? Is the ambiguity intentional? How can we tell?

What is clear, though, is that Mater is asserting a relationship between the oil industry, which has transformed Saudi society and continues to dominate its economy, on the one hand, and the act of suicide, on the other. Mater, who was born in a small farming village, has referred to himself as "the son of this strange and scary oil civilization." He has also remarked that "in ten years our lives changed completely. For me it is a drastic change that I experience every day."[20] From Mater's perspective, the oil industry and the petrodollars it has generated have had a destructive effect on Saudi society. It is also this very oil wealth that the Saudi government has used to promote the world-wide spread of Wahhabism, one of the fundamentalist approaches to Islam of the kind that the extremists of al-Qaeda and the Islamic State have invoked to justify the death and destruction they have wreaked in Saudi Arabia and elsewhere around the world.

This critique of the oil industry is not the only taboo subject that Mater confronts in *Evolution of Man*. The prohibition on the depiction of the human form, which constrains much Islamic art, continues to restrict contemporary Saudi artists. By using x-rays, Mater draws from the scientific and technological world of his career as a physician to work around this restriction. At the same time, he is able—literally—to see beneath the skin of Saudis who have lived through the cultural changes that oil has brought and reveal their inner worlds. In this way, Mater documents the psychological power with which oil is able to colonize people's minds. *Evolution of Man* raises two other subjects that are taboo in Saudi culture: the act of suicide, which is strictly forbidden in Islam, and the Darwinian theory of evolution, which is widely regarded, not simply as false, but as heretical in Saudi Arabia and many other parts of the Muslim—and the Christian—worlds.

"Through my art," Mater says, "I am clearly making a critique. I am also acting as a witness to the changes and taking part with an opinion and a voice. I believe the artist's role is to expose the truth."[21]

ABDULNASSER GHAREM: THE VOICE OF HIS SOCIETY

Adbulnasser Gharem, another cofounder of Edge of Arabia, made Arab art history in April 2011 at Christie's Dubai, when one of his works sold for $842,500, the highest price ever paid for the work of a living Arab artist. Suddenly Gharem, who agreed to donate all the proceeds from the sale to Edge of Arabia to help nurture a new generation of Saudi artists, had become "the Rock Star of Arab Art."[22] Like his close colleague Ahmed Mater, Gharem is from a small mountain village in the Asir region and studied at the al-Meftaha Arts Village in Abha. He attended secondary school there with two of the fifteen Saudi citizens who participated in the attack on the World Trade Center in New York on September 11, 2001. He is now a major in the Saudi army.

Gharem is a conceptual artist best known for his performance works and his site-specific installations. A monograph on his work, which has been exhibited in Berlin, Venice, and London, was published in 2011. In interviews, Gharem has discussed what it means to him to be an artist working in Saudi Arabia:

The strict traditions that have been passed on through generations have put a taboo on art. That has been one of the biggest challenges for me. But thanks to Allah, these challenges have taught me how to be more patient and tolerant. Things have changed though in a kind of slow motion. Art is a tool for making positive changes in the community. In simple words, an artist is the voice of a society. Artists can play a bigger role by constructively criticizing the ills of the society to render it as beautiful as it can be.[23]

One of Gharem's most controversial and powerful works had its origins in a disastrous accident that occurred in 1982 in a ravine near a village in the rugged mountains south of Abha, not far from the Yemeni border. After heavy rains, authorities warned of flash floods. Villagers placed their faith in concrete and steel, and took refuge with their vehicles and livestock on a large bridge that had recently been built across the ravine. Tragically, the bridge was washed away, and many people were swept to their deaths. Huge pieces of the roadway can still be seen in the riverbed downstream from what is left of the bridge. As often happens, the disaster was never reported in the Saudi media. A legend has it that the bridge was built by the Binladin Group. When a company official boasted that the bridge would last a hundred years, he forgot to say "Mashallah"—"Allah has willed it"—and the destruction of the bridge was Allah's punishment for this act of disrespect.[24]

In 2003, after driving past the site of the disaster for years, Gharem, with the help of twenty-four assistants, spent four days and three nights painting the word *siraat*—"path" or "way"—thousands and thousands of times in white spray paint all over the roadway of the stump of the bridge that projected out over the river bed (see fig. 8). Gharem also made a short film documenting the project. With a night vision video camera, he filmed two men spray-painting the cracked asphalt. Dimly lit by several hand-held flashlights, Arabic script spreads over the roadway. The camera follows the double yellow line in the center of the road until it stops suddenly at the jagged end of the damaged bridge. With the camera, we peer over the edge and see the headlights of cars driving along the gravel road in the bed of the ravine below. Somber piano music and ghostly voices can be heard in the background. And in the strangest touch of all, a herd of goats wander back and forth across the road.

Siraat remained secret for years. Then in 2008, Edge of Arabia planned to display Gharem's still photographs and film of the project for the first time at an exhibition in the Brunei Gallery in London. But this was not to be. According to one report, a false rumor spread that Gharem had blasphemously written verses of the Quran on the surface of a road, which had been defaced by car tires and people's feet. According to another report, curators decided not to include the work in order to avoid offending one of the exhibition's major sponsors. In any event, just three weeks before the opening of the exhibition Gharem learned that *Siraat* would not be shown.[25]

When he returned to Saudi Arabia after the show, Gharem mounted a successful publicity campaign to rehabilitate his reputation. In 2011, when *Siraat* was finally exhibited at the Fifty-fourth Venice Biennale, the Saudi minister of culture and information saw it and responded positively. Since then, *Siraat* has been shown in Berlin and Istanbul; it has also been purchased for the collections of the Victoria and Albert Museum in London and the Los Angeles County Museum of Modern Art. Gharem has provided details of the location of *Siraat* on his website and occasionally art tourists travel to the mountains of Asir to visit it.

Like much of even the most avant-garde contemporary Saudi art, *Siraat* draws its meaning and power from the Quran. In this work, Gharem is clearly making reference to the *siraat al-mustaqim*—the straight path, the path that pleases God, the path of Islam—that is mentioned in the first sura of the Quran, where Muslims pray to Allah: "Guide us along the straight path—the path of those upon whom Thou hast bestowed Thy blessings" (1:6–7). This phrase is repeated many times every day by Muslims when they pray.

"Al-Siraat" is also the name of the bridge over Hell, well known in Islamic tradition, that all humans must cross before they enter paradise. This bridge, this path, is "thinner than a hair and sharper than a sword." Believers will cross over it in the blink of an eye, with the speed of lightening, while the wicked, snared by thorns and hooks, will fall off and burn in the fires of hell for eternity.

Asir villagers took refuge on a bridge recently built of concrete and steel by the Saudi government. This bridge, however, was not strong enough to save them from being washed away by a flood. These villagers were on a path connecting life and death; their worlds were destroyed. But by water, not by fire. With the act of writing—an act of graffiti or an act of calligraphy?—Gharem commemorates an unwritten, and therefore unknown, tragedy. He brings religious imagery and sacred texts to bear—literally—on the site of a terrible accident by writing on it. In this way he explores our relationships with the human structures and the natural forces that surround us. He calls into question the relationship between Saudi citizens and their state, as well as the relationship between devout Muslims and their God, Allah.

The Athr Gallery is located in the Serafi Mega Mall on Tahlia Street in Jeddah, in a neighborhood of popular shops and restaurants named after a huge desalinization plant that stands nearby. Founded in 2009, Athr is widely considered the leading art gallery in the Kingdom. In addition to representing many of the best contemporary Saudi artists, the gallery provides a public space for lectures, seminars, and workshops designed to generate dialogue on important issues facing Saudi society.

We had come to the Athr Gallery on the last day of our stay in Saudi Arabia to participate in a workshop led by Saddek Wasil, a young Saudi artist whose first solo exhibition, They Will Not Cease to Differ, had recently opened there.[26] The exhibition's title is from the Quran (11:118): "And if your Lord had so willed, He could have made mankind one community; but [He willed it otherwise, and so] they will not cease to differ." Wasil seems to be suggesting that this passage from the Quran provides divine sanction for the celebration of the extraordinary linguistic and cultural diversity that characterizes humanity, the people of Saudi Arabia, and the pilgrims who come as "guests of God" to the Holy Mosque in Mecca.

At the entrance to the gallery, we found ourselves face to face with a row of five *dallah,* the brass coffee pots with long spouts used for serving Arabic coffee in the traditional ritual of Saudi hospitality. These *dallah,* however, looked nothing like the ones we had seen at Desert Designs in al-Khobar at the beginning of our trip. These *dallah* stood on a huge, hand-made bumper of a jeep or truck that was hanging from the ceiling against a white gallery wall. Each *dallah* had been transformed in a different way; each of them *differed* from the others. One was wearing a gas mask; another was wearing headphones; another was completely covered in red packing tape with "Fragile" written all over it. Is the traditional vessel of Saudi sociality at risk of being broken by violence and rapid social change?

When we entered the gallery, we were surrounded by intense, even grim, works of industrial art. *Faces of Tin* contained row after row of blue spray cans—cans of starch—flattened out to form strange, elongated metal faces. In a similar work, these eerie metal faces and a battered stop sign were locked behind a grid of metal bars. On another wall hung a series of metal "African masks"—distorted faces made from gears, tangled chains, and coiled steel bands.

Saddek Wasil is a large man with short black hair and a neatly trimmed mustache and goatee. His face testifies to his family's origins in Central Asia; his grease stained clothes and hands to the years he's spent with hammer and blowtorch creating strong, hard art from the scrap metal and used car parts he found in his father's garage in Mecca. His father can't believe the junk he makes is art.[27]

Wasil worked individually with Bates students and with several young Saudi women wearing *abaya*s and *niqab*s, who were also attending the workshop. After giving each of them safety glasses to wear, he set out his tools and art materials on the floor: a hammer, a power drill, a rectangular block of wood, a thick art book, a handful of huge nails, and a pile of heavy steel screws.

With the help of a translator, Wasil began by telling the first volunteer, a female student from Bates, to hammer the book onto the block of wood.

"Your anger is going into the art," he said. "That's why art is full of energy. You have to have powerful feelings in order to make strong art. Hit it again! Hit it again!"

But Olivia mishit the nail, bending it over to one side.

"You had too much anger," Wasil said. "You didn't focus on the art. You need to balance energy and control. It takes time."

Olivia's next nail entered the wood straight and true. We all applauded.

After the book was securely nailed to the block of wood, a young Saudi woman knelt down, took the power drill nervously in her hands, and started to drive the heavy hex-head screws into the wood to form a shiny metal frame around the book.

"Don't be scared!" Wasil encouraged her. "When you're scared, it's not art. Use both hands! Good! Good! It's a different energy with a power tool. You're just directing it. With the hammer, you use physical effort."

A student asked Wasil why he worked with metal.

"It's pure," he said. "It's strong. Art gives me strong feelings, the feeling that I can change things. It gives me the chance to meet different people, have them see my art, and communicate my emotions to them."

As students gained more confidence and began working on their own, Wasil shared more of his thoughts with us.

"Women are often afraid of tools. Then they learn how to drill, and they feel good, and they smile. If you don't have the courage to do things like this, what kind of life will you have? If you're afraid, it's hard to be brave. But fear is like a dog following you. You run faster than you ever thought you could.

You feel fear with the first nail. With the second, there's still some fear. When you feel no fear at all, you don't have any focus, and you loose everything. Fear is in all of us—fear of the future, fear of getting lost, fear of death. But with fear comes change."

At the end of the workshop, the manager of the gallery gave each of us a copy of the exhibition catalog. The students all wanted Wasil to sign their copy. Initially he hesitated, but then he agreed; he'd sign it for them as a gift. I told him he had already given them a gift, a much greater gift—his art. Moved, Wasil said he wanted to give me a gift. But first, I must promise to accept it. I did. Then he took my head in his hands, bent it toward him, and kissed me on the forehead.

FOUR

Finding Science in the Quran

CREATIONISM AND CONCORDISM IN ISLAM

Thousands of fossils show that rabbits have always been rabbits. The evident fact revealed by fossils is that living species did not evolve; God created them.[1]

THE NATIONAL MUSEUM OF SAUDI ARABIA, the centerpiece of the King Abdulaziz Historical Center in Riyadh, was built in 1999 as part of the centennial celebrations (calculated according to the Islamic, or Hijri, calendar) commemorating the capture of the city by Abdulaziz ibn Saud, the first king of Saudi Arabia, in 1902. The museum's gently curved, dun-colored west wall faces the old Murabba Palace and was designed to evoke the canyon walls of the dry Najd highlands that dominate the central region of the Arabian Peninsula.

At the entrance to the first gallery, which is called "Man and the Universe," stands a large meteorite that was discovered by H. St. John Philby, a British Arabist and explorer, during his travels in the Rub al-Khali desert, the Empty Quarter, in southeast Saudi Arabia. Just behind the meteorite is a small booth containing a diorama depicting the Big Bang—swirling nebulae of red, blue, and purple stellar dust and gasses. A small plaque contains a passage from the Quran (7:54): "Your Guardian Lord is Allah, Who created the heavens and the earth in six days; then He established Himself on the Throne. He draweth the night as a veil over the day, each seeking the other in rapid succession. He created the sun, the moon, and the stars, governed by laws under His command."

Other exhibits in the gallery are devoted to the solar system, plate tectonics, fossils of extinct animals, and, of specific interest to many Saudis, the domestication of the camel. After several galleries introducing the pre-Islamic cultures of Arabia, visitors enter a dark tunnel representing the Jahiliyya period, the "Age of Ignorance" that preceded the coming of Islam. The clashing swords and the cries of pain and agony of Muhammad's desert warriors and their enemies fill the tunnel. At the end of the tunnel, an escalator leads up to a large, brightly lit hall devoted to the "Prophet's Mission."

In the center of the room, encased in glass, is a beautiful handwritten, leather-bound copy of the Quran. The walls of the room are bathed in a rainbow of colored light and covered with panels full of detailed information about the life of the Prophet. The rest of the galleries in the museum deal with the history of Islam in the Arabian Peninsula, the Saudi state, King Abdulaziz himself, and the Hajj.

Even more impressive than the National Museum in Riyadh is the Museum of Science and Technology in Islam on the campus of the King Abdullah University of Science and Technology. KAUST was built in 2009 on the Red Sea coast, an hour's drive north of Jeddah, the most cosmopolitan city in the country. The museum takes advantage of the latest technology—multitouch tables, automated scale models, and an intimate big-screen video theater—to celebrate the extraordinary accomplishments of Muslim scientists, inventors, and engineers who lived during the golden age of Islam between the seventh and the seventeenth centuries. The nine "clusters" into which the museum is organized explore the contributions Muslim scholars have made to the fields of architecture, astronomy, chemistry, and mathematics. The "Life and Environmental Sciences" cluster contains exhibits on geology, biology, botany, and animal biodiversity.

We visited the Museum of Science and Technology in Islam at KAUST on May 16, 2012. Our guide was Ibrahim, a young Saudi who had recently graduated from the University of Washington with a degree in economics. The lobby of the museum was dominated by a six-meter-tall sculpture of a molecule of DNA. Running horizontally between the strands of this huge double helix were several clear plastic tubes, representing the backbones of the DNA molecule, each of which contained a sample of nature's biological diversity—a lizard, a fish head, a sea shell, a bird beak. This "Spiral of Life" symbolized the disciplines of bioscience and bioengineering, two of the main fields of teaching and research at KAUST.

A short film introduced visitors to the museum and to the university as a whole. King Abdullah directed Saudi Aramco to build KAUST to serve as a "Modern House of Wisdom," "an Arab MIT," that would spark a revival of science and technology in the Muslim world and contribute in important ways to the benefit of all humanity. Ibrahim showed us sextants, water clocks, and chemistry labs from the golden age of Islam; he described the contributions of Muslim scholars like the Persian mathematician al-Khwarizmi, whose Latin name al-Goritmi is the source of the English word "algorithm." Ibrahim emphasized that Islam was not opposed to science, the way Christianity was, and he contrasted the support that early Muslim religious authorities gave scientists with the persecution of Galileo by the Catholic Church.

"Muslim scholars laid the foundations for the Renaissance in Europe," he said. "I'm not trying to proselytize you, I'm just telling you our history."

Ibrahim also told us that according to Prophet Muhammad, when it comes to religion, you should believe and not ask questions, but when it comes to science you can ask anything you want. I decided to take advantage of the opportunity and asked Ibrahim what he thought about evolution.

"As a Muslim," he said, "I'm told that no matter what, I'll never find anything that contradicts Islam. I haven't found a conclusive answer about evolution that conflicts with my faith. Nothing in science discounts what I believe as a Muslim. These things don't affect me as a man of faith.

"How do we know that God didn't create life and destroy it many times?" he asked. "The problem with science is that it becomes so aggressive and attacks religion. Science drags Islam into conflict. The modern world brought that conflict; science was never heretical in the Islamic world before.

"We believe blindly everything written in the Holy Book. If it's written, it's a true fact. When God says it, it's true. If we don't accept the word of the Quran, it's a big problem. As Muslims, it's not our job to decipher everything. The key issue is: 'Will it make me a good human being?' All other questions are unimportant. Religion is supposed to guide the way we live, but science has to control everything. Scientists are trying to disprove religion, but I believe that science and faith can coexist at different levels."

Some Bates students were beginning to look uncomfortable as my conversation with Ibrahim became more intense, but I decided this was an appropriate time to push the issue. After all, I was talking to an official guide in a university museum of science and technology. I asked Ibrahim if he believed that human beings and great apes were descended from common primate ancestors.

"You mean do I believe that early human beings were apelike? No! I believe in Adam and Eve. Being a person of faith, I believe that God created all genetic material in Adam and Eve. Evolution's just a theory. It's widely believed, but it's just a hypothesis; it's not scientific fact.

"Evolution from a western perspective claims that nonhumans evolved into humans. It also says that we share 98 percent of our DNA with apes. This to me shows that the clay God used to make Adam and Eve is the common material of all life. Using clay, God made all beings from the same material. I believe in *khalq*—that's Arabic for 'creation.' I believe in intelligent design."

After we left the museum, Halah, one of the young Saudis who had helped organize our program, was angry at me for confronting Ibrahim on the subject of evolution. She said I should have paid more attention to the exhibits on the history of science in the Muslim world. Halah said her religion teaches her to think logically and rationally. That's how she approaches everything, and that's how she approaches evolution. She just hasn't been convinced by the scientific arguments for evolution.

When I suggested that her attitude toward evolution had been influenced by her religious beliefs, Halah grew even more angry.

"My religion doesn't have anything to do with it," she said. "I hate it when I tell people I don't believe in evolution and they call me a stupid Muslim."

I was upset. Had I been insensitive? Was I wrong to express what I feel is my legitimate opposition to the teaching of creationism in American public schools while I was visiting a university science museum in Saudi Arabia? I wasn't sure; I felt conflicted. I thought about the science museums I had visited in the United States. Was the Boston Museum of Science actually the Boston Museum of Science in Christianity? Should the Museum of Natural History in New York really be called the Museum of Christian Natural History?

STEPHEN J. GOULD'S OVERLAPPING MAGISTERIA

What is the relationship between science and religion? Can these two very different ways of understanding the world coexist, or does a commitment to one render the other invalid? What conceptions of God are compatible with science? And what are the religious implications of the Big Bang and Darwinian evolution?

People in different cultures and at different historical moments have offered different answers to these difficult questions. In some cultures, a dichotomy between science and religion doesn't exist. Where it does, surveyors of the boundary between the two domains often reach very different conclusions about exactly where the border should be located. An "age of science" can be preceded *or* followed by an "age of religion." And while the existence of some Gods may be threatened by the latest discoveries in biology or astronomy, the existence of others may not. It may even be confirmed.

In *Rock of Ages: Science and Religion in the Fullness of Life*, Stephen Jay Gould offers some very thoughtful responses to these questions. Gould argues that the relationship between science and religion should be governed by what he calls "the principle of non-overlapping magisteria." He uses the term *magisteria* (from the Latin *magister,* "teacher") to refer to "a domain of authority in teaching." Gould defines the principle of nonoverlapping magisteria as a "principle of respectful noninterference—accompanied by intense dialogue between the two distinct subjects, each covering a central facet of human existence."[2]

According to Gould, the domain of science encompasses human attempts to understand the natural world by gathering factual knowledge about this world and developing theories to explain it. Scientists employ techniques that have been validated by previous success and that are well suited for describing and explaining the facts of the natural world. The domain of religion, on the other hand, is concerned with human attempts to establish moral bases for our actions and in this way to construct meaningful lives. Matters of ethics, moral principles, and values—the meaning and purpose of life—are the concern of religion.

Gould is forceful in his insistence that people working on either side of the border between these two magisteria should respect the limits imposed on them by the boundary and refrain from trespassing on the territory of the other. Expertise in one domain does not entitle people to make claims in the other; that lies beyond their purview. Scientists, in other words, should refrain from using their specialized knowledge to assert moral claims or to attempt to validate (or refute) other people's religious beliefs. Arguments about the existence of God, angels, human souls, and miracles lie outside the compass of scientific explanation. "The facts of nature," Gould writes, "are what they are, and cannot in principle, resolve religious questions about God, meaning, and morality."[3]

Religious thinkers, on the other hand, are equally responsible for respecting the boundaries of *their* magisterium and for not trespassing on the domain of science. God and souls have no place in the world of science, and religious belief in their existence cannot alter what scientists know about the natural world. In Gould's words, religious belief must not "dictate specific answers to empirical questions or foreclose the acceptance of documented facts." The principle of nonoverlapping magisteria places equally binding restrictions on those operating in both domains; it sets out a "logically sound, humanely sensible, and properly civil way to live in a world of honorable diversity."[4] Biologists have no more right to promote atheism than religious fundamentalists have to deny evolution.

Gould invites people working in both magisteria to participate with mutual respect in a dialogue across the border where the two domains meet. He understands how difficult this task can be and how bitterly contested the territory on either side of the boundary often is. There is no hope for some false fusion of science and religion, only the wisdom that comes from the ability to integrate these two different domains into a single coherent worldview.

In one of his most controversial claims, Gould rejects the conventional wisdom that the relationship between science and religion has generally been characterized by irreconcilable conflict. While acknowledging his focus on the relationship between science and the Judeo-Christian tradition, Gould argues that the so-called "war between science and religion" is a myth, a superficial and ultimately false characterization of the relationship between the two domains. Gould offers a more careful reading of the history of this relationship, one that specifically addresses the cases of Columbus, Galileo, Newton, and Darwin. He demonstrates that this is not a conflict between science, on the one hand, and religion as a whole, on the other, but a conflict between science and mainstream religious thought, on the one hand, and a small and (until recently at least) relatively marginal tradition of Christian fundamentalism, on the other.

Gould believes that if his principle of nonoverlapping magisteria were respected, the conflict between science and religion wouldn't exist. He argues that the recent efforts of Christian fundamentalists to introduce Biblical creation, intelligent design, and the ultimate oxymoron, "creation-science," into the American system of public education is the result of their failure to show proper respect for the domain of science. These efforts, he notes, have been condemned by virtually all scientists and by most religious authorities, including Pope Jean Paul II. While Gould insists he has "enormous respect for religion," he does, on at least one occasion, refer to creationism as "palpable nonsense."[5] Clearly then, the boundary between science and religion needs to be more carefully surveyed; its location more precisely defined. All areas of overlap between the two magisteria have not been eliminated, and full wisdom remains to be achieved.

There was certainly no conflict between science and religion during the golden age of Islam, when Muslim scientists in the Middle East made impressive contributions to the fields of mathematics, astronomy, and medicine—as we learned from our visit to the Museum of Science and Technology in Islam on the KAUST campus. For the last century or more, however, the relationship between science and Islam has been much more contentious. While a small group of Muslim scholars continue to explore productively the relationship between the two, for the majority of people in the Muslim world science and Islam do not coexist at all comfortably.

The conservative forms of Islam that pervade many societies in the Middle East in the early twenty-first century have adopted extremely critical, if not outright hostile, attitudes toward modern science. Muslims who believe that the natural world is the manifestation of supernatural agency and design frequently reject what they see as the mechanistic and materialistic approach of western science. Many conservative Muslims see a moral void in science and the secular humanism that accompanies it; they see modern science as a threat to their spirituality and their faith. Paradoxically, this extreme skepticism toward science often coexists with eager enthusiasm for many of the new products that scientific and technological advances have made possible. A result of the negative attitude toward science that exists in many Muslim countries is often a lack of government support for scientific education and research and a dramatic proliferation of organizations that promote a variety of pseudoscientific and antiscientific ideas.[6]

The explanation for this profound contrast between the position of science in western Europe and the United States, on the one hand, and the Middle East, on the other, does not lie entirely in the nature of the Judeo-Christian and the Islamic religious traditions themselves. Both traditions are extremely diverse systems of belief; both contain some approaches that are compatible with modern science and others that are not. The difference between the positions that science occupies in these two parts of the world can be understood in light of the very different historical experiences they've had and the very different political systems that have governed them.

The hostility toward science that exists in much of the Muslim world today can be attributed in large part to the experience of European colonialism and to the rapid modernization and westernization that followed. The economic, political, and military dominance that Europe, and more recently the United States, has exerted over countries in the Middle East has contributed in fundamental ways to the pervasive poverty, corruption, social inequality, and lack of democratic institutions that characterize them. To many people in the Muslim world, modern science is simply another European ideology imported from the West—Darwinism, Marxism, materialism, atheism, the list is long—that are seen as existential threats to some forms of traditional Islam.

The rejection of modern science is part of the process of decolonization and the assertion of cultural integrity that accompanied independence movements in much of the Middle East after World War II. The challenge facing Muslim societies in the region is to preserve their traditional cultural and religious values in the face of the dramatic transformations that have been brought about by recent developments in western science and technology. One manifestation of this rapid and destructive social change has been the rejection of science by many people in the Muslim world.

In *Islam and Science,* Muzaffar Iqbal searches for some remedy for the malaise that pervades the region. "What," he asks, "are the ways open to more than one billion Muslims who live on this planet to find their rightful place in a world dominated by modern science and its numerous products without losing all sight of their spiritual tradition? How should Islam be related to modern science?"[7] In his struggle to answer these difficult questions, Iqbal invites serious Muslim scholars who have been educated in scientific *and* Islamic traditions and who recognize the limits of both to examine modern science in light of the religious truths of the Quran. His goal is the creation of a "new nexus" between Islam and science. I suggest that a genuine understanding of this nexus involves precisely what Stephen Jay Gould has called the *wisdom* that comes from articulating an appropriate relationship between the two great magisteria of science and religion.

EVOLUTION: AN ANTI-ISLAMIC THEORY?

Evolution has become a flashpoint in the relationship between science and religion in many parts of the Muslim world, as it has in many parts of the Christian world. In much of the Middle East, it is not just members of fundamentalist minorities who reject Darwin's ideas; many in the mainstream, even members of intellectual elites, do so as well. The rejection of evolution there is part of the more general resistance to the legacy of European colonialism. More specifically, Darwinian evolution is understood as a denial of God's role in creation and a denial of the unique position of human beings in the natural world. It is a direct threat to the truth of the Adamic creation myth presented in the Quran in passages like this: "O mankind! Reverence your Lord, who created you from a single soul" (4:1); and, "Allah is the one God who made all things he created excellent; and He began the creation of man from clay.... He fashioned and breathed into him of His spirit" (32:7–9). Many Muslims see Darwinian evolution as some kind of corrosive acid eating away at their religious beliefs.

When it comes to managing the controversial relationship between the teaching of evolution and the practice of Islam, members of Muslim societies in the Middle East have adopted a variety of solutions, many of them involving very difficult compromises. This should come as no surprise, given the different forms of Islam and the different educational and political systems that exist throughout the Middle East.

In Saudi Arabia, all educational policies must be in conformity with the strict tenets of the fundamentalist Wahhabi school of Islam. Evolution, therefore, is completely absent from Saudi school curricula at all levels, even in the biology courses taught in medical schools. The Saudi Ministry of Education promotes the teaching of Islamic creationism with regard to the origin of life in general and the origin of human life in particular. Saudi science books claim that adaptation is evidence of divine creation as described in the Quran, and they denounce evolution as an anti-Islamic theory. Twelfth-grade biology texts describe the direct creation of human beings by Allah and discredit Darwinian evolution as an erroneous and blasphemous western theory introduced to Muslim countries as part of a colonialist policy of domination and control.

In Iran, the situation is very different. In spite of the fact that the Islamic Republic of Iran is governed by a theocratic constitution and a supreme leader, who is a Shia cleric, science in Iran is not subordinated to religious ideology; it is treated as a separate and independent domain of knowledge. Schoolbooks deal openly with the Darwinian concepts of adaptation and natural selection. One Iranian textbook acknowledges straightforwardly that virtually all contemporary biologists accept that Darwinian evolution is able to account fully for the diversity of life on earth. Although human evolution is not dealt with specifically in its school curricula, Iran presents the subject of biological evolution in a more serious manner than most other countries in the Middle East. The reasons for the different treatment of evolution in Iran and Saudi Arabia are not difficult to discern. Since the mid-nineteenth century, Iran has had a secular, western-style educational system, and for much of the twentieth century under the Pahlavi dynasty, Iranian society has experienced a significant degree of secularization and westernization.

In Turkey, evolutionary theory has also enjoyed a relatively secure position—until recently at least. After the defeat of the Ottoman Empire in World War I and the establishment of Turkey as a modern, secular, European nation-state by Kemal Ataturk in 1923, the teaching of evolution was fully incorporated into the Turkish educational system. There was little effective resistance, and the situation remained relatively stable, until the 1970s, when Islamist political parties gained increasing influence over Turkish society. In the early twenty-first century, with the rise to power of the Justice and Development Party, which is often described as "mildly Islamist" or "Islamic-leaning," controversy over the teaching of evolution has grown more intense. Now Turkey is the center of an aggressive Islamic creationist movement that has spread throughout the entire Muslim world.[8]

The undisputed leader of Islamic creationism is Adnan Oktar, a bizarre figure with no scientific or religious training, who writes under the pen name Harun Yahya. Oktar and some of his supporters reportedly believe he is the Mahdi, the Muslim messiah; but critics describe him as a charismatic charlatan who has built a cult following through a well-funded media campaign of self-promotion. In 1996, a book entitled *The Holocaust Deception* appeared under his name, and in 2008, he was sentenced by a Turkish court to a three-year prison sentence "for creating an illegal organization for personal gain."[9]

The Science Research Foundation, founded by Oktar in Istanbul in 1990, sponsors conferences and produces a seemingly endless supply of books, CDs, DVDs, magazines, and websites promoting Islamic creationism. By far the most sensational media outlet for Oktar's work has been *Building Bridges,* a daily television show that appears on an Istanbul station owned by Oktar, whose four hostesses—with their tight clothes, dyed blond hair, heavy eye make-up, and bright red lipstick—have been called Oktar's "Barbies," his "Versace harem," "Turkey's antievolutionist showgirls," and "TV's Islamic Creationist TV babes."[10]

Many of Oktar's antievolutionist claims draw on material produced by the Institute for Creation Research, a Christian organization based in Texas that sponsors work in Biblical creationism, creation science, and intelligent design. In books like *The Evolution Deceit* and *The Dark Face of Darwinism* available for free online, Oktar argues that evolution is the product of a godless conspiracy of Freemasons, atheists, Marxists, and Jews, who are all out to destroy Islam. He even claims that Darwinism is somehow responsible for the 9/11 attacks on the World Trade Center. Oktar calls evolution a "feeble and perverted ideology contradicted by the Quran," and says that its dominance in the West is the result of the "ruthless power of the system of the Antichrist." According to Oktar, evolutionary biologists like Stephen Jay Gould believe that "aliens" produced the first proteins and that "our forefathers were microbes."[11]

Oktar's most impressive work to date is *The Atlas of Creation,* a huge eight-hundred-page volume that weighs twelve pounds, measures eleven inches wide by fifteen inches tall, and is full of beautiful, high-quality color photographs of an astonishing variety of plant and animal life. Published in Istanbul in 2007 and translated into fifty-seven languages, *The Atlas of Creation* has been distributed free of charge to tens of thousands of scholars in the United States and Europe. The book is Oktar's attempt to prove beyond any possible doubt that none of Darwin's claims are supported by scientific evidence and that all the research that's been done on evolution since Darwin's time has actually refuted the theory of evolution that bears his name.

In Oktar's *Atlas of Creation,* large photographs of beautiful fossils spread over two pages, while small photographs of similar living species are set in a corner. Short texts present the ages of the fossils and then point out the obvious conclusion: evolution has not taken place. Page 158: "Thousands of fossils show that rabbits have always been rabbits. The evident fact revealed by fossils is that living species did not evolve; God created them." Page 313: "This fossil, typical of the cockroaches alive 108 to 92 million years ago, is the same as ones living today, which shows that the theory of evolution is invalid." And page 366: "Fossil bats millions of years old refute the claim that living things underwent evolution. Fossils like this reveal that God created living things" (see fig. 9).

Species by species, country by country, the same argument is repeated over and over again for hundreds of pages. Phasmid nymphs, aphid larvae, and scuttle flies from Poland; wolf, tiger, and rhinoceros skulls from China; garfish, pipefish, and lantern fish from the United States. "They have been the same for millions of years"; "they have never undergone evolution"; "evolution is a big lie."[12]

Occasionally Oktar presents other more fanciful images to refute Darwin's work on evolution. In a drawing at the top of one page, a crocodile stands facing a chipmunk. Between them, emerging from large eggs, are four young animals intermediate in form between the two. Over them is stamped a big red *X* and in large capital letters the word "FALSE." According to the caption: "There exist no fossils belonging to any strange creature partly resembling a crocodile and in other parts a squirrel. . . . Squirrels have always remained squirrels, and crocodiles have always remained crocodiles. All these facts reveal that the theory of evolution . . . is simply a product of imagination."[13]

The evolution of human beings from their primate ancestors is singled out for particular scorn. According to Oktar, all hominin fossils ever found can be attributed to extinct species of ape or extinct races of human beings: "no evolutional changes have occurred in the skulls of men." He dismisses *Australopithecus afarensis* and *Homo habilis* as extinct species of ape, while *Homo erectus* and Neanderthals are identified as extinct races of human beings. And he cites the Piltdown hoax as evidence of the deceitful practices of paleontologists in order to dismiss out of hand well-known fossil discoveries like Lucy, Turkana Boy, and the Laetoli footprints.

Oktar argues desperately that Darwinian evolution is a myth and that it has been completely discredited by recent scientific discoveries. He claims that human beings are not descended from primate ancestors, that the scientific theory of evolution is not able to explain the complexity of the biological world, and that Darwinism is the greatest fraud ever perpetuated in the history of science. Finally, Oktar closes the *Atlas of Creation* with a statement of his own personal religious beliefs—"Our Almighty Lord has created all living things in the finest form"—and a quotation from the Quran—"God is the Creator of everything and He is Guardian over everything. . . . It is those who reject God's signs who are the losers."[14]

Needless to say, scholarly responses to Oktar's *Atlas of Creation* have been devastating. A group of European scientists have characterized the book as preposterous, absurd, intellectually dishonest, breathtakingly inane, and "more like a primitive theological treatise than a scientific refutation of the theory of evolution." One biologist described it as a "ludicrous pseudoscientific joke"; another reported being "astonished at what a load of crap it was."[15]

CONCORDISM: CAN SCIENCE PROVE THE QURAN
IS THE WORD OF GOD?

In the conflict between evolution and creationism, whether in its Christian or its Islamic form, Stephen Jay Gould argues that religious thinkers have made the mistake of overstepping the boundary between the two nonoverlapping magisteria, science and religion. Creationists, in other words, have failed to recognize the proper limits of the domain of religion and have trespassed onto territory belonging to the domain of science. Gould's critics, on the other hand, argue that when it comes to the origin of human life the magisteria of science and religion *do overlap,* and to quite a significant degree. Managing this boundary dispute is the challenge.

Another very different approach to negotiating the relationship between science and religion has become popular in the Muslim world. *Concordism* is a doctrine that seeks to integrate science and religion by demonstrating that religious knowledge revealed to humans by God at some point in the distant past corresponds with much more recent scientific discoveries. Concordists claim that religious knowledge in ancient sacred texts must be true if it is confirmed by modern science. Rather than rejecting scientific knowledge, as creationists do, concordists coopt science and use it as a tool to legitimate their religious beliefs. They try to prove scientifically the divine truth of revelation. Concordism, like creationism, is a part of the larger effort by leaders of the Muslim world to assert their traditional religious values against the ever-present threats of cultural imperialism, westernization, and modernization.

Concordists identify particular passages in their sacred texts with the discovery of specific scientific facts. They claim that the parallels—the *concordances*—that exist between the two realms subordinate science to religion and prove the ultimate truth of religious knowledge. Attempts by geologists to prove that the flood described in Genesis actually occurred and efforts of amateur archaeologists to find the remains of Noah's ark high on the slopes of Mount Ararat on the Turkish-Armenian border exemplify the best—or the worst—of concordism.

An early proponent of Islamic concordism was Maurice Bucaille, a French surgeon who learned Arabic in order to read the Quran, which he came to believe had been divinely revealed to the Prophet Muhammad. In *The Bible, the Quran, and Science,* published in 1978, Bucaille argued that the Quran, unlike the Bible, was in basic agreement with scientific facts, that the points of agreement between the Quran and modern science constituted a divine miracle, and that the Quran was therefore the word of God.

In his introduction, Bucaille writes that it is "impossible to explain how a text produced in the seventh century could have contained ideas that have only been discovered in modern times." He claims that this miracle conveys an important message about the relationship between science and religion: "in a century where for many people, scientific truth has dealt a deathblow to religious belief, it is precisely the discoveries of science that, in an objective examination of the Islamic scripture, have highlighted the supernatural nature of revelation and authenticity of the religion which it taught."[16]

The Bible, the Quran, and Science has become one of the most popular works on science in the Muslim world. It has been translated into many languages, sold millions of copies, and spawned an entire "concordist industry" that has produced a deluge of books, television shows, DVDs, and websites claiming that modern scientific discoveries prove that the Quran is in fact the word of God. While Bucaille's work is dismissed out of hand by virtually all serious scientists, it is warmly embraced by many young educated Muslims eager to promote their Islamic heritage in the face of the onslaught of western culture. It is also fully endorsed by Muslims who want to reconcile the conflicts they experience between their deeply held religious beliefs, on the one hand, and their careers in engineering and science, on the other.[17]

Bucaille has enjoyed particular prestige in the world of Islamic concordism because he was a western scientist who underwent a conversion experience and devoted the rest of his life to describing the "scientific miracles" in the Quran. Unlike Muslim creationists, Bucaille argues that there is no conflict between science and Islam. For Bucaille, science is not a threat to the Quran, but a means to demonstrate that the Quran was divinely revealed to the Prophet Muhammad by God. According to claims made by some of Bucaille's followers, after his return to earth Neil Armstrong recognized the mysterious sounds he had heard while walking on the moon as the Muslim call to prayer and promptly converted to Islam.

According to the majority of western scientists, Islamic concordism, like its Christian counterpart, involves little more than projections of scientific facts onto vague statements in the Quran. From this perspective, creative translations and imaginative interpretations form the basis for most concordist claims. Most serious scientists find nothing of value in concordism and charge its practitioners with engaging in futile efforts to accomplish an impossible task: using science to validate religion.

Islamic concordism has also been the target of criticism from *Christian* concordists, who argue that the Bible contains more accurate scientific information than the Quran. They charge Bucaille and his followers with looking only for concordances between science and Islam when they read the Quran, and of looking only for discordances between science and Christianity when they read the Bible. Christian concordists, of course, are guilty of doing just the opposite. Muslim critics have leveled an even more devastating charge against Islamic concordists, accusing them of seriously misreading the Quran by treating it as a book of scientific facts about the natural world, rather than a book about religious questions of meaning and morality. To these Muslim critics, Islamic concordism is a gross profanation of the Holy Quran.

SCIENTIFIC MIRACLES: OCEANOGRAPHY, ASTRONOMY, AND EMBRYOLOGY

The International Commission on Scientific Signs in the Quran and Sunnah was founded by Sheikh Abdul Majeed al-Zindani in Saudi Arabia in 1984 to promote Islamic concordism throughout the world. Al-Zindani, described by CNN as "a provocative cleric with a flaming red beard," has been named a "Specially Designated Global Terrorist" by the U.S. Treasury Department on the grounds that he once served as spiritual advisor to Osama bin Laden.[18] The commission raises several hundred thousand dollars a year on its own; it also receives a generous subsidy from the Muslim World League, one of the largest Islamic NGOs in the world. The Muslim World League, founded in 1962 by then Saudi Prince Faisal and based in Mecca, encourages the peaceful spread of Islam, promotes Islamic solutions to contemporary social problems, and advocates for the adoption of sharia law by governments around the world.

The explicit mission of the commission is to promote Islamic concordism by demonstrating that the Quran contains a wealth of facts that have been documented by recent scientific discoveries. The Quran must, therefore, be the product of divine revelation and the Prophet Muhammad the messenger of God. In a wealth of websites and other publications, the commission argues that there are over a thousand verses in the Quran that are "of a scientific nature" and that are compatible with the facts of modern science. The existence of this information in the Quran constitutes a miracle and proves that Islam is the one true religion.

The presentation of this material in booklets like *This Is the Truth* and *The Quran and Modern Science* follows a very consistent pattern. Specific verses from the Quran are presented, as are the corresponding "scientific facts." Then the "scientific miracle" is explained and documented. According to the Quran (25:61), for example, "God (Allah), the Almighty said: Blessed is He who has placed in the sky great stars and placed therein a burning lamp and luminous moon." Scientists have discovered that the energy of the sun is generated by the burning of hydrogen, which is transformed into helium in a nuclear reaction under great pressure and at temperatures reaching fifteen million degrees Celsius. It is a "scientific miracle" that the Quran contains information that modern astronomers discovered hundreds of years later after the invention of the telescope. "Who could have informed Prophet Muhammad of this," the pamphlet concludes, "except Allah, the Most High!" This pattern is repeated over and over again with examples from geology, oceanography, and biology. The conclusions to be drawn are inescapable: "science and religion are compatible"; "the conflict between science and religion experienced by the West does not exist in Islam"; and finally, "Allah is the source of the one true religion."

Of all the activities of the International Commission on Scientific Signs in the Quran and Sunnah, the most controversial has been the series of conferences it has sponsored over the past three decades in cities throughout the Muslim world. Prominent non-Muslim scientists from Europe and the United States were offered inducements to attend these lavish events—large honoraria, luxury hotel rooms, first-class plane tickets, and palace dinners with government officials. They were assured that the commission was a neutral, scholarly organization open to all new scientific discoveries. Much to their dismay, however, they soon learned that this was not the case. At some point during the conference, they were presented with verses from the Quran and asked to comment on their accuracy. While they were being videotaped, they were pushed to acknowledge the divine origin of the Quran. The commission then posted these videos on YouTube and other websites like Islamicity.com as evidence that distinguished western scientists believed that the Quran was the word of God.

In *This Is the Truth,* Professor William Hay, an oceanographer from the University of Colorado, replies to questions posed to him at one of the commission's conferences in Jeddah. When asked about verses from the Quran containing descriptions of what could be interpreted as boundaries between undersea currents, Hay replies: "I find it very interesting that this sort of information is in the ancient scripture of the Holy Quran, and I have no way of knowing where it would have come from."

"Then you have flatly denied it to be just from a human source," the interviewer concludes. "Who do you think is the original source of such information?"

"Well," Hay is quoted as replying, "I would think it must be the divine being!"[19]

Several years later, in an interview conducted with *The Rationalizer,* a blog associated with the Richard Dawkins Foundation for Reason and Science, Hay claimed that he had really said that if there had been absolutely no other possible source for the information, then it could only have been a divine revelation. He also told *The Rationalizer* that at the conference he had stated that proof of divine intervention would be required and that he did not believe that divine intervention had been involved. Hays went on to say that the original video was "a misrepresentation." He told another journalist: "I fell into a trap."[20]

A YouTube video available at the website "Quran and Science" opens with exotic "Oriental" music and a deep male voice reciting the Quran. Then Professor Alfred Kroner, a geologist at the Johannes Gutenberg University in Mainz, Germany, addresses the conference in Jeddah: "I think it is almost impossible, that [Muhammad] could have known about things like the common origin of the universe, because scientists have only found out within the last few years with very complicated and advanced technological methods that this is the case. Somebody who did not know something about nuclear physics one thousand four hundred years ago could not, I think, be in a position to find out from his own mind that the earth and the heavens had the same origin."

The video ends with a dramatic image of the earth set against the darkness of interplanetary space as an open Quran sweeps down through the sky like a shooting star toward the Holy Mosque in Mecca (see fig. 10). Kroner, like Hay, later told *The Rationalizer* that his comments at the conference had been taken out of context and that he had never meant to suggest that the Quran contained divine revelation.

Professor Tom Armstrong, an astronomer at NASA, seems to have been the only scientist invited to the conference in Jeddah who resisted the temptation to make statements sympathetic to his hosts' religious beliefs that he would later regret. When asked his thoughts on the similarities between the Quran and modern scientific discoveries, Professor Armstrong replied carefully:

> I am impressed how remarkably some of the ancient writings seem to correspond to modern astronomy. I would like to leave it at that. There may be something beyond what we understand as ordinary human experience to account for the writings that we have seen. It is not my intention or my position to provide an answer to that. I have said a lot of words without, I think,

expressing exactly what you want me to express, but it is my job as a scientist to remain independent of certain questions, and I think that is one of the reasons that I better stop just a little bit short of giving you the complete answer that you might desire.[21]

Professor Gerald Goeringer, a biologist from Georgetown University, who also attended this conference, refused to endorse the commission's concordist views. "It was mutual manipulation," he said frankly. "We got to go places we wouldn't otherwise go to. They wanted to add some respectability to what they were publishing."[22]

The poster child for Islamic concordism—the western scientist who has done the most to promote the goals of the International Commission on Scientific Signs in the Quran and Sunnah—is Professor Keith Moore, an embryologist at the University of Toronto. In the 1970s Moore, the author of several well-respected anatomy textbooks, was invited to join the Embryology Committee of the King Abdulaziz University in Jeddah on a study of the relationship between the Quran and modern embryology. Moore soon became an ardent proponent of the idea that the Quran contains a wealth of scientifically accurate information about the development of the human embryo and is therefore a product of divine revelation.

In a video entitled *Holy Quran: Top Scientists Comment on Scientific Miracles in the Quran,* Moore enthusiastically endorses the commission's work: "It is clear to me that these statements [in the Quran about human development] must have come to Muhammad from God or Allah because almost all of this knowledge was not discovered until many centuries later. This proves to me that Muhammad must have been a messenger of God or Allah." Moore's interview is illustrated with dramatic images of the tiny face of a fetus floating peacefully in amniotic fluid to the accompaniment of a male voice reciting the Quran.[23]

Moore presents his views in greater detail in an article he wrote for the *Journal of the Islamic Medical Association of North America* entitled "A Scientist's Interpretation of References to Embryology in the Qur'an."[24] According to the Quran, he writes, Allah "creates you in the wombs of your mothers, in stages, one after another, in three veils of darkness" (39:6). Moore suggests that these "three veils of darkness" refer to the anterior abdominal wall, the uterine wall, and the amniochorionic membrane.

The Kindle version of the ninth edition of Moore's textbook, *The Developing Human: Clinically Oriented Embryology,* published in 2013, is easily available from Amazon for just under forty-five dollars. The third edition, entitled *The Developing Human: Clinically Oriented Embryology with Islamic Additions,* was published in hard copy in 1983 in Saudi Arabia. But it is not available anywhere. It is not to be found in the British Library or in the U.S. Library of Congress. It *is* for sale at Online-Islamic-Store.com, but it is listed as "out of stock." The "Islamic additions" to Moore's book, which received Moore's full approval, were written by Sheikh al-Zindani himself. One of the people al-Zindani thanks in his acknowledgments is Osama bin Laden, who apparently developed a strong interest in concordism after hearing one of al-Zindani's lectures. Bin Laden also helped pay for the publication of Moore's book.[25]

The Islamic edition of Moore's embryology text, with its alternating chapters of standard scientific information and passages from the Quran, has been the target of fierce attacks by many scientists. On his highly rated science blog, one of Moore's most persistent and harshest critics, biologist Paul Myers, describes Moore as "an idiot" who publishes "ridiculous claims" supporting the notion that the Quran is a divine source of information. "Remember," Myers warns, "ancient holy books are sources of lies and misinformation, not science."[26]

SCIENCE PROVES HOMOSEXUALITY IS AGAINST THE WILL OF GOD

One morning near the end of our stay in Jeddah, we visited the offices of the Ladies' Section of the Islamic Education Foundation, a nonprofit founded in 1997 to encourage both Muslim and non-Muslim women to deepen their understanding and appreciation of Islam. We entered an attractive courtyard and walked around a small freestanding wall that shielded the front door of the building. Once inside we were greeted by several women wearing black *abaya*s and *hijab*s; some also wore *niqab*s. They greeted the female students with warm embraces; they did not shake hands with the males in our group. On a table in the foyer, I noticed copies of Oktar's *Atlas of Creation* and the Islamic edition of Moore's *The Developing Human*.

We were introduced to Dr. Fatima Naseef, a well-respected scholar of Islam and one of the few female Saudi religious authorities to occupy the prestigious position of sheikh. Naseef was born in 1944 in Jeddah to a wealthy merchant family, whose house in the old city is now a well-known museum and cultural center. She attended the first girls' school in Jeddah, which was founded by her mother; later she received a B.A. in Arabic language and literature from King Abdulaziz University in Jeddah, an M.A. in linguistics from the School for Oriental and African Studies at the University of London, and a Ph.D. in Quranic studies from Umm al-Qura University in Mecca. Naseef teaches and lectures on Islam in Saudi Arabia and abroad. She is also the author of *Women in Islam: A Discourse in Rights and Obligations,* published by the International Islamic Committee for Woman and Child in Cairo.

We also met Dr. Lamya Shahin, a physician who serves as director of outreach programs and lecturer in comparative religion at the foundation. She had just returned from Oxford, where she had participated in an interfaith dialog on the relationship between science and religion. Shahin gave us a passionate introduction to Islamic concordism, a powerful religious performance in which she testified to her belief that science proved the Quran was the word of God. First she read PowerPoint slides that contained English translations of verses from the Quran; then she chanted the original Arabic. Next she presented dramatic images of natural phenomena—pulsars and black holes, embryos and fetuses, volcanoes and tsunamis. Then she described the latest discoveries in various scientific fields, which proved that Allah had revealed the Quran to Muhammad, His Prophet. "Muhammad didn't have a microscope or a telescope," she said, "but he did have access to God."

Shahin ended her talk with a discussion of the Muslim perspective on homosexuality, which drew heavily on the work of Ron Wyatt, the Biblical pseudoarchaeologist, best known for his "discovery" of Noah's ark on Mount Ararat. Shahin presented detailed geological evidence (including satellite mapping and geochemical analysis) demonstrating that balls of sulphur and fire from nearby volcanic eruptions had destroyed the ancient cities of Sodom and Gomorrah. This, she said, proved scientifically that homosexuality was against the will of God and that gays and lesbians were evil. This explains, she added, why the anal mucosa does not protect people from the AIDS virus.

It was clear to me that several of the students in our group were very troubled by what they had heard, but they hesitated. They were unsure how to respond. After a short, but awkward silence, Eliza asked the first question.

"Do you mean to say that gay men and women deserve to die of AIDS?"

"Yes," Shahin replied. "Homosexuality is a sin."

Two other students firmly challenged Shahin's claims. Sam said that his gay uncle, his male partner, and their adopted child formed a very loving family. Shahin replied that in her opinion homosexuality destroyed the fabric of society and violated natural law. Ana then said that her parents were two gay women, that she had two mothers.

It was then my responsibility to speak.

"I know of no evidence," I said, "psychological, sociological, or anthropological, that shows that homosexuality is harmful or unnatural in any way."

Shahin concluded her presentation saying that it was clear we had very different views on the subject.

As we said goodbye, we were each given a bag full of small books, pamphlets, and a little jar of holy water from the Zamzam Well in the Holy Mosque in Mecca. Without thinking, I extended my hand to Shahin in a gesture of goodwill. I immediately realized my mistake, when she declined to shake it. Not because of my views on homosexuality, but because I was a man.

As we returned to our hotel, several students tried to express the strong emotions they had struggled to hold in check until then. Eliza was in tears; she was afraid she had offended Shahin by challenging her views. I assured Eliza that she had expressed her views in a perfectly appropriate manner. Another student was furious at the offensive things Shahin had said. I told her that if she hadn't wanted to hear views like this, she shouldn't have come to Saudi Arabia.

Ahmed, the young Saudi university graduate taking time off from his job with General Electric in Bahrain to accompany us on our trip, was angry too. But not at Shahin. At us.

"I thought you were here to learn about Saudi culture," he said. "You just focused on a few of the things she said. She wasn't attacking anyone; she was being diplomatic. Some of the comments you made were offensive. The Quran isn't bad or wrong just because of the way she interprets it. There are lots of other ways to interpret the Quran. Don't forget, she doesn't represent all Muslims."

Ahmed was right, of course. Shahin did not represent all Muslims. She did, however, represent a great many.

Our confrontation with creationism and homophobia in Saudi Arabia challenged values that I hold dear, as did our confrontation with other disturbing aspects of Saudi culture—religious intolerance, restrictions on the freedom of women, the violation of basic human rights, and the absence of democracy. How can we navigate between the extremes of ethnocentrism— my culture, my values, are superior to those of other people—and cultural relativism—I have no right to judge the culture, the values, of others? Is it possible to define a universal set of moral values that allows us to avoid both the lack of respect for other cultures that comes with ethnocentrism, on the one hand, *and* the moral paralysis that comes with cultural relativism, on the other?

Our experiences in Saudi Arabia did not provide answers to these difficult questions, but they did force us to confront them directly and personally. And this is the blessing bestowed on us by encounters with cultures that are not our own.

FIVE

Roads of Arabia

ARCHAEOLOGY IN SERVICE OF THE KINGDOM

Saudi Arabia is not a country that was invented with the discovery of the first oil well.[1]

QASR AL-FARID, "THE CASTLE that stands alone," was carved into a huge monolith of red sandstone two thousand years ago. It is one of over 130 monumental tombs in the necropolis that surrounds the ancient Nabataean city of Hegra, now known as al-Hijr or less formally as Madain Saleh. Hegra is located four hundred kilometers north of Medina in an area where the high basalt plateaus of the volcanic Hijaz Mountains drop down through formations of eroded sandstone to meet the desert. The towering outcrop into which Qasr al-Farid was carved stands cut almost in half; rough natural rock curves out around the smooth flat plane of the tomb's facade like the hood of a cobra. The facade itself—twenty meters tall and fifteen meters wide—is ornately carved in high relief. Four pilasters with Nabataean horned capitals flank the central door, while perched on the peak of the triangular pediment above, a sandstone eagle stands watch over the tomb (see fig. 11).

Qasr al-Farid is isolated—it stands alone—for several reasons. Although it is a UNESCO World Heritage Site, and even though an author of the Lonely Planet guide to Saudi Arabia calls it "one of most extraordinary ancient sites anywhere in the world," Madain Saleh receives hardly any international visitors. Saudi Arabia is not open to foreign tourism; the government does not issue tourist visas.[2]

Madain Saleh does not receive many Saudi visitors either, since visiting ornate tombs built by polytheists during the pre-Islamic, or Jahiliyya period, the Age of Ignorance, is strongly discouraged by the Kingdom's Wahhabi clerics on the grounds that such activities pose a threat to the absolute monotheism they demand. In addition, Madain Saleh, a world-class archaeological site on a par with the Acropolis or the Pyramids, is located in Saudi Arabia, a country where, until recently at least, the practice of archaeology has not been welcome.

Jabal Ithlib, at the eastern edge of the four-thousand-acre site of Madain Saleh, is a maze of irregularly shaped and deeply eroded sandstone formations—mushrooms, domes, and spires—varying in color through a range of reds, oranges, and golds. The tombs below are surrounded by desert scrub, an occasional thorn tree, and the dry waterbed of the Wadi al-Hijr, where a Nabataean well, groves of date palms, and ancient residential areas are located. To the west, more mountains rise in the distance fading away to the horizon in the sandy haze.

The tombs at Madain Saleh stand in rows carved into the sides of long sandstone ridges in groups of up to twenty. Their facades exhibit an impressive mix of Assyrian, Babylonian, Egyptian, and Greco-Roman architectural elements, testament to the close ties that linked Nabataean Hegra to the cultural centers of the Mediterranean and the Middle East. The tops of the facades are decorated with stair-step patterns rising from complex sets of friezes, cornices, and architraves, which rest in turn on pilasters and columns that flank the doors of the tombs. Adorning the doorways is a wonderful assortment of lotus flowers, serpents, lions, sphinxes, and eagles.

In the center of the facades above the doors, the Nabataeans carved foundation inscriptions. The inscription on one of the tombs in the Qasr al-Bint group makes a bold announcement:

> This tomb was built by Kahlan al-Tabib bin Wail for himself, his children, and his descendants by legitimate right to endure forever. It is forbidden to anyone who inherits this tomb to sell, rent, or lease it. Anyone who writes [something] additional on it must pay 3,000 harithis to Dhi al-Shira and the same to our lord the king. This was written in the month of Ayyar in year 35 of the reign of Harithah, King of the Nabataeans, who loves his people. This tomb was carved by the sculptors Aftah bin Abd al-Madah and Khalaf Allah.[3]

The walls inside the cool, dark tombs are textured with the marks of the tools that Nabataean stonemasons used to carve them out of the soft sandstone. Some of the burial chambers have small rooms off to the side accessible through low doors. All the chambers have long shallow rectangular niches cut in the walls—and occasionally in the floor—where the bodies of the dead were placed. On average there are six or seven graves per tomb, but one of the largest contains sixty-four niches stacked four or five high on each wall. The individual graves were closed with stone slabs and sealed with mortar.

Madain Saleh is surrounded by an aura of frightening myth and legend. It is, after all, a huge cemetery, and for many Saudis it has been, and still is, an accursed place full of dangers, haunted by the spirits of the pagan dead who were buried there. This is one of the reasons why the site has so few Saudi visitors.

The popular name Madain Saleh, which means "the cities of Saleh," refers to an ancient prophet, who lived three thousand years before Mohammad and whose story has entered Arab popular culture from its original source in the Quran.

The tribe of Thamud, which had settled at al-Hijra, was full of idol worshippers. Allah sent his prophet Saleh to condemn their idolatrous ways and persuade them to repent and convert to the worship of Allah, the one, true God. But the people of Thamud were not convinced; they demanded that Saleh perform a miracle as a sign of his divine authority. They challenged him to bring forth a pregnant camel from the rocky walls of Jabal Ithlib.

Just then the mountain cried out in pangs of labor and from its "rocky womb" gave birth to "a she-camel ten months gone with young." Instead of caring for her, as they should have, the wicked people of the tribe of Thamud killed the camel as soon as she had given birth. The newborn camel immediately cried out and ran back into the mountain. The young camel was announcing that Allah would punish the tribe by destroying their city in three days.

At this point, the people of Thamud repented, but it was too late. "There fell a fearful wind, the earth shook, a voice was heard from heaven." The idolaters "were found lying upon their faces, all dead corpses, and the land was empty of them as [if] it had never been inhabited." Saleh and a few believers were saved, but for many years they mourned the destruction of their tribe for sinning against the will of Allah.[4]

At the beginning of the third century B.C.E., the Nabataeans, who had formerly been nomadic pastoralists and traders, established a kingdom of settled agricultural communities extending from Syria in the north to the Red Sea coast of the Arabian Peninsula in the south. By the first century B.C.E., the Nabataean Empire, with the spectacular Hellenistic city of Petra as its capital, controlled the valuable caravan routes that transported incense, spices, and other luxury goods in a trading network that linked the Indian Ocean, Mesopotamia, and the Mediterranean Sea. During the first century C.E., the Nabataeans came under Roman rule, and Hegra became the second city of the Nabataean Empire with a population of several thousand.

Aside from its remarkable necropolis, the main feature of ancient Hegra was a large residential area surrounded by mud-brick walls, whose inhabitants practiced an oasis-based system of irrigated agriculture that drew water from a series of 130 wells to produce crops of wheat, olives, grapes, and dates. The cosmopolitan nature of the city is suggested not only by the different architectural styles that decorate its tombs, but also by the many languages of the inscriptions that have been discovered there. One of the few Latin inscriptions found in the entire Arabian Peninsula records the restoration of the walls of Hegra by Roman legionnaires in 177 C.E., during the reign of Marcus Aurelius. The religious life of ancient Hegra was diverse as well, and its inhabitants worshiped a variety of gods. On the walls of a narrow gorge in Jabal Ithlib, they carved dedicatory inscriptions to their principal god, Dhu Shara, while they also called on gods named Allat, Manat, and Hubal to protect their tombs from desecration.

Sometime during the late pre-Islamic period, Hegra was abandoned, not to be permanently resettled until the nineteenth century. In his 1888 *Travels in Arabia Deserta,* Charles Doughty, the first European to explore the tombs of Madain Saleh, found inside them fragments of bone, cloth, and leather, as well as "loathsome insects" and "mummy odors." He describes the nearby peasant village as "a place of fear and danger." The villagers told him the old story of the prophet Saleh; they said they couldn't sleep at night because of the spirits—the jinn—that still inhabited the tombs. In 1908, Madain Saleh became a stop on the Hijaz Railway, which was built by the Ottoman sultan to transport pilgrims traveling from Damascus to Medina and then on to Mecca for the Hajj.

The first archaeological research at Madain Saleh was carried out by two Dominican fathers, Antonin Jaussen and Raphael Savignac, in the first decade of the twentieth century. Their *Mission archéologique en Arabie* remains a valuable source of information on the site. After that, Madain Saleh attracted little attention from the outside world until the end of the 1960s, when the Saudi government began to settle Bedouin nomads there in order to take advantage of the ancient wells and irrigation canals that were still functioning. But in 1972, when al-Hijr was designated an official archaeological site, the Bedouin were resettled outside its boundaries. In 2001, the French Ministry of Foreign Affairs and the Saudi Ministry of Antiquities and Museums reached an agreement for long-term archaeological excavations to be carried out jointly between the Centre national de la recherche scientifique and the Department of Archaeology at King Saud University in Riyadh.

In 2008 al-Hijr / Madain Saleh became the first site in Saudi Arabia to be inscribed on the UNESCO World Heritage List. In its application, the Saudi

Commission for Tourism and Antiquities (SCTA), wrote that the Kingdom of Saudi Arabia was committed to doing everything necessary "to ensure the conservation of the site . . . and to guarantee as much as possible the protection of this cultural heritage for future generations."[5]

More recently the SCTA has made additional efforts to develop the potential of Madain Saleh as a tourist destination. Since Saudi Arabia does not issue tourist visas, the main audience for this campaign has been Saudis and the small expatriate community living in the Kingdom. One of the main obstacles to this campaign has been the religious taboo surrounding a site associated with polytheism, idolatry, and death.

In February 2013, two advisors to the Saudi Royal Court visited Madain Saleh and made public comments explicitly aimed at allaying these fears. His Excellency Sheikh Abdullah bin Mohammad bin Abdul Rahman al-Motlak praised the SCTA's efforts to preserve Madain Saleh as an example of "the miracles and warnings" of Allah that are described in the Quran. His colleague, His Excellency Sheikh Abdullah bin Sulaiman bin Mohammad al-Mani, stressed that visiting archaeological sites like Madain Saleh was fully "in accordance with Sharia law" and that Saudis visiting these sites can learn important lessons that will "further strengthen their faith in God All Mighty."[6]

THE POLITICS OF THE PAST

Archaeology is always practiced in a political context. With their ability to control the awarding of excavation permits, governments have the power to determine which sites will be explored and which will not, which artifacts will be discovered and which will remain buried in the ground. It is all too easy for powerful segments of society to exploit archaeology and other scholarly disciplines like linguistics, folklore, and history to advance their own political goals. Archaeology is particularly well suited to facilitate the process of nation building by providing the raw materials necessary for the construction of national cultures and histories. Archaeologists discover the material remains of a nation's past; they literally exhume the bodies of ancient ancestors. From archaeological excavations emerge the objects that constitute a nation's heritage.

This process can be quite complicated. Some aspects of the past must be remembered; others must be forgotten. Different groups have different understandings of the past and are usually interested in promoting different versions of history. With revolutions, military coups, and other political transformations, new governments place new demands on the past, and archaeologists are often charged with resolving competing claims over who controls it. The ancient past is a valuable resource that archaeologists are in a unique position to access.

With the development in the 1980s of critical archaeology, some archaeologists turned their attention away from an exclusive focus on the past to explore the political environments in which they work. As David Fowler points out in his aptly named essay, "Uses of the Past: Archaeology in Service of the State," archaeologists have always been "immersed in, and conditioned by, the economic, political, and governmental institutions of nation states," and they have often "analyzed and interpreted the past to fit the ideological requirements of those states." Fowler goes on to argue that archaeologists have an obligation to explore the ways political leaders "have manipulated the past for nationalistic purposes, both ideological and chauvinistic, and to legitimize their authority and power."[7]

According to Bruce Trigger, another archaeologist interested in the politics of his discipline, nationalist archaeology is generally "directed towards strengthening patriotic sentiments" and often receives "substantial government patronage." The main purpose of nationalist archaeology, he continues, "is to bolster the pride and morale of nations or ethnic groups. It is probably strongest amongst peoples who feel politically threatened, insecure or deprived of their collective rights by more powerful nations.... [And it tends] to draw attention to the political and cultural achievements of ancient civilizations."[8]

Just as some archaeologists have turned a critical eye toward the politics of their own discipline, so have some scholars in the field of museum studies. Archaeological discoveries are generally made available to the public in two different ways: by opening sites to visitors and by putting artifacts on display in museums. Like government decisions to support the excavation of certain sites and not others, government decisions to support museums that exhibit certain objects from certain periods, and not others, shape in crucial ways the versions of the past that become known to the public. Museums, therefore, are sites for negotiations over who will control the history and the identity of a nation.

In *Museum Politics,* Timothy Luke explores the display of cultural power in modern museums, places that increasingly function as "secular cathedrals," "guardians of shared history," and "storehouses of national treasures."[9] Luke argues that museums serve as tools in culture wars, both at the level of domestic politics and the level of international diplomacy. In the case of "blockbuster" exhibitions that involve the loan of valuable artifacts from one country to another, the political goals of both countries must be accommodated. And the exhibitions, far from being apolitical "cultural exchanges," become important components of the diplomatic relationships between the two countries.

Museum curators have the authority to chose objects for exhibition and determine how they will be displayed. The politics of this process is masked by the transformation of historical objects into "works of art," aesthetic artifacts that have supposedly been purified of all political significance. This transformation hides the fact that art is often used intentionally as an ideological instrument to challenge or legitimate different versions of national histories and cultures.

Different kinds of museums play different roles in the political conflicts they become involved in. National museums usually enjoy the greatest prestige. During the eighteenth and nineteenth centuries, as part of the nation-building process, European countries built national museums; they were seen as necessary components of the modern nation-state. In the twentieth century, many countries in the third world followed suit, in order to identify ancestors and heroes for new national canons.

When visitors walk through a national history museum, they are traveling through a nation's past. Each museum has an entrance and an exit, just as each nation's history has a beginning and an end. The texts and labels on museum walls constitute the script that frames and interprets what visitors see. Docents, museum guides, and pre-recorded audio tours stage performances that enact national narratives.

As George Orwell observed in *1984*, "he who controls the past controls the future, and he who controls the present controls the past."

ARCHAEOLOGY, MUSEUMS, AND TOURISM

With the exception of some early European and American antiquarians, the practice of archaeology in Saudi Arabia began in 1963, when the Saudi Council of Ministers established a Department of Antiquities and Museums under the auspices of the Ministry of Education. During the 1970s, Saudi and foreign archaeologists began long-term cooperative projects that included conducting topographical surveys, registering and preserving archaeological sites, and cataloging and restoring archaeological artifacts. In 1977, the first issue of *Atlal: The Journal of Saudi Arabian Archaeology* was published, and the following decade saw the beginning of several large-scale excavations at important sites such as Qaryat al-Faw, Tayma, Dedan (al-Ula), and Madain Saleh.

In what proved to be a significant administrative reorganization, in 2003 the Department of Antiquities and Museums was incorporated into the Supreme Commission for Tourism, which had been established just three years earlier. Then in 2008, the new organization, now officially named the Saudi Commission for Tourism and Antiquities (SCTA), announced a five-year plan to bring the country's archaeological sites up to international standards. The SCTA also tried to promote broader public interest in the archaeological heritage of the Kingdom. Its president, Prince Sultan bin Salman, a member of the royal family and the first Saudi in space—he flew on the U.S. space shuttle *Discovery* in 1985—is the person generally credited with these important changes.

Although many of these preservation and development efforts have focused on fortresses and palaces associated with the recent history of the Kingdom and its founder, King Abdulaziz ibn Saud, pre-Islamic and early Islamic sites have benefited from increased attention as well. Other examples of greater openness in Saudi archaeology are the improved cooperation between Saudi archaeologists and their European and American colleagues, the increased freedom Saudi archaeologists have to publish the results of their excavations, and the lifting of restrictions on media coverage of archaeological discoveries. Saudi efforts to bring archaeology and tourism under one administrative umbrella had what was undoubtedly their greatest success when Madain Saleh was declared a UNESCO World Heritage Site in 2008.

Attracting young Saudis to their discipline is one of the greatest challenges facing Saudi archaeologists. King Saud University in Riyadh is the only university in the country with a Department of Archaeology. The KSU department, the oldest in the Gulf, is part of the College of Tourism and Archaeology, which was established in 2005 in order to meet the growing demand for qualified graduates in tourism, archaeology, and both hotel and heritage management. Students enrolled in the college choose from a variety of courses, including subjects such as ancient epigraphy, introduction to museology, travel agency operations, and managing tourism crises.

The history of museums in Saudi Arabia closely parallels the history of archaeology there. In 1967, a small archaeological and heritage museum was established at KSU by the Department of Antiquities and Museums. Now managed by the College of Tourism and Archaeology, the museum is used primarily for training students. It is open on weekday mornings, Saturday to Wednesday, for men only. There are no visiting hours for women or families.

The most important museum in Saudi Arabia is the National Museum in Riyadh. It was built in 1999 with the input of museum consultants from around the world, and now is a major source of national pride and one of the top attractions for tourists visiting Riyadh, the vast majority of whom are Saudi. The National Museum, together with the King Abdulaziz Foundation for Research and Archives, constitutes the King Abdulaziz Historical Center, an impressive area in central Riyadh surrounded by parks and plazas.

In an *Aramco World* review, the National Museum was lauded as "history's new home in Riyadh."[10] The biggest challenge facing the team of international experts who served as consultants during the design process was the embarrassing fact that the new museum's collection of actual artifacts was too poor to stand on its own. Instead of displaying actual archaeological and historical objects, curators were forced to create replicas, dioramas, and video installations in order to accomplish the educational goals of the museum.

The National Museum presents a chronological account of the prehistory and the history of the Arabian Peninsula with an emphasis on the role of the Kingdom of Saudi Arabia in the worldwide dissemination of Islam. The names of the eight halls indicate fairly clearly the scope of the museum: Man and the Universe, Arab Kingdoms, Pre-Islamic Era, the Prophet's Mission, Islam and the Arabian Peninsula, the First and Second Saudi State, the Unification of the Kingdom, and the Hajj and the Two Holy Mosques.

The second most important museum in Saudi Arabia is the Museum of Science and Technology in Islam on the campus of the King Abdullah University of Science and Technology, north of Jeddah. In addition to these two major museums, there are many smaller regional museums located in cities throughout the country, the majority of which have been built since the 1980s. Most of these local cultural heritage museums are located in former palaces of King Abdulaziz and are frequently devoted to specific topics like the Two Holy Mosques Museum in Mecca, the Hijaz Railway Museum in Medina, and the Museum of Currency in Riyadh. Finally, there are several private museums that house collections assembled by wealthy individuals from distinguished families. One of the best of these is the museum of Safeya

Binzager in Jeddah, which contains both her own paintings and her collection of traditional Saudi clothing and furniture; another is that of Munira Ashgar in Dhahran, which houses her collection of Saudi folk art.

The future of museums in Saudi Arabia can be glimpsed in the plans for the King Abdulaziz Center for World Culture, a joint project of the Saudi government and Saudi Aramco that was begun in 2008 and is still in the planning stages. When completed, the center will serve as a Saudi version of the Smithsonian Institution. Its seven story Knowledge Tower, part of a futuristic building complex to be constructed in Dhahran, will house a museum, library, auditorium, cinema, classrooms, and other educational facilities that are not available anywhere else in the Kingdom. The museum will contain galleries devoted to Islamic civilization, natural history, national heritage, and contemporary culture.

Planning for the center is taking place in cooperation with international partners like the Victoria and Albert Museum in London and the Boston Center for Adult Education. Some people involved in designing the teacher training, community enrichment, and children's summer programs want all activities to be open to mixed groups of men and women; others oppose the idea of men and women learning together. As one spokeswoman put it when we visited the center, "We want to go forward cautiously with respect for the Kingdom's government and religion and with mindfulness honoring our traditions."

Tourism is a new concept in Saudi Arabia. It was not until 2000 that the Supreme Commission for Tourism was established in order to plan and develop the tourism sector of the Saudi economy. When it became the Saudi Commission for Tourism and Antiquities (SCTA) in 2008, its goals broadened to include the promotion of archaeology, museums, and an interest in Saudi history and culture more generally—all in the interests of encouraging the growth of tourism in the country. These developments clearly signaled an awareness on the part of Saudi authorities that archaeological sites had the potential to become important tourist attractions.

At the same time, according to a publication entitled *Tourism Investment in Saudi Arabia,* authorities recognized that any Saudi tourist industry would have to be developed in a manner consistent with the values and principles of the conservative Wahhabi form of Islam that has such a pervasive influence over Saudi society. Any plan to promote the growth of tourism in the Kingdom, therefore, confronts serious conflicts and contradictions. It is difficult to promote tourism in a country where significant hostility exists to the presence of non-Muslims, where alcohol is banned, and where women's dress is tightly regulated.

What's more, Saudi travel policies are some of the most restrictive in the world—so restrictive in fact that it is virtually a "closed country," as one SCTA official we met at Madain Saleh put it. Except for citizens of other Gulf States, it is very difficult to travel to Saudi Arabia. The Saudi government began issuing tourist visas in 2006, but even then they were only available from a small number of travel agencies, for people traveling in groups, on guided tours, organized by licensed tour companies, and following approved itineraries. Visas required a sponsor, took several weeks or months to process, and had to be obtained before entering the country.

In 2010, the Saudi government suspended the issuing of tourist visas entirely, and since then none have been issued. The only visas currently available for travel to Saudi Arabia are diplomatic, student, and work visas; visas for family visits or official government business; and religious visas for pilgrims performing Hajj. All visas to Saudi Arabia indicate whether visitors are Muslims or non-Muslims. The SCTA has declined to comment on this new policy, but its chairman acknowledged that people working in the tourism sector were angered by the decision. It obviously presents a severe impediment to investment in the tourist industry.[11]

Possible reasons for the decision include concerns for the safety and security of international visitors, the desire to minimize the disruptive influence foreigners would have on conservative segments of Saudi society, and the difficulty of preventing people who enter the country on tourist visas from traveling to Mecca and Medina and creating problems for the authorities responsible for the Hajj. Since 2010, therefore, virtually all tourism in Saudi Arabia has been domestic, with the minor exception of expatriates, citizens from other Gulf countries, and Muslims who enter the country on Hajj visas and then "overstay" to explore the country as tourists.

In an interview with the BBC, Prince Sultan bin Salman, president of the SCTA, expressed the hope that "interest in the past will encourage tourism in the future." "Within the next three years," he added, "Saudis will wake up to knowledge about their own country that has been missing throughout their lives."[12] In another interview with the *Smithsonian* blog, Prince Sultan bin Salman adopted a more realistic tone, admitting that at present Saudi Arabia is "not even open for tourism."[13] Many archaeological sites in Saudi Arabia, he added, even the most famous ones like Madain Saleh, are not yet ready for increased tourism. Anyone planning to visit one must arrange with a local hotel or tour operator to obtain an official government permit at least a week ahead of time. And in a sign that tourist visas to travel to Saudi Arabia may not be available any time soon, the March 2013 edition of the *SCTA Newsletter* announced that knowledge of English or any other foreign language was no longer a requirement for applicants for the job of tour guide.

American and British news reports of archaeological discoveries in Saudi Arabia have recently appeared with attention-grabbing headlines: "Saudi Arabia's War between God and Archaeology"; "Google Earth Finds Saudi Arabia's Forbidden Archaeological Secrets"; "Saudi Archaeology: A Contradiction In Terms"; and "Digging Up the Saudi Past: Some Would Rather Not." Articles like these focus more on the conflict between Saudi archaeologists and conservative Saudi religious authorities than they do on the new information archaeologists have discovered about the history of the Arabian Peninsula. This conflict, which presents serious challenges for archaeologists working in Saudi Arabia, is part of the much broader conflict between conservative Wahhabi Islam and the more liberal forces challenging the Saudi government.

Conservative religious opposition to the practice of archaeology in Saudi Arabia takes many forms. While Saudi archaeologists are allowed to publish in scholarly journals, the results of their excavations are not covered in the Saudi media. An SCTA official told a reporter from the Associated Press that all archaeological sites in Saudi Arabia are treated equally and that archaeologists are free to discuss their findings in academic venues. Nevertheless, many archaeologists still hesitate to discuss their work with the press.

OBJECTS THAT SHOULD NOT BE EXCAVATED OR PUT ON DISPLAY

The hostility of Saudi religious authorities has been directed primarily, but not exclusively, at archaeological research on the Jahiliyya period. One well-known Saudi cleric insisted that anything associated with the pre-Islamic period "should be left in the ground." "Any ruins belonging to non-Muslims," he added, "should not be touched. Leave them in place, the way they have been for thousands of years!"[14] In 1994, a group of Saudi clerics reportedly issued a fatwa stating that the excavation and preservation of ancient sites "could lead to polytheism and idolatry," both of which are crimes according to the Saudi version of sharia law.[15]

Some non-Saudi commentators have expressed fear that pre-Islamic arti-facts and ruins discovered in the Kingdom might be vandalized or even destroyed like the Buddhas of Bamiyan, the colossal statues in central Afghanistan that were dynamited by the Taliban in 2001. These concerns are often accompanied by references to "Islamofanatics" and "mad mullahs" who want to "cleanse the land of infidel influences" by blowing up "ancient ruins and museum displays to remove their polluting presence from holy Arabia."[16] The fear that archaeological interest in the Jahiliyya period might somehow undermine the strictly monotheistic Wahhabi form of Islam that pervades Saudi culture has in the past restricted access to ancient sites for both Saudi and foreign archaeologists, and for tourists as well. Over the past decade, however, the Saudi government has become significantly more supportive of archaeological research in the Kingdom.

A revealing instance of the politicization of Saudi archaeology involves what has come to be known as the Jubail Church, a Nestorian Christian church built in the sixth or seventh century near the industrial city of Jubail, 110 kilometers north of al-Khobar on the Persian Gulf. A number of histori-cal studies have convincingly shown the existence of a large Christian popu-lation in the region during the pre-Islamic period. There were also areas in the southwest of the country that were inhabited predominantly by Christians until some time between the seventh and the tenth centuries, when they were either driven out or converted to Islam.

According to an article published in 1994 by John Langfeldt in *Arabian Archaeology and Epigraphy*, a young Saudi driving in the dunes west of Jubail in 1986 became stuck in the sand. As he tried to dig himself out, he discov-ered a wall. He contacted local officials, who sent a contractor to excavate the site. When they discovered several crosses incised on the walls of the build-ing, they notified the Saudi Department of Antiquities, who instructed them to build a fence and post guards around the site. When Langfeldt visited, he was not allowed to enter the site or take photographs, but officials did let him use binoculars to examine the ruins of the church from a distance.

In 1987, the Saudi Department of Antiquities conducted excavations at the Jubail Church and discovered additional crosses impressed in the plaster on either side of the main doorway. Several months later someone contacted Langfeldt to tell him he'd found three flat stones near the church, each of which was inscribed with a cross. Afraid that the stones would be destroyed if he left them at the site, the man took them home. Langfeldt suggested he photograph them, return them to their original location, and then notify the Department of Antiquities.

In his article, Langfeldt published these photographs, as well as his own. He presented convincing evidence that the main building at the site was a Christian church and that located nearby were Christian burials and a small monastery. By 1992, the crosses on the wall of the church had been obliterated. Because many Saudis "vociferously deny" a past Christian presence in their country and are eager "to minimize the significance of the Jubail church," Langfeldt emphasized that there has been long and extensive Christian presence in what is now Saudi Arabia and that Christian communities persisted there until at least the eighth century. Langfeldt concluded his article with an optimism that has proven unfounded: "We eagerly await the excavation reports of the General Department of Antiquities and Museums of Saudi Arabia." To date Saudi archaeologists have published nothing at all about the church at Jubail.[17]

According to other accounts of the Jubail Church, Saudi officials will not reveal any information about the site—not even its exact location—nor will they issue permits for anyone, including foreign archaeologists, to visit it. The reason, they say, is that the site is still "under excavation." An amateur archaeologist, a Saudi, wrote an article about the church for a local newspaper, but the editor refused to publish it. From a conservative Wahhabi perspective, the existence of a Christian church on Saudi territory, even one sixteen hundred years old, presents a threat to the Islamic purity of the Kingdom. The case of the Jubail Church confirms the opinion of some western scholars that Saudi officials have refused to allow the excavation of Christian sites because they do not want to acknowledge a Christian presence in their country. One non-Saudi archaeologist summed the situation up by describing the attitude of Saudi officials as "completely anti-Christian."

The Saudi government and the religious authorities that support it also oppose the expression of any archaeological or historical interest in the country's early Islamic heritage. They are concerned that early Islamic shrines or tombs could become sites for the worship of figures other than Allah and in that way encourage the practices of idolatry and polytheism. Saudis committed to architectural and historic preservation have strongly protested these policies, especially when they affect the two holy cities of Mecca and Medina. According to some estimates, in the past twenty-five years the Saudi government has demolished 95 percent of Mecca's historic buildings, many of which were over a thousand years old, in order to make room for luxury hotels, apartment blocks, and parking lots.

One of the recent battlegrounds in the conflict over Mecca's architectural heritage involved the seventeenth-century Ottoman portico of the Holy Mosque, which was destroyed as part of an expansion project to make room for the ever increasing number of pilgrims who come there to pray. In 2002, the Saudi authorities destroyed an eighteenth-century Ottoman fortress on a hill above the mosque in order to build the Mecca Royal Clock Tower, a Fairmont Hotel, which at seventy-six floors, stands as one of the world's tallest buildings. The Turkish minister of culture accused the Saudi government of committing an "act of barbarism." According to a Saudi historian based in the United Kingdom; the policies of the Saudi government amount to nothing more than "cultural vandalism." Dr. Sami Angawi, a prominent Sufi leader of the Hijaz and a highly respected Saudi architect, lamented that we were witnessing "the last few moments of the history of Mecca."[18]

Conservative Wahhabi religious beliefs also have a dramatic impact on Saudi museums. From a strict Wahhabi perspective all art is blasphemous, particularly art that depicts the human form. Many Saudis suspect that the Museum of Contemporary Islamic Art, which was originally planned as part of the King Abdulaziz Historical Center in Riyadh, has never opened because of clerical opposition, even though the collection has already been assembled and the building to display it has already been built.

Saudi museums in general display few pre-Islamic artifacts. One Saudi archaeologist told me that this is primarily because of religious sensitivity. The Jahiliyya Era Hall in the National Museum in Riyadh emphasizes the ignorance and darkness that, from a Wahhabi perspective, characterize everything associated with this period. Prominently displayed near the entrance to the hall is a passage from the Quran (16:36) that draws a sharp distinction between Muslims, who serve Allah and accept the Truth, on the one hand, and non-Muslims, who refuse to submit to Allah and deny the Truth, on the other. According to a consultant involved in planning the exhibits at the National Museum, officials decided that pre-Islamic artifacts could not safely be displayed there because of opposition from religious conservatives. As a compromise, curators decided to include photographs and murals of pre-Islamic sites, but no actual artifacts from the period. No Saudi museum, in fact, has any Christian or Jewish artifacts on display. One conservative cleric justified this omission with an interesting rhetorical question: "How can crosses be displayed when Islam doesn't recognize that Christ was crucified? If we display them, it's as if we recognize the crucifixion!"[19]

The conflict between conservative religious forces and more progressive elements in Saudi society has significantly interfered with the growth of archaeology and the expansion of tourism. Over the past few decades, however, important liberalizing trends have begun to emerge. The Saudi government has invited foreign archaeologists to join their Saudi colleagues in excavating pre-Islamic sites; it has also started to promote domestic tourism more actively. The phrase "evolution, not revolution," a staple of Saudi conversations about social change, applies as well to the developments taking place in the intersecting worlds of archaeology, museums, and tourism.

ROADS OF ARABIA: ARCHAEOLOGY IN SERVICE OF THE KINGDOM

Roads of Arabia is the epitome of the international "blockbuster" exhibition that makes appearances at prestigious European and North American art museums, complete with long lines of visitors, glowing reviews, and lavishly illustrated catalogs. Roads of Arabia was the product of an extensive history of cooperation and exchange between France and Saudi Arabia. In 2004, during a visit to the Kingdom by French President Jacques Chirac, the head of the Louvre and Prince Sultan bin Salman, the nephew of King Abdullah and president of the SCTA, signed an agreement to foster closer ties between their two countries.

A year later, Saudi Prince al-Waleed bin Talal donated 17 million euros to the Louvre for the construction of a new wing of exhibition halls to be devoted to Islamic art. In 2006, the Louvre loaned 150 masterpieces from its collection of Islamic art to the National Museum in Riyadh for an exhibition there that attracted a half a million visitors. According to Ali Ibrahim al-Ghabban, vice-president of antiquities and museums at the SCTA and co-curator of the exhibition, Roads of Arabia was an important part of a long-term Saudi strategy "to use antiquities to promote the country and build tourism." The exhibition, said al-Ghabban, "will help Saudis to be proud of their heritage."[20]

Roads of Arabia was jointly conceived and curated by officials at the Louvre and the SCTA. The selection of the specific objects to be included in the exhibition was the subject of protracted negotiations. The main sponsors of the Louvre exhibition were Saudi Aramco, ExxonMobil, Saudi Arabian Airlines, Boeing, and several other Fortune 500 corporations based in Saudi Arabia and the Middle East. At the opening of the exhibition in Paris on July 14, 2010, rumors circulated as to why King Abdullah had failed to attend. Was he offended at an article in the French press quoting him as saying that Israel and Iran didn't deserve to exist? Or was he just tired after a long trip to Washington?

CNN's account of the opening was typical of the positive media response that Roads of Arabia generated: "A groundbreaking new exhibition of rare artifacts from Saudi Arabia's ancient past—some which have never been shown abroad—has opened in the Louvre, Paris. The world-famous museum is hosting *Roads of Arabia: Archaeology and History of the Kingdom of Saudi Arabia,* a traveling exhibition showcasing 300 archeological treasures found in the Gulf country, many pre-dating the birth of Islam."[21] After closing at the Louvre in September, 2010, Roads of Arabia traveled to the Vittoriano Museum in Rome, the Hermitage in St. Petersburg, and the Pergamon Museum in Berlin. According to the SCTA, more than a million and a half people saw the exhibition over the course of its European tour.

On November 17, 2012, Roads of Arabia began the American portion of its world tour with a grand opening at the Arthur M. Sackler Gallery on the National Mall in Washington, DC. The Sackler and the nearby Freer Gallery are the Smithsonian Institution's national museums of Asian art. At the opening ceremonies, the secretary of the Smithsonian and the director of the Sackler and Freer Galleries, in their dark suits, welcomed the Saudi ambassador to the United States and the president of the SCTA, who were wearing long brown *bisht*s trimmed in gold and white *shemagh*s over their heads. Filming the event was KSA2, the English-language Saudi television channel.

The festivities continued with a Family Day Cultural Celebration that included performances of classical and modern Arab music, a film screening of *Arab Shorts,* traditional Arab cuisine, and workshops in Arabic calligraphy for children to be held in the "ImaginAsia classroom." At a scholarly symposium entitled "Crossroads of Culture," archaeologists discussed the results of recent excavations and some of the challenges facing their work in Saudi Arabia. When the exhibition closed at the Sackler in February 2013, it continued its U.S. tour with shows in Houston, Chicago, and San Francisco.

Standing at the entrance to the Roads of Arabia exhibition at the Sackler, were three anthropomorphic funerary stelae dramatically lit from above and mounted in front of a jet-black background on pedestals that placed them at human height. Carved from the same roughly textured, light brown sandstone, all three had been found in northwest Saudi Arabia, and they all dated from the fourth millennium B.C.E. These stelae have been described as "highly abstract," "surprisingly modern," and "hauntingly mysterious."[22] The low, square head of one was separated from his torso by two curves, one suggesting his jaw line, the other the neckline of his clothing. From his belt hung a double bladed dagger. The large oval head of another stele, with its round, projecting ears and deeply carved mouth and eyes, tilted pensively—or perhaps sadly—to the side (see fig. 12).

Covering the curved wall to the right of the entrance was a huge black-and-white photograph of rock outcrops, like those around Madain Saleh, rising from the desert. The wall to the left announced the title of the exhibition and the names of its major sponsors, while a short text promised archaeological discoveries that have "radically transformed our understanding of the region" and offer "a timely glimpse into the Arabian Peninsula's richly layered and fascinating past." In a small room to the left, a short introductory film took viewers on "a fascinating and unexpected journey" to explore both the "incense roads" that crisscrossed the Arabian Peninsula before the birth of Islam and the "pilgrimage roads" that brought Muslims from all over the world to the holy cities of Mecca and Medina. The most striking scenes in the film, however, presented exotic, Orientalist images of Arabia that would not have been out be out of place in a tourist brochure: camels walking in single file across the desert; a minaret against a red sky with the call to prayer sounding in the distance; and a white-robed man standing at the top of a sand dune holding out his arm to release a falcon against the backdrop of a huge orange sun.

Display cases in the first room of the exhibition were filled with prehistoric tools providing early evidence for the existence of humans in the Arabian Peninsula—Neolithic blades of flint, Acheulean scrapers of andesite, and Oldowan choppers of quartzite. The next room contained a delightful menagerie of sandstone animals from the seventh millennium that had been discovered by a camel herder while digging a well in the desert. Among the heads of a sheep, an ostrich, and a hunting dog, lay the head and body of an equid—a horse, ass, or onager—whose muzzle and shoulders bore markings suggesting the presence of a bridle and reins. This discovery raised the exciting possibility that the domestication of the horse, previously thought to have occurred in Mesopotamia around 3,500 B.C.E., had actually taken place on the Arabian Peninsula three or four thousand years earlier.

Highlights of the next few rooms included the "al-Hamra cube," a pedestal or altar decorated with religious scenes—stars, crescent moons, bull heads with solar discs between the horns—from Tayma dating back to the fourth or fifth centuries B.C.E. and a gold funerary mask and glove from the grave of a young girl who died in the city of Thaj during the first century C.E. Later rooms contained several large sandstone heads and three colossal headless statues of Lihyanite kings from the third or fourth centuries B.C.E., which had been found in Dedan, the modern al-Ula, a short distance south of Madain Saleh. The skin of some figures had been painted red, while that of others had been covered with black tar. The rigid posture—left foot forward, stiff arms, and clenched fists—suggested Egyptian or Syrian influence. Other rooms contained ceramics, wall paintings, and statues imported from Greece and Rome. Most striking was a bronze statuette of Hercules holding a lion skin and club.

A few feet to the right of Hercules, a doorway led from the pre-Islamic period to the Islamic period. As visitors crossed the threshold, they passed from the first part of the exhibition, "the incense roads," to the second part, "the pilgrimage roads." They were now in "Mecca/Makkah."[23] On one wall was an account of the rise of Islam: the birth of the Prophet Muhammad, His flight to Medina, His conquest of Mecca, and the transformation of Islam into a multicultural religion as Christians, Jews, and people who had worshiped other local deities all became Muslims.

On another wall hung a video panel presenting an animated history of the Holy Mosque in Mecca from the building of the Kaba through the mosque's twentieth-century expansions. Against a third wall stood an impressive three-and-a-half-by-two-meter door of the Kaba, built in the workshops of the Imperial Palace in Istanbul, donated by the Ottoman Sultan Murad IV, and installed in 1635–36 after a major flood had damaged the Holy Mosque. This door, made of wood and gilded silver leaf, had stood in place in the Kaba until sometime between 1937 and 1947, when it was replaced by the present door in a gesture proclaiming King Abdulaziz ibn Saud guardian of the most holy site in the Muslim world.

By far the most moving objects in the room from my perspective were eighteen tombstones from the al-Mala Cemetery in Mecca; they ranged in date from the ninth to the sixteenth centuries. Inscribed on the flat surface of irregularly shaped blocks of gray, green, and pink basalt were epitaphs identifying the deceased by name, occupation, and family ties (see fig. 13). The epitaphs included the *bismillah* ("In the name of God, the Compassionate, the Merciful"), passages from the Quran, and prayers in memory of the deceased, many of whom had died in Mecca while on the Hajj. The variety and quality of the calligraphy and the architectural and floral ornamentation framing the epitaphs were striking.

The epitaph on the tombstone of Yusuf, son of Abdallah, who died in June 1199, read in part:

> Oh, you who find fault with me, be gentle; oppress me not.
> I refuse to be blamed.
> Had Fate struck you as it did me,
> You could only have let your tears flow.
> The blows of Fate tore me apart;
> I have fallen prey to laments and grief.
> Destiny parted us from our beloveds;
> I ought [to] have been the first to die.
> Death, oh death, you left me no companion with whom I could find
> consolation; not a friend is left to me.[24]

The next room of the exhibition explored the "pilgrimage roads" that Muslims from all over the Arab world took on their journeys to Mecca and Medina. Maps on the walls illustrated the four main routes to the Holy Cities from Egypt, Damascus, Yemen, and Iraq; display cases contained personal objects pilgrims had brought with them on their journeys from faraway Baghdad and Samarkand—soapstone incense burners, delicate blown glass, and silver coins. A video monitor showed archival footage of scenes from the Hajj: veiled women drawing water from wells, pilgrims crossing the desert in camel caravans, and still more pilgrims disembarking from the Hijaz Railway in Medina or from ships and planes in Jeddah.

The last room of the exhibition celebrated King Abdulaziz ibn Saud, who seized Riyadh in 1902, conquered Mecca and Medina in 1925, and founded the Kingdom of Saudi Arabia in 1932. Displayed here were a formal black-and-white photograph of the king taken in 1910 when he was thirty-four years old, the wood and leather stand for his prized falcon, his brown and gold *bisht,* his gold-hilted sword, and his Quran.

On a wall nearby hung a large Saudi flag—a sword and the text of the *shahada,* the testimony of faith, emblazoned in white against a bright green background. Around the room were books and maps illustrating the early exploration of Arabia, information about the history of archaeology in the region, and on either side of the exit a collection of photographs documenting the "Foundations of a New Nation"—the desert, old Riyadh, groves of date palms, the Hijaz Railway, and a historic photograph of King Abdulaziz meeting with President Franklin Delano Roosevelt on February 14, 1945, on the American destroyer *USS Quincy* in the Great Bitter Lake in Egypt's Suez Canal.

REBRANDING SAUDI ARABIA

The Roads of Arabia exhibition at the Sackler was an important artistic and cultural event. It was also an important political and diplomatic event that contributed to the maintenance of the "special relationship" that exists between Saudi Arabia and the United States. In addition, the exhibition served more broadly to promote the interests of Saudi Arabia on the international stage. The political context in which Roads of Arabia took place and the role it played in the diplomatic relationship between Saudi Arabia and the United States were too obvious to be concealed behind the discourse of high culture and fine art that surrounded it. Roads of Arabia is an example of archaeological diplomacy at its best.

Part of the Smithsonian Institution, the Sackler Gallery is administered by the U.S. government; it is located on the National Mall in Washington, the most symbolically important and politically charged site in the United States. While there are policies and guidelines—like Smithsonian Directive 603—designed to avoid conflicts of interest and limit the degree to which exhibitions at the Smithsonian are politicized, it is impossible, and in some respects undesirable, to eliminate all political influence on the Smithsonian.

In 2009, in fact, the U.S. State Department assigned a foreign service officer to the Smithsonian to serve as senior advisor for international affairs to the undersecretary for history, art, and culture. This advisor, who works in the Smithsonian's Office of International Relations, acts as liaison between the State Department and the Smithsonian in order to help the State Department "gain greater access to the Smithsonian's fabulous resources" and "use the Smithsonian's expertise and collections" to serve the diplomatic goals of the United States.[25] As the Foreign Service officer who served in this capacity while Roads of Arabia was at the Sackler told me, "The State Department needs to use every tool in its tool box, and the Smithsonian is a great tool."

From the Saudi perspective, the political utility of the exhibition was also clear. A diplomat at the Saudi Embassy in Washington coordinated negotiations between the SCTA and the Smithsonian and helped organize the celebration that opened the exhibition. The Saudi diplomatic presence at the opening ceremonies impressed one reviewer, who wrote: "Art exhibits rarely come with their own diplomatic entourage, but the new groundbreaking show at the Sackler *Roads of Arabia* does."[26] The Saudi embassy also sponsored a congressional reception that took place at the Sackler on January 22, 2013, the day I visited the exhibition. In an effort to maintain at least some distance between art and politics, curators—at least so I was told—are generally not invited to diplomatic events like this.

One specific political goal of exhibitions like Roads of Arabia is to create a new brand for the country sponsoring it, to redefine the country's identity and reposition it in the world marketplace of cultures, nations, and states. This process often involves an elaborate public relations campaign to erase old, negative associations and replace them with new, more positive ones. Efforts to market a new brand for a country may serve a variety of political and economic goals: enhancing its international reputation, developing its global trading networks, advancing its diplomatic interests, and promoting tourism. The audience for these rebranding campaigns is often both domestic and international. A particularly effective way for a country to rebrand itself is to mount an international art exhibition that will showcase its national heritage at leading museums around the world.

Saudi Arabia is a country with a serious image problem; it is in desperate need of rebranding. In the early twenty-first century, the Saudi "brand" is associated with camels, deserts, and oil; with a decadent monarchy, the oppression of women, and the violation of human rights; and with religious extremism and terrorism. The rebranding effort of which Roads of Arabia is part was designed to fight the legacy of 9/11 and the attacks on the Twin Towers of the World Trade Center, which have inextricably linked Saudi Arabia with the export of suicide bombers in particular and Islamic terrorists more generally. With Roads of Arabia, the Saudi government is trying to associate the Kingdom instead with ancient civilizations, high culture, and fine art.

In a 2012 issue of the *Saudi Voyager,* a magazine published by the SCTA, whose slogan is "Discover! Saudi Arabia," His Royal Highness Prince Sultan bin Salman said that Roads of Arabia shows conclusively that "from early times Saudi Arabia has always played an important role in the Middle East. It has existed as a bridge between the East and the West. The first dialogue of civilizations finds its origins in the Kingdom, which has historically had a strong communication with the rest of the world. Indeed a role Saudi Arabia is playing until today."[27] In an interview with the *Washington Post*, Sultan bin Salman added: "We've always be been at the crossroads of civilization, and we are now at the crossroads of international and economic affairs." Saudi Arabia, he emphasized, is "not a country that was invented with the discovery of the first oil well."[28]

The newly rebranded Saudi Arabia has a long history linking its present with an ancient past. Roads of Arabia demonstrates that in antiquity Saudi Arabia was the center of a vital trade network that brought together many different civilizations of the ancient world. It was a place where different cultures came together and peacefully coexisted. It was open to the influences of other cultures, not isolated or closed off; it was a diverse, a cosmopolitan, even a multicultural region, a "meeting place of civilizations." As a result of the continuity that characterizes Saudi history—at least according to this new Saudi marketing campaign—these same qualities characterize modern Saudi Arabia as well. Prince Sultan bin Salman's claim that the first "dialogue of civilizations" took place in the Kingdom is an unmistakable reference to the national and international "dialogues" promoted by King Abdullah, the "King of Dialogue."

In some of the publicity material for Roads of Arabia, this rebranding campaign was acknowledged in a surprisingly direct manner. In an interview published on Smithsonian.com, Julian Raby, the director of the Sackler, openly conceded the political goals of the exhibit, noting that the Saudi government hoped to redefine the Kingdom as an open and dynamic land, just as it had been in antiquity. Ali al-Ghabban also admitted that one of the exhibition's goals was to create a new image for his country: "Most Westerners believe that Saudi Arabia is only a desert land with oil wells. They don't know that the country was a bridge between the East and the West. We played this role in the fourth millennium B.C.E., and we continue to play it. In the outside world, we should correct the wrong image of our country."[29]

The *National Review* was much more critical. Cleverly titled "The Saudis' PR 'Roads' Show," its review of Roads of Arabia referred to the exhibition as a "lavish attempt to throw sand in the eyes of the West," arguing that it was part of an "assiduously waged public-relations campaign" mounted by the Saudi royal family since 9/11 "to improve its image by sponsoring major cultural initiatives in the West." The review also took sharp exception to al-Ghabban's claim that the exhibition demonstrated that "we [Saudis] are not closed. We were always open. We are open today." Finally, the review argued that in light of Saudi Arabia's atrocious record on human rights, the exhibition constituted little more than a disinformation campaign designed to promote a positive image of an open and tolerant country that could not be further from the truth. "In the face of this reality," the review concluded, "the Saudi PR efforts take on a decidedly sinister cast."[30]

WORKS OF ART OR PAGAN IDOLS?

The first part of Roads of Arabia, which dealt exclusively with the pre-Islamic period, posed the greatest challenge to efforts to rebrand Saudi Arabia as an open, tolerant country known for its rich archaeological heritage, as opposed to an isolated, intolerant country where all non-Muslim forms of religious belief and practice are forbidden. It is also with the presentation of the pre-Islamic period that the image of a homogeneous, strictly Muslim society constructed by Saudi religious authorities for domestic consumption, on the one hand, conflicts most sharply with the image of a diverse, multicultural society constructed by Saudi archaeologists and tourism officials for international consumption, on the other. In spite of skillful attempts to mask these contradictions, the efforts of the SCTA to market this new positive image to a global public are unlikely to succeed in supplanting the negative images that are already in wide circulation.

The pre-Islamic section of Roads of Arabia presents the Arabian Peninsula of the time as a multicultural region inhabited by an incredible variety of people speaking many different languages and worshiping many different gods. This land was multilingual and polytheistic with a vengeance. Among the tribes, kingdoms, and empires that inhabited Arabia during this period, were the Dedanites, Himyarites, and Lihyanites; the Minians, Nabataeans, and Sabeans; the Babylonians, Egyptians, and Persians; and the Greeks, Romans, and Byzantines. Among the Babel of languages spoken there were Hadramatic, Hagaric, and Hismaic; Qatabanic, Safaitic, and Thamudic; Aramaic, Syriac, and Taymaic; Greek, Hebrew, and Latin.

In testament to the wondrous creativity of the religious imagination, the people of the Arabian Peninsula in the pre-Islamic era worshiped as many as a hundred different deities: Ara, god of the sun; Athtar, god of the morning star; and Hubal, god of the moon; Dhu Ghaba, lord of the grove; Dhu Samawi, lord of heaven; and Dhu Shara, lord of the mountains; the three daughters of Allah: Allat, Al Uzza, and Manat; and more: Aabit, Almqah, and Ara; Salm, Sayin, and Suwa; Bayta, Manaf, and Ruda; and Mar, Qais, and Wadd.

Many of the most spectacular objects in the pre-Islamic rooms of the exhibition, such as the three anthropomorphic funerary stelae and the colossal sandstone statues and heads from al-Ula, offer dramatic proof of the practice of what conservative Saudi religious authorities would condemn as idolatry. The same is true for many smaller artifacts in the exhibition: the bronze and terracotta figurines of the Egyptian child god Harpocrates, the Greek goddess Artemis, and the Egyptian goddess of fortune, Isis-Tyche. The valuable works of art on display at the Sackler are, in the eyes of conservative Wahhabi religious officials, nothing more than pagan idols.

Because of this religious sensitivity and the close relationship between Wahhabi officials and the Saudi government, it has been difficult to incorporate these objects into the canon of Saudi national culture. Some of these artifacts—works of art or pagan idols?—have never been displayed publicly in prominent Saudi museums. Some of them can be found in small, local museums scattered around the country; some remain in storage, hidden from public view. Presenting these objects to a domestic audience in Saudi Arabia would create controversy, but shipping them abroad, Saudi officials hope, will create a more positive image for the country on the international stage.

The official SCTA website on the exhibition contains no images of works of art from the pre-Islamic period, nor does it contain a single image of a sculpture of a human figure. None of the most impressive objects in the exhibition, therefore, none of the anthropomorphic stelae, none of the colossal statues, none of the small figurines, are included anywhere on the website. It's not at all surprising, then, that young Saudis studying in the United States who came to see Roads of Arabia at the Sackler told reporters they had no idea that their country's archaeological heritage included such wonderful works of art. One surprised young Saudi said he'd learned more about his country's history visiting the exhibition in Washington than he had during all his years of schooling in the Kingdom.

Notably absent from the pre-Islamic section of Roads of Arabia are any Christian works of art. Some would claim that no Christian artifacts worthy of inclusion have ever been found in Saudi Arabia. Others would argue that displaying objects acknowledging a Christian presence in the Kingdom would be beyond the pale for the Saudi curators, that it would have been much too sensitive an issue for curators at the Louvre to even bring up. Still others would insist that some of the few Christian artifacts that *have* been found—simple crosses incised on funerary stelae, for example—or at least some *photographs* of Christian artifacts, could have been included. Among the many Roads of Arabia on display in the exhibition, there is not a single Christian "road" to be found.

From a Wahhabi perspective, the term *Jahiliyya,* the Age of Ignorance, has strong negative connotations. It is used to refer to the "ignorance of divine guidance," to refer to nonbelievers and enemies of Allah, people who refuse to be guided by the will Allah as revealed in the Quran. Jahiliyya is a state of corruption and immorality characterized by *shirk,* the sin of paganism, idolatry, and polytheism. A person who lives in a state of Jahiliyya is a *mushrik,* a person who commits *shirk,* or a *kafir,* a nonbeliever, an infidel, someone who refuses to believe in Allah.[31] In some contexts, Jews and Christians are included in this category; in others they are identified as "people of the Book," who have a great deal in common with Muslims.

From a conservative Muslim perspective, people living in the Jahiliyya period were wicked and corrupt; they practiced immoral sexual acts; they committed female infanticide and human sacrifice; they ate carrion and drank blood; they practiced usury, gambled, and consumed alcohol; and worst of all, they worshiped ancestors, demons, and gods made of wood and stone. It was the divine revelation of the Quran that rescued humanity from this state of depravity and barbarism.

There are interesting parallels between the opposition described here between two chronological periods—the Islamic era and the Jahiliyya period—on the one hand, and the opposition that exists in the present between two groups—Muslims and non-Muslims—on the other. The dichotomy between Muslims and non-Muslims, in other words, has both a temporal and a spatial dimension. The temporal boundary that separates the Islamic era from the Jahiliyya period corresponds to the conceptual boundary that distinguishes Muslims from non-Muslims and the geographical boundaries that exclude non-Muslims from space that is sacred to Muslims.

In sharp contrast to this negative image of the Jahiliyya period promoted by conservative Saudi religious authorities, stands the positive image of the period, referred to more neutrally in Roads of Arabia as the pre-Islamic period, promoted by officials of the SCTA and the non-Saudi curators of the exhibition. Roads of Arabia celebrates the diversity of languages, religions, and cultures that characterized the Arabian Peninsula before the time of Muhammad. While the conservative religious view of the Jahiliyya period denies any link between it and the Islamic period, educational material produced by the SCTA in conjunction with Roads of Arabia claims just the opposite. It emphasizes the continuity, not the lack of continuity, that characterizes the relationship between the two periods.

To anyone familiar with conservative Islamic discourse on the Jahiliyya period, the following passage from a booklet published by the SCTA and available at the opening of Roads of Arabia may come as quite a shock. "Antiquities are the seeds of historical continuity. . . . Although the Kingdom of Saudi Arabia is renowned for Islamic traditions and values, Islam did not appear in a vacuum. On the contrary, it was founded upon layers of civilization and arose in a society which was characterized by openness and mobility. . . . Islam acknowledged the existence and importance of the great Pre-Islamic civilizations of Arabia, respected the great revealed religions which had preceded it."[32]

Some of the statements made by SCTA officials involved in Roads of Arabia explicitly reject the negative view of the Jahiliyya period endorsed by conservative religious authorities. When asked about the destruction of the Buddhas of Bamiyan by the Taliban in Afghanistan or about threats by Egyptian fundamentalists to destroy the Sphinx, Dr. al-Ghabban of the SCTA said, "It's stupidity. The first Muslims did not do the same. I think we need to understand deeply our religion, and I can guarantee you there is no contradiction between protecting the human heritage and Islam." Prince Sultan bin Salman agreed: "Islam came as a very proud religion, but it identified with these ancient civilizations and did not demean them. We would be doing a disservice to Islam if we thought Islam came to a void, to a clean sheet of paper, to a people who had nothing else."[33]

Most reviews of Roads of Arabia simply glossed over the contradiction between these two very different perspectives toward artifacts from the pre-Islamic period. Reviewers attributed their sudden appearance in international museums not to the fact that their existence had previously been suppressed by Saudi authorities, but to the fact that they had just been lying for centuries lost and forgotten in the desert sand. Publicity material for the exhibition simply referred to these works as part of the "untold story of Saudi Arabia's past" without offering any explanation as to why this particular story of this particular past had remained untold for so long.

One account of the exhibition was more explicit; it described Saudi archaeological heritage as having been "eradicated from collective memory."[34] A particularly perceptive reviewer observed that many of the objects on display were considered "controversial" and even "blasphemous" from the perspective of "the strict Wahhabi brand of Islam enforced throughout Saudi Arabia since the rise of the Saud dynasty at the beginning of the twentieth century." In spite of this, the reviewer continued, "the Saudi government is utilizing these artifacts in an attempt to cultivate a new and improved international persona for the country and the Saud family."[35]

It is ironic that the same stone figures condemned domestically as objects of pagan worship by religious officials representing the king as "Custodian of the Two Holy Mosques," are celebrated abroad as part of ancient Saudi cultural heritage by officials of the SCTA representing the king as ruler of a modern state. These stones are either idols or archaeological artifacts, and therefore their worship—litholatry, the worship of stones—is either idolatry or archaeolatry. What pagans worship literally, archaeologists worship figuratively. The same is true for the locations where these objects were found. Madain Saleh is either an evil place cursed by the prophet Saleh to be avoided by good Muslims, on the one hand, or a tourist destination worthy of being designated a World Heritage Site, on the other.

TOMBSTONES TO VENERATE, DESTROY, OR PUT ON DISPLAY?

The same paradox that characterizes this contradictory treatment of archaeological artifacts from the Jahiliyya period also characterizes the treatment of some of the material from the early Islamic period on display in the exhibition. Among the most impressive objects in the rooms devoted to the Islamic period are the tombstones from the al-Mala Cemetery in Mecca. In text on the gallery wall, the Sackler curators write that the "hundreds of tombstones of the now *destroyed* al-Mala Cemetery north of Mecca" put "a humble, yet noble face" on the many Muslims who died and were buried in Islam's most holy city.

In her essay for the exhibition catalog, Carine Juvin, a medieval historian in the Department of Islamic Art at the Louvre, provides additional information on fate of the tombstones: "The cemetery was the burial place of some of the leading figures of the early days of Islam. In the course of centuries it became renowned as a site for religious visits linked to the pilgrimage until it *vanished* in the twentieth century, as a result of expanding urbanization and construction work in the holy city."[36]

A comparison of the descriptions of the al-Mala Cemetery offered by the Sackler curators and by Juvin raises some interesting questions: What actually happened to the al-Mala Cemetery? Was it destroyed or did it vanish? If it was destroyed, who destroyed it and why? And how can a cemetery just vanish?

The al-Mala Cemetery in Mecca, one of the two most important cemeteries in the Islamic world, is where Muhammad's mother, wife, grandfather, and other ancestors were buried. A photograph of the cemetery taken in 1880 shows the many mausolea and shrines of martyrs and saints that had been built there over the centuries. In 1925, all these structures were demolished by King Abdulaziz ibn Saud when he captured the Hijaz from the Hashemite Sharif of Mecca. This was the same year the king ordered the destruction of the mausolea and shrines in the equally important al-Baqi Cemetery in Medina.[37] Since then, Muslims throughout the world have expressed their outrage at these acts of desecration. Many Muslims—especially Shia, for whom early Muslim sites like these are particularly sacred—continue to mourn the destruction of these sites with great sorrow.

Some of the tombstones on display in Roads of Arabia were preserved in situ in the al-Mala Cemetery until 1984, when they were removed and taken to a small museum in Jeddah housed in the historic Khuzam Palace, a former royal residence of King Abdulaziz. There they were kept in storage in poor conditions, lying on the ground covered in dust, until Carine Juvin discovered them, recognized their importance, and successfully lobbied for their inclusion in the Roads of Arabia exhibition. These tombstones could have been removed from the al-Mala Cemetery to prevent them from being destroyed by vandals or because they were an affront to conservative Wahhabi ideology.

According to Saudi religious authorities, all vestiges of early Islamic funerary structures should be eradicated in order to prevent them from becoming sites of unacceptable religious practices and to keep those buried in them from becoming objects of worship as martyrs or saints. The ambivalent attitude many Saudi officials have toward these objects is revealed by an incident that took place at the opening of Roads of Arabia at the Louvre that was described to me by an archaeologist who attended the event. When a Saudi prince learned that the tombstones were from the al-Mala Cemetery in Mecca, he simply turned his back and walked away.

Now the al-Mala Cemetery consists of large areas of brown gravel surrounded by low white-washed walls. All the graves in it are identical; each one is marked by a small, nondescript white stone or group of stones that bears no name, no date, and no epitaph. This is typical of contemporary Saudi cemeteries. The government forbids the placement of names or any other identifying marks on graves in order to prevent them from becoming the site of proscribed rituals. Saudis are not allowed to pray in cemeteries; Saudi women cannot even enter them. Wahhabi religious leaders condemn these practices as "heathen aberrations," "wicked stratagems of Satan," and "abominable innovations contrary to the guidance of the Prophet." That is why during the nineteenth and early twentieth centuries Wahhabis "destroyed almost all burial sites that they could lay their hands on," including, "most regrettably," those in Mecca and Medina.[38]

The destruction of the al-Mala Cemetery in Mecca, like the destruction of al-Baqi Cemetery in Medina, is part of the wider campaign that has long been waged by the Saudi government to destroy any site associated with early Islam that could possibly become a place of worship. Among those sites that have been destroyed as part of this campaign are the house of Muhammad's wife Khadija (now a public bathroom); the house of Muhammad's father-in-law Abu Bakr (now a Hilton Hotel); and the Prophet's own birthplace (formerly a cattle market and now a public library).

By destroying its mausolea and removing its tombstones, Saudi authorities have transformed the al-Mala Cemetery into a homogeneous and anonymous Wahhabi cemetery. In this way, the Saudi government has severed the relationship between contemporary Saudis and an important element of their early Islamic heritage, just as it has severed their relationship with their pre-Islamic heritage. Ironically the Saudi government is using this same heritage to rebrand the Kingdom abroad and assert a living continuity between contemporary Saudi culture and both its pre-Islamic and its early Islamic pasts. By removing tombstones from the graves they mark and putting them on display in museums abroad, the Saudi government has transformed sacred religious objects into secular archaeological artifacts and works of art. Objects that were once part of a living religious tradition that was forbidden by King Abdulaziz are now celebrated as part of Saudi cultural heritage in an international exhibition whose patron is the son of King Abdulaziz and whose final room is devoted to the unabashed worship of King Abdulaziz himself.

THE PROPAGANDA ROAD

Roads of Arabia concludes with what can only be described as a shrine to King Abdulaziz ibn Saud, the founder of the Kingdom of Saudi Arabia and the father of Abdullah, the present king, custodian of the Two Holy Mosques, and patron of the exhibition. This final room celebrates King Abdulaziz's role as founder of the Saudi state and father of the Saudi nation; it glorifies both his diplomatic skills and his military prowess. From a political perspective, this display is of central importance. It marks the Al Saud dynasty as the proprietor of the Kingdom of Saudi Arabia and therefore the actual *owner* of all the objects in the exhibition.[39] The preface to the catalog published in conjunction with the exhibition in Berlin acknowledges this relationship of possession when it describes "the Royal House of Al Saud" as presenting "the rich history and culture of *its* country."[40]

From an archaeological and an art historical perspective, however, the material on King Abdulaziz and the founding of the Kingdom is of very little interest. Massumeh Farhad, the curator of Islamic art, ended her tour before even entering the room; she simply had nothing to say about it. And a docent at the Sackler Gallery referred to the last room of the exhibition as an "add-on." Both the Louvre website devoted to the exhibition and the review of it in the *New York Times* ignored the room completely.

The Roads of Arabia catalog published in conjunction with the exhibitions at the Louvre and the Sackler contains one chapter on King Abdulaziz and one on the founding of the Kingdom; both were written by Fahd al-Simari, the general secretary of the King Abdulaziz Foundation for Research and Archives in Riyadh. They present a fawning account of the king's glorious career. We learn, for example, that the King's strong character was forged from "the inherent hardships of Bedouin life" and that he "was known to all for his piety, courage, gentlemanly spirit, and great generosity, as well as his far-sighted political savvy." We read that he was "a wise man who had learned the lessons of history" and who was "always motivated by a concern for the public interest and the rights of his subjects." Finally, as the caption of the famous photograph tells us, we learn that his 1945 meeting with President Franklin Roosevelt and Winston Churchill bears witness to his "political influence and farsighted positions."[41]

Scholars who have worked in Saudi Arabia have different opinions about the material on King Abdulaziz presented in both the exhibition and the catalog. Many agree with a European archaeologist who told me that the inclusion of this material was "a political, a diplomatic, act." Another non-Saudi archaeologist involved in the exhibition said, "Of course it was a very political exhibition. We had to be very careful and to accept the final royal section." Then he added somewhat defensively, "but it was a great opportunity to show all these almost unknown treasures." A third archaeologist told me unambiguously that the articles by al-Simari about King Abdulaziz were included in the catalog at the express wish of the Saudi officials involved in the exhibition.

As might be expected, Saudi officials *were* very pleased with the material on King Abdulaziz. In an email message he sent me, al-Ghabban argued that the personal possessions of the king in the last room were "completely connected" with the ancient material in the first part of the exhibition: "We view Saudi Arabia of today as a continuation of a long sociocultural history, and each historical period has a diachronic relationship with the preceding and the following events." More surprisingly perhaps, a non-Saudi archaeologist I contacted expressed a similar opinion. This archaeologist defended the inclusion of the material on the king and denied the existence of any conflict between scholarship and politics in the exhibition: "The country is centered on the Saud family. The exhibition reinforces the link between the antiquities and the country, and the country and the royal family. I couldn't imagine them showing the antiquities of the country without showing the unification of the country by the King."

Still other non-Saudi scholars seemed resigned to this politicization of their academic work. One archaeologist I spoke with grudgingly accepted the need for this material: "I take it with a grain of salt. It doesn't bother me; I just ignore it. I have a friend who is incensed by it, by the propagandistic, tendentious tone of the last room. He criticizes the Louvre and the Smithsonian for going along with it. But I accept it as the price to be paid. I think one learns to put up with portraits of emirs and sheikhs in this sort of thing when working in the Arabian Peninsula and to just cut to the parts that really matter academically."

While most reviews of Roads of Arabia have been extremely positive, several have been explicit in their criticism of the politics of the exhibition. A reviewer for the *Wall Street Journal* noted that "the thumbnail story of Saudi Arabia's formation" at the end of the exhibition "feels odd, almost like a plea to secure for this oil-rich kingdom a spot on the world cultural map. Unnecessary, really: The art already has done that."[42]

Another reviewer was "unsettled" by the description of the king "as a great mediator, natural and peaceful leader, and unifier of the Arabian peoples," and by the reference to Wahhabism as "representative of peaceful Islam." She interpreted "this re-writing of Saudi history" as a clear attempt by the Saudi government to promote Saudi Arabia as "the religious center for Muslims the world over, and THE authority of Islam." Expressing deep disappointment "at the blatant propaganda embedded in the exhibition," she concluded that "the historical artifacts, up to but *not* including the modern Saud family, hold immense historical value and are well worth seeing."[43]

A third reviewer described this last room as "an unfortunate distraction from the beauty of the exhibition and a reminder that the business of politics and public relations lurks behind every artifact." In a humorous, but decisively positive note, she concluded: "It's a shame to end the exhibition with the Propaganda Road, because until then the exhibition is a triumph."[44]

TOWARD A MORE MODERATE SAUDI IDENTITY

From an artistic and scholarly perspective, Roads of Arabia was without doubt a wonderful success. This success, however, is tarnished by the fact that it was used by the Saudi government for political and diplomatic purposes. The exhibition and its catalog not only presented an overly flattering portrait of King Abdulaziz ibn Saud, the founder and father of all successive rulers of a country that has an extremely poor record on religious freedom, democracy, human rights, and the treatment of women and foreign workers. The exhibition and the catalog also glossed smoothly over the fact that many of the very objects offered here for display in the world's finest museums are regarded very differently in Saudi Arabia itself.

With Roads of Arabia, the Saudi government was seeking to rebrand Saudi Arabia by exporting for international consumption objects from the Kingdom's pre-Islamic and early Islamic past and presenting them as evidence of the long, continuous history of an open and diverse culture. Within Saudi Arabia, however, these same objects are attacked by conservative religious authorities as evidence of idolatrous, pagan practices of the Jahiliyya period and its immediate aftermath. To some, this is little more than false advertising, a hypocritical public relations campaign designed to cast Saudi Arabia in a new, more favorable light. To others, it represents something more positive—a genuine sign of change, in which the Saudi government has begun to adopt a more tolerant and liberal stance toward its past, as well as its future. In either case, as a review in *Le Monde* optimistically, but realistically concludes, the Kingdom of Saudi Arabia seems to be turning "anew toward its past with a willingness to move beyond the inertia and the conservatism of certain religious figures. This effort is worthy of praise and is part of an attempt to construct a more moderate Saudi identity."[45]

Despite—or perhaps because of—the best efforts of its Saudi and non-Saudi curators, Roads of Arabia exposed the tensions that continue to trouble efforts to rebrand the Kingdom of Saudi Arabia on the world stage.

SIX

Saving Jeddah, the Bride of the Red Sea

I will speak with a little bit of heartache about the destruction of
the old houses of Jeddah.[1]

TO MANY OF ITS LONG-TIME residents, Jeddah, the second largest city
and the principal port of the Kingdom of Saudi Arabia, is a woman. She is a
bride, the "Bride of the Red Sea," because of her location on the Kingdom's
west coast a short 130 miles away from Egypt and Sudan. She is also a grandmother. According to one popular etymology, her name is derived from
jaddah, the Arabic word for "grandmother." Legend has it that Jeddah is the
burial place of Eve, "the grandmother of mankind." After Eve was driven out
of the Garden of Eden, people say, she descended to earth and came to
Jeddah. She was buried where she died, on her way to Mecca, a half-hour by
camel outside the main gate of the city.

For centuries Eve's grave was a regular stop for Muslim pilgrims on the
Hajj and for anyone seeking divine assistance, especially barren women praying for children. Richard Burton, the famous nineteenth-century British
traveler who visited Jeddah in 1853, described Eve's grave as a low white-
washed structure, two hundred meters long, marked by a headstone, a foot-
stone, and in the center, a small domed tomb. According to another nineteenth-century visitor, the inside walls of the tomb were covered with prayers
and passages from the Quran. Under a green drape stood a sacred stone
known as al-Surrah, the navel of the earth.

In 1928, Eve's tomb was destroyed by King Abdulaziz ibn Saud when he
conquered the Hijaz during his campaign to gain control of the Arabian
Peninsula. According to the severe Wahhabi form of Islam promoted by the
Saudi king, worshiping or even praying at graves was strictly forbidden. In
1975, the Saudi government sealed the site of Eve's tomb under a layer of
concrete as part of its continuing effort to discourage these evil, idolatrous
rites.

Jeddah owes its specific location to the fact that just offshore from the natural lagoon that formed its early harbor lies a gap in the coral reefs that line the shore of the Red Sea. A short distance inland lies a parallel gap in the steep coastal mountains that allows easy travel inland to Mecca. Archaeological excavations have revealed that Jeddah was established as a fishing village in the fourth or fifth century B.C.E. In 647 C.E., fifteen years after the death of the Prophet Muhammad, Uthman ibn Affan, the third caliph, designated Jeddah the official port of arrival for Muslim pilgrims traveling to the holy cities of Mecca and Medina.

A tenth-century Arab traveler described Jeddah as "well fortified and well populated," adding, "The people are traders and are wealthy. The town is Makkah's treasury and Yemen's and Egypt's emporium."[2] In 1229, an Arab geographer described the two walls that surrounded the city; the outer one was ten meters thick, the inner one five meters thick, and they were made of limestone blocks dressed with gypsum mortar. A huge moat outside the walls was filled with seawater, transforming the city into an island. Inside the city were hundreds of cisterns. During the Hajj, the city was home to great crowds of people who gathered there from all corners of the Muslim world on their way to and from Mecca.

Until the early sixteenth century, Jeddah was ruled by a series of caliphs and emperors. Then the city, together with the surrounding region of Hijaz, came under the control of the Ottoman sultans, who in 1525 rebuilt the city walls in order to defend it from the Portuguese. In the first half of the nineteenth century, a British merchant wrote "a guide to trade and commerce" in Jeddah for the British East India Company. He cataloged the many currencies in circulation there—Gingelees, Missirees, and Zirmabobs; Razeens, Stamboles, and Zelottas; Gubbers, Pestareens, and Turahs—as well as the principal commodities traded in the city's markets—betel-nut, cardamom, lead, musk, opium, quicksilver, saltpeter, sandalwood, turmeric, and vermillion. A French merchant added other goods to the list: ambergris, dates, elephant tusks, licorice, mastic, ostrich feathers, pearls, and sulphur.[3]

In 1869, the opening of the Suez Canal brought about a dramatic expansion of trade and rapid growth in the size of the city's merchant class. Inside the city gates, the number of caravansaries and consulates increased dramatically, the former to house pilgrims visiting Mecca, the latter to house representatives of European governments seeking to expand their influence in the Arabian Peninsula. In 1916, Sharif Hussein of Mecca revolted against the Ottoman Turks, but Abdulaziz ibn Saud lay siege to the city and finally captured it in 1925. Then in 1932, the city of Jeddah with the entire Hijaz was incorporated into the newly established Kingdom of Saudi Arabia.

During the second half of the twentieth century, as oil wealth transformed the Kingdom, the city of Jeddah grew tremendously—from a small city of thirty thousand inhabitants at the end of World War II to a huge urban center of over four million people at the beginning of the twenty-first century. The old city walls, which had enclosed an area of less than one square mile, were torn down in 1947, as the city expanded to its present area of almost six hundred square miles. The modern city of Jeddah is a major industrial center that boasts world-class skyscrapers, universities, and port facilities, as well as one of the largest desalinization plants in the world.

Jeddah has become one of the wealthiest and most cosmopolitan cities in the Middle East. It is inhabited by Muslims from all over the world, who originally came as "guests of God" to perform the Hajj and worship at the Holy Mosque in Mecca. Jeddah is perhaps best known for three of its most impressive architectural monuments. The white, Teflon-coated, fiberglass tents of the Hajj Terminal at the King Abdulaziz International Airport were designed in 1981 to accommodate the arrival of eight hundred thousand pilgrims a year. The twenty-mile-long Corniche, a seaside promenade with beaches, restaurants, and amusement parks, is graced with an open-air gallery of modern sculpture. And King Fahd's Fountain, whose 260-meter-high jet of Red Sea water is illuminated at night, can be seen from everywhere in the city.

The architecture of al-Balad, the old city, has long impressed western travelers. Carsten Niebuhr, who visited Jeddah in 1761 with the Danish Arabia Expedition, wrote: "The walls are still standing but are now so ruinous that a person may, in many places, enter over them on horseback."[4] In 1909, A. J. B. Wavell, a British military officer and explorer, found Jeddah in "very dilapidated condition." "The high narrow houses," he wrote, "seem to totter on their foundations—the minarets of the mosques are all yards out of the plumb. A slight earthquake would reduce both places to a heap of rubble."[5]

T. E. Lawrence, who visited Jeddah in 1917 while serving in the Arab Bureau of the British Foreign Office, found Jeddah a "remarkable town."

> The streets were alleys, wood roofed in the main bazaar, but elsewhere open to the sky in the little gap between the tops of the lofty white-walled houses. . . . There was no glass in Jidda, but a very profusion of good lattices, and some very delicate shallow chiselling on the panels of window casings. . . . House-fronts were fretted, pierced and pargetted till they looked as though cut out of cardboard for a romantic stage setting. Every storey jutted, every window

leaned one way or the other; often the very walls sloped. It was like a dead city, so clean underfoot and so quiet. . . . The atmosphere was oppressive, deadly. There seemed no life in it. . . . One would say that for years Jidda had not been swept by a firm breeze: that its streets kept their air from year's end to year's end, from the day they were built for so long as the houses should endure.[6]

Over the past century the process of decay has continued, accelerating greatly in the 1960s and 1970s. As the Kingdom grew wealthier, Jeddah began expanding to the north, and the old merchant families left their homes in al-Balad for modern housing in newer parts of the city. Floods and fires have accomplished what years of neglect and abandonment had not.

THE DESTRUCTION OF THE OLD CITY: "IT TOUCHES MY HEART"

One morning in May 2012, we met Dr. Adnan al-Yafi at the Jeddah home of a colleague and friend. After receiving his Ph.D. from the University of Texas, al-Yafi served for many years as deputy director-general of the Hajj Research Center in Mecca, an organization devoted to improving the services the Saudi government provides to the millions of pilgrims who visit the two holy cities every year. He specializes in the fields of land use, traffic analysis, and pilgrim accommodation.

After we enjoyed the generous hospitality of our host—tea, dates, Arabic coffee, and Krispy Kreme donuts—al-Yafi talked proudly about his family history and his love for the old city. The seventh-generation descendent of a prominent philosopher and Sufi poet, al-Yafi was born in al-Balad in 1950. His father had a shop on a main street next to a big grocery store that was owned by a Greek family who had come to Jeddah from Alexandria by way of Port Sudan.

"I will speak with a little bit of heartbreak about the destruction of the old houses in Jeddah," al-Yafi said.

"In 1964, the first home to be demolished to make room for the new highway was ours. Two years before I was born, the city still had a wall around it, but they demolished it too. When I was young, the homes were all four or five stories tall. Each family had one floor. We lived on one; my uncle lived on another; my grandparents on another. My grandfather's father built the house; my grandfather lived there his whole life. He said that they'd have to demolish the house on top of his head.

"'I was born here,' my grandfather said, 'and I want to die here.' He delayed the process as long as he could. When my grandfather died, we mourned for three days. On the fourth day, the tractors started tearing down the house. It touches my heart."

More than anyone else, another of al-Yafi's colleagues, Dr. Sami Nawar, personifies recent efforts to preserve the old city of Jeddah. Nawar is a short, intense man with wire-rimmed glasses and a neatly trimmed black mustache. Dressed in an immaculate white *thobe* and *shemagh,* he speaks passionately about his love for al-Balad. Nawar is both the general director of culture and tourism for the municipality of Jeddah and a professor at a small women's school, where he teaches courses in architecture and historic preservation. He is also the author of a book on the city, *The Legacy of Jeddah,* and the founder of the Saudi branch of the International Council on Monuments and Sites, a global NGO dedicated to the conservation of the world's archaeological and architectural heritage.

As he often does when visitors to Jeddah express interest in the old city, Nawar offered to take us on a short tour. Our first stop was Bayt Nasseef, the Nasseef House, built in the 1870s by Omar Nasseef Effendi, governor of Jeddah at the time and a member of one of the oldest and wealthiest families in the city. When King Abdulaziz captured the city in December 1925, after a year-long siege, he used the house as his royal residence, until he moved the capital of the new Kingdom to Riyadh. For years, Bayt Nasseef was known as "the House with the Tree" because of the large *neem* tree—an Indian lilac—that grew just to the left of the main entrance. As late as 1920, people said it was the only tree in the old city.

At seven stories high, with over a hundred rooms, Bayt Nasseef was the tallest building in Jeddah until 1970. The view from the flat open rooftop over the parapets out to the Red Sea is still impressive. The steps of the large central stairway are wide and low. Nawar told us this was so that camels laden with supplies could mount directly to the kitchen on the fourth floor. Since 1999, the fully restored Bayt Nasseef has served as a museum and cultural center, where lectures and exhibitions on the history and culture of Jeddah, Medina, and Mecca are held. During Ramadan, traditional Hijazi games, music, and living history performances take place there.

The old houses of Jeddah were built with large blocks of soft coral lime-stone excavated from inshore reefs; they were faced with stucco that was either whitewashed or painted in light pastels. For added stability, teak logs were embedded horizontally in the walls. Projecting out over the streets on each floor were cantilevered wooden balconies and bay windows made of delicately carved latticework in faded shades of turquoise blue, light green, and reddish brown. They provided privacy and kept out the sun, while at the same time allowing breezes off the Red Sea to circulate through the houses (see fig. 14).

Grand entrance halls and large reception rooms occupied the ground floor, while the upper floors contained living quarters and women's areas. The flat roofs surrounded by crenelated parapets, were used for sleeping, laundry, and children's play; they also collected rainwater, which was channeled down to cisterns built underneath the houses. According to a popular couplet, pedestrians in the streets below used to call out to the owners of the old mansions:

> Greetings, O you seated in the latticed balcony
> And exalted high above all people.[7]

During our visit to Jeddah, the narrow streets of al-Balad were crowded with people from all over the Muslim world—"whatever the Red Sea washed ashore." Barefoot Somali children played soccer in small squares. Their mothers stood watching from doorsteps dressed in long brightly colored skirts and *hijabs* that contrasted sharply with the jet-black *abayas* and *hijabs* that Saudi women wore. Construction workers from Bangladesh and Pakistan sat drinking coffee on low cinderblock walls; and Yemeni men in white *thobes* and round white caps played backgammon squatting cross-legged on carpets spread out on the cobblestone streets. Men walked by wearing gold-and-white embroidered turbans in traditional Hijazi style, another contrast with the white and checkered *shemaghs* of Saudi men.

When I asked Nawar about the identities of some of the people who filled the streets, he looked around and said, "There are no Saudis here." A moment later he pointed out three women hurrying along the sidewalk. He recognized them as Saudis by the expensive black *abayas* they were wearing.

PRESERVING THE OLD CITY AND REVIVING THE SOCIAL FABRIC

The social problems facing the people of al-Balad are just as pressing as the architectural problems facing its old houses. The majority of the population consists of "overstayers," people from Somalia, Yemen, Afghanistan, and other troubled parts of the Muslim world, who enter Saudi Arabia on Hajj visas and then, when they have completed their pilgrimage to Mecca, remain in the country illegally, melting easily into the diverse and unregulated population of the old city.

Some undocumented immigrants throw their identity cards away so that Saudi officials can't deport them to their country of origin. Many live as squatters in the old abandoned houses of al-Balad. They aren't allowed to work; their children can't enroll in school; and neither they nor their children—nor anyone else for that matter—can apply for Saudi citizenship. Many "overstayers" are forced to survive in the underground economy by engaging in drug dealing and prostitution, problems that are only expected to grow worse in the near future.

One evening on a street corner near the North City Gate, we met Malak Baissa, the mayor of the district of Al Sham Wal Mazloom in the old city. A tall, handsome man in his mid-forties with a neatly trimmed gray beard, Baissa dresses in the traditional Hijazi style with a gold and white turban and a white vest over a long white *thobe*. He is from a well-known Jeddah family; his father also served as mayor. Every evening in his office, Baissa holds a traditional *majlis*, an informal city council meeting, where his male constituents come together to discuss the social and political problems that concern them.

Baissa was eager to tell us about the challenges he faced as he worked to improve the lives of the residents of the old city. Among the most pressing problems confronting his administration were illegal immigration, unauthorized construction, an inadequate sewage system, and traffic congestion.

"Ninety-percent of the people living here are not Saudis," he said through a translator. "Somalis are the biggest group, then Yemenis, then Egyptians. There's no social fabric here. We're trying to revive the social fabric. We're trying to give people what they're missing, to provide them with sports facilities, health care, and a better education. We need to build sidewalks, bathrooms, and parks. There are a thousand Somali children in the old city. We've started awareness programs for disadvantaged youth. In fifteen years, they'll be part of the city. I want to get the 'overstayers' papers so they can become legal citizens.

"The stereotype is that the Somalis are all trouble makers. Saudis treat them as if they were criminals; they want to send them all back to Somalia. We need to deal with them as human beings. We started a program to help the children feel more comfortable, to give them a sense of belonging. We're trying use social media to present a positive image of the Somalis to the Saudi community.

"Some people want to commercialize the old city with malls and expensive stores, to promote tourism. I want to find people jobs and bring back the old inhabitants of the city. I want to preserve the community, as well as the buildings. I have the support of some people, but I'm pushing the boundaries of Saudi society."

Efforts to save al-Balad are broad-based and involve the participation of local, national, and international organizations. The scope of the challenge is immense. In old Jeddah, there are over a thousand historic structures in urgent need of preservation and restoration. The Saudi government has allocated 15 million dollars to help in the preservation efforts. The Saudi Commission for Tourism and Antiquities became involved in the process with the hope of promoting tourism in the area, but these efforts have been handicapped by the fact that Saudi Arabia no longer issues tourist visas. Preservation efforts have also been taking place at the local level. In 1991, local activists founded the Jeddah Historical Preservation Society, and in 2007 the Jeddah Urban Development Company was formed. Two hundred buildings have already been scheduled for preservation, and there are plans to involve members of the city's old families to restore the beautiful old homes they abandoned many years ago.

In June 2014, efforts to preserve the old city of Jeddah culminated in the announcement by Prince Sultan bin Salman, president of the SCTA, that the UNESCO World Heritage Committee meeting in Doha, Qatar, had just designated al-Balad a World Heritage site. During his speech, the prince attributed this good news to the King Abdullah Project for the Care of Cultural Heritage, a government program dedicated to the preservation and restoration of the country's archaeological and historical monuments.

THE CORNICHE: THE FLOATING MOSQUE, THE BICYCLE, AND THE DALLAH FOUNTAIN

Jeddah is famous for its Corniche, a recreational area that extends for twenty miles along the city's Red Sea coast. It includes international hotels and restaurants, beach resorts, athletic facilities, playgrounds, malls, and museums. There are lush green spaces for picnicking, walking, and enjoying open views of the Red Sea. Two of the most popular locations on the Corniche are the

Gift of Allah Happy Land Park, with its outdoor rides, bowling alley, and ice skating arena, and the Waterfall Theme Park with a pirate ship, a ride through an "Amazon jungle," and the fifteen-meter-high waterfall for which the park is named. Another popular location along the Corniche is the Fatima al-Zahra mosque, generally known as the "Floating Mosque" because it was built on stilts out over the Red Sea. At high tide, it seems to be resting on the surface of the water.

The most impressive single feature on Jeddah's Corniche is undoubtedly King Fahd's Fountain, also known simply as the Jeddah fountain. The highest fountain in the world, it stands taller than the Eifel Tower. This gift to the city from the late King Fahd shoots a jet of water weighing eighteen tons three hundred meters into the air at a speed of over three hundred kilometers per hour. At night, illuminated by five hundred spotlights, it is visible from all over the city.

Jeddah's Corniche is the site of one of the world's largest collections of open-air monumental sculpture. In the 1970s and early 1980s, Mohamed Said Farsi, the mayor of Jeddah at the time, established this extensive outdoor gallery in order to beautify the city, introduce modern art to its inhabitants, and gain the city an international reputation. Farsi, an architect and urban planner, was committed to creating parks, gardens, and public art at a time when rapid population growth and increasing traffic congestion had already begun to damage the quality of life of the Jeddawi, as the people of the city are known.

Farsi sought to bring to Jeddah the work of well-known international artists, such as Alexander Calder from the United States, Henry Moore from the United Kingdom, Jean Arp from France, and Joan Miro from Spain. But he was also eager to promote the work of Arab artists and to help them develop new and distinct forms of Arab art. Farsi was constrained in his efforts to bring contemporary art to Jeddah by the need to respect the conventions of Saudi culture and avoid representations of the human form. Farsi commissioned works that focused on traditional Saudi material culture, the industrial past of the city of Jeddah, and the scientific achievements of the Muslim world.

One of Jeddah's best-known landmarks is the *Monument to the Unknown Cyclist,* which is located in the center of a rotary at Bicycle Square. Built by Julio Lafuente, a Spanish sculptor born in 1921, out of scrap metal from an old marble factory owned by Mohammed bin Laden, the sculpture stands fifteen meters high and twenty-five meters long, simple and austere, stripped to its essentials. At night, it's bathed in floodlights that constantly change color.

Lafuente has over thirty other sculptures along the Corniche, many of them inspired by Arab and Islamic themes. Some of his works are calligraphic sculptures. Near the entrance to the Royal Terminal of the King Abdulaziz International Airport stands the *Verse Boat,* a twenty-ton bronze work in which the smoothly flowing lines of the bow of a traditional Arab dhow morph suddenly into tightly curved lines of Arabic script. The quotation from the Quran reads: "My Lord, lead me in with a just ingoing, and lead me out with a just outgoing." Another powerful sculpture by Lafuente, entitled *Shahadat al-Tawhid*—the Muslim affirmation of monotheism, "There is no God but Allah"—is a three dimensional Kufic inscription made of gray granite that rests on a base of gray boulders in the shallow sea just in front of a small white mosque built on an artificial island.

Many of Lafuente's works explore traditional Arabic material culture. Of these, one of the best known is the *Mameluke Mosque Lanterns,* four monumental lanterns made of steel with blue, red, and yellow panels of colored glass that are illuminated at night from within. Another of these works, *Dallah Fountain,* consists of two dozen huge bronze coffee pots standing on tall granite pillars tilted at different angles as if caught in the act of pouring coffee into an equal number of small coffee cups standing on short granite pillars around the fountain.

With *Science and Religion,* Lafuente acknowledges the contributions of Muslim astronomers: on a base set in an ornamental lagoon stands an obelisk made of four columns of two-ton marble moons. Each column rises eighteen moons high; each moon frozen at a different phase of the lunar cycle. With other sculptures Lafuente strikes a lighter, more contemporary note. In *Clouds,* an old Douglas DC3, the plane that revolutionized air travel in the 1930s, seems to fly over a traffic circle skimming the top of a bank of billowy, white concrete clouds. And in *Accident!* five cars project at jarring angles from a huge white cube of cinder blocks, a comment perhaps on the danger of driving in Jeddah traffic.

Among the Muslim Arab artists Farsi commissioned to produce work for Jeddah's Corniche was Mustafa Senbel from Egypt. *The Seagull,* one of his most impressive works, is an abstract sculpture made of marble and reinforced concrete that stands over fifty meters tall. It consists of two curved arcs—the gull's wings? water splashed up by a gull's dive?—and a taller, vertical column on which are carved verses from the work of four well-known

Hijazi poets. With two other works Senbel acknowledges two British-made desalination plants that provided fresh water for the city of Jeddah during the first half of the twentieth century. *Desalination Pipes I,* consists of a group of cement and reinforced-plastic pipes—the same kind that were used to construct the city's new water mains—set together vertically to form a tower that evokes the spiral ramp of the Malwiya Minaret of the Great Mosque of Samarra in Iraq.

By 2012, the condition of many of the sculptures on the Jeddah Corniche, especially those made from bronze, granite, and local stone, had deteriorated significantly because of a combination of factors: sun, wind, sand, salt, and the harshest of all—neglect. To remedy the situation, a major restoration project was undertaken by Abdul Latif Jameel Community Initiatives, the social responsibility arm of the ALJ Company, the largest independent distributor of Toyota and Lexus vehicles in the world. Members of the Jameel family have served as important patrons of Islamic art in general, and Saudi art in particular, at both the national and the international levels. They have contributed to a thriving contemporary art scene in the Gulf region through the establishment of the Jameel Gallery for Islamic Art at the Victoria and Albert Museum in London and through their sponsorship of the arts initiative Edge of Arabia. The Jameel family's efforts to restore the public sculptures on the Corniche mark an important step in the revitalization of the city of Jeddah.[8]

STRENGTHENING CIVIL SOCIETY

Not all efforts to improve the quality of life of the residents of Jeddah have been focused on rebuilding the old city. There are also programs devoted to the welfare of the poor and disadvantaged of Jeddah, who live in other parts of the city where there is no interesting architecture and where tourists will never set foot. These programs demonstrate the significant contributions that NGOs can make to the general social welfare in a country where civil society is poorly developed and where local and national governments have been unable to provide their citizens with a satisfactory standard of living.

Fatin Bundagji is the owner and president of the Think 'N' Link Cooperation, a small management and development consultancy in Jeddah. After finishing high school in Switzerland, Bundagji returned to Jeddah, married, and had children. When she turned thirty, she was eager to begin a life of public service. She began by studying English, politics, and management; then she embarked on a career in journalism. Soon she decided to dedicate herself full-time to improving the lives of women, immigrants, and the poor. During the ten years she worked for the Jeddah Chamber of Commerce, Bundagji directed the Women's Empowerment and Research Center.

In 2004, in an address to the Third Arab International Women's Forum, Bundagji spoke of her deep commitment to empowering Saudi women so that they could participate more fully in the economic and social development of their country.[9] She elaborated on her goals in an interview that was published online by the Carnegie Endowment for International Peace: "The problem lies in raising and reshaping awareness, and here we have to go back to education, the importance of concentrating on the concept of citizenship, ... and on the cause of women's rights and their role in public life.... Women's participation in the decision-making process is necessary to ensure proper and balanced strategic planning that takes into account the social and economic needs of Saudi women."[10]

When we met Bundagji one morning at her office in Jeddah, she was wearing a black *abaya* and *hijab,* a large silver watch, and bright red lipstick. I asked her to describe her early involvement in public life.

"I was itching for something to do," she said. "When I was thirty-nine, I applied to head a training program in 1999 run by the Jeddah Chamber of Commerce. Before that I had never interacted with men. I'd always resorted to books, books about women in leadership and management. Then in 2004, I decided to participate in the municipal council elections. Only two women in the whole country ran. It was taboo; it was a brand new concept. No one understood it. Westerners were intrigued that women wanted to run for office, but locally there was total silence about their candidacies. The issue isn't about law or religion; it's about culture. People who don't want their daughters exposed to the public versus people who want women to progress.

"I'd go walking on the waterfront. There were no paths, no walkways. There were advertisements and billboards and kiosks. It was terrible. I started taking photographs—just to document it. There were no benches, no public bathrooms. The municipality was violating my rights by selling space to kiosks on the sidewalks so people couldn't walk on them.

"I convinced the youth to get organized. We documented eighteen city violations and went to the municipal council. There were fundamentalists on it; they wouldn't meet us because we were women. We lobbied the mayor, and we documented more violations. For a whole year nothing happened. Sewage was just being flushed into the sea. The water was stagnant; it had turned green. It was dangerous to swim. The fish were dying; people were getting infections.

"Some women said, 'Go to the Prince.' Others said, 'No, don't bother. He'll just say "Follow the system."' We spent a whole year lobbying and working hard. People said, 'Who are these women?' Then we organized a program called Muwatana, which means 'citizenship.' Our focus was 'Man, Space, and the Rule of Law.'"

On November 25, 2009, Jeddah was struck by a disastrous flood. Three and a half inches of rain—twice the yearly average—fell on the city in just four hours. It was the worst flooding Saudi Arabia had experienced in over twenty-five years. The city had an inadequate sewer system and no storm drains at all. The streets were covered in three feet of water. Over a hundred people were killed, and over three hundred were missing. Twenty-two thousand people were displaced from their homes, eight thousand buildings destroyed, and three thousand vehicles swept away. Total losses were estimated at 270 million dollars. To make matters worse, the rains had come on the first day of the Hajj, when several million pilgrims were passing through the city. All the disaster relief efforts were focused on providing emergency care for the pilgrims; nothing was left for the people of Jeddah.

During the recovery efforts that followed, Bundagji and the other members of Muwatana worked tirelessly to help the survivors. One of their most valuable contributions to the relief effort was a video documenting the scope of the disaster and the inadequacy of the government's response. The video, which we watched during our visit to Bundagji's office, showed frightening scenes of flooded streets, cars buried in mud, and rats fleeing the rushing water. Standing amid the devastation, angry residents were shouting at overwhelmed government officials: "No one is helping us! We have no assistance!"

Six days after the flood, little had changed. Whole neighborhoods were underwater, and many roads were still impassable. The civil defense forces were doing nothing. Twenty-two days after the flood, Bundagji and a group of women wearing black *abayas*, work gloves, blue surgical facemasks, and brightly colored baseball caps over their black *hijabs* were shoveling trash with young men from the devastated neighborhoods.

Muwatana began to attract national attention for its work. In the meantime, men on the Jeddah Municipal Council in their clean white *thobes* were giving speeches outlining their plans to provide residents of the city with food and clean water. As rats, cockroaches, and flies began to multiply and fears of an epidemic spread, the Ministry of Health set up a few makeshift clinics, but nowhere near enough. Municipal workers cleaned up the mud and trash from one street and just dumped it on another. Newspaper headlines screamed: "King Orders Investigation!"

After we'd finished watching the video, Bundagji spoke more about the flood and her efforts to provide relief for the people of Jeddah.

"The floods were worst in Gueza," she said. "That's the poor area where disasters always happen. The people who live there used to be Bedouin. The municipality said they couldn't build houses there, but the Bedouin found corrupt officials who gave them permission. A few years later the area was full of slums and shantytowns. Then the floods hit.

"To the south of the city there's a whole area where the police don't go. It's full of overstayers from Afghanistan and Africa. There's a lot of disease and drugs there. Poor kids and rich kids were working together on the cleanup. Seventy percent of our volunteers were wealthy. They were wearing their Nike shoes, their Armani jeans, and driving their big four-by-fours and SUVs.

"We heard poor children say, 'We never thought rich kids were so decent.'

"The Chamber of Commerce set up a coordinating committee. Representatives of all sectors of society were sitting there in the boardroom.

"'You keep talking,' I said. 'I need authority. I want to go to work.'

"We had on our hard hats and our T-shirts. No civil society organizations were allowed to operate in the Kingdom, but we did. The Muwatana did. We went to the prince and talked to him about the floods. Then we produced a written report with pictures and the video; we sponsored the whole thing ourselves. Our royals didn't know what was happening; otherwise they would have done something.

"This was a critical point in our history. Business leaders and young people came together to hold people in government ministries accountable. The whole society was mobilized. The government spent a year investigating the disaster. A year later in a YouTube interview, the prince spoke with reporters about the investigation. It was the first time in our history that's ever happened."

On January 27, 2011, a second flood devastated Jeddah. The eastern portion of the city was completely inundated, and floodwaters coursed through the main streets toward the Red Sea. Some fifteen hundred people were rescued from flooded homes and housed in temporary shelters.[11] Damage from this second flood was estimated at 4.5 billion dollars. This time the Saudi government immediately assigned responsibility for repairing the damage and improving Jeddah's inadequate infrastructure to Saudi Aramco. Promptly and efficiently Aramco engineers conducted detailed hydrological studies, constructed a series of dams outside the city, and built a network of discharge channels to drain floodwater safely into the Red Sea.

Since the floods, Bundagji has continued her efforts to strengthen civil society in Jeddah and in the Kingdom more generally. She has concentrated on empowering members of local communities, encouraging social entrepreneurship, and establishing links between the public and the private sectors. She has also organized programs to train young adults to serve as leaders and mentors for other young people. One training session was held at the Jeddah Coast Guard Station. Bundagji described the look on people's faces, people who had spent their whole lives being threatened and intimidated by the police and the military. Now for the first time, they were being welcomed to a government facility and invited to work together with members of the military for the common good of Saudi society.

Toward the end of our meeting, a student asked Bundagji about the challenges that the strict separation of men and women posed for her efforts to promote the growth of civil society in Saudi Arabia.

"During the floods," she said, "women played a major role. Men did the visible work, but women were working behind the scenes. Some families didn't want men to enter their houses. So women volunteers went inside, while men worked in the streets. Some families wouldn't let men into their homes even if someone in the family were dying. People said: 'But women can't work with the Coast Guard. Their families would object, and they'd be publically scorned.'

"It's a new thing in Saudi Arabia for men and women to work together. We've taken the first steps, but we want to do more. *Inshallah,* God willing."

FRIENDS OF JEDDAH PARKS

To learn more about the efforts civil society organizations were making to improve the lives of the people of Jeddah, we met with Ziad Jarrar, the head of communication at the al-Aghar Group, a nonprofit think tank founded in

2007. Al-Aghar is dedicated to the study of the many economic, social, and cultural challenges facing the Kingdom. Its goal, Jarrar said, is to transform Saudi Arabia into "a highly productive and internationally competitive knowledge society by engaging stakeholders in a dialogue to provide strategies and options." The al-Aghar Group conducts conferences and publishes studies on topics such as "the future of public education in the Kingdom," "youth think tank initiatives," and "empowering innovation to serve development."

Jarrar is a young man with very short hair; he grew up in Toronto and speaks English with a Canadian accent. His frequent quotations from the Quran testify to the profound role Islam has played, and continues to play, in his life.

"We focus on youth, education, religion, and development," he said. "We also work on water and renewable energy projects. Our goal is to develop social initiatives to improve family life and strategies to develop the human potential of the country. We hold workshops and focus groups that involve academics, members of the private sector, government officials, and members of the royal family. The whole country is engaged in national and religious dialogue. Abdullah is the 'King of Dialogue.' We focus on interreligious dialogue, but what we really need is Sunni-Shia dialogue and even dialogue among Sunnis.

"We need to diversify the economy and become less dependent on oil. Our oil minister said, 'The stone age didn't end because we ran out of stone, and the oil age won't end because we run out of oil.' We need to leap frog ahead; the world won't wait for us. We need to nationalize non-Saudi brains and help shift Saudi society to a knowledge society.

"The message of God in the form of the Quran is for all Muslims," he stressed. "There is one Quran for everyone. We need to translate that message into everyday life and make it work, but cultural factors come into play. Many people look to scholars to learn how to be Muslims; they want sheikhs to interpret things for them. But Islam needs to belong to everyone, not just the few. If you give Islam to the people, they'll be more open and tolerant. It's important to give the message of Islam back to the people and empower them."

Several days later Jarrar took us to meet the leaders of Friends of Jeddah Parks. He has contributed a great deal to the organization and is proud of its success. Operating officially under the auspices of the Chamber of Commerce, Friends of Jeddah Parks is a nonprofit organization dedicated to the notion that parks provide important social and economic benefits to the city: they reduce crime, empower young people, and build communities. A group of women from several old Jeddah families founded the organization. They set up a male board of directors—family friends and business leaders—who could be relied on to raise a lot of money. They plan to work with the corporate social responsibility programs of large Saudi companies to encourage them to contribute to their cause.

We visited the Faisal Zahid Sports Park, the first park built by the Friends of Jeddah Parks. It's located in the al-Qoriat district of the city, a poor working-class area inhabited by both Saudis and immigrants—many undocumented—from Yemen, Africa, and Asia. The park was built in 2007 at a cost of 4 million dollars. Jarrar said that the largest donation to the park—over 1.5 million dollars—had been given by Mohammed Zahid in honor of his late son Faisal, who had died in a car accident. The Zahid Group is a multinational corporation based in Jeddah with interests in mining, agriculture, construction, real estate development, and the generation of electricity.

"Everything with the blessing of Allah," said Jarrar, visibly moved by the memory of this generous gift.

The Faisal Zahid Sports Park provides a safe place for constructive activities for over thirty-five hundred children every week. The park boasts a colorfully decorated graffiti wall, a soccer field, and courts for volleyball and basketball. But the emphasis is not all on athletics. In a small classroom building, Internet access is available, and classes are offered in time management, youth leadership, career counseling, and job training. The walls of the office are covered with photographs of King Abdullah meeting with young men who have won prizes for their accomplishments in activities sponsored by the park.

At the end of our visit, I walked out onto the soccer field to speak with some of the young men playing there. They were in their late teens and early twenties; their fathers worked at the airport or the Toyota factory, for the phone company or the military. Most of them were unemployed. Each of them told me that what he needed most of all was a job.

Later that afternoon Jarrar took us to Amira Park in the Anusla neighborhood of Jeddah, a low-income area where many government employees live. This park had been built by local volunteers on an empty block of sand and gravel that had been used as a parking lot for large trucks. Originally planned as an ungated family park for men, women, and children, it was turned into a gated park exclusively for the use of women and children because young men had been harassing the women and girls relaxing there. That's why boys over fourteen are not allowed in the park any more. Amira is the only park in the entire Kingdom reserved exclusively for women.

Just inside the entrance gate, we saw an old orange Volkswagen bus. The writing on the open side door identified it as "Maktabati"—My Library. Ten children sat on a blanket on the grass nearby as a young woman of African descent read aloud to them. Palm trees, playgrounds, and benches made the park an attractive sanctuary in a crowded, dusty city.

Amira Park has a stage for children's theater productions and a prayer area for women. It's open free of charge all week. On the weekends over a thousand people visit the park. During school holidays, a traditional Hijazi clown and Sponge Bob Square Pants entertain the children, while Aladdin Adventures provides inflatable slides and bounce houses for the children's enjoyment. Young volunteers wearing green sashes clean up litter. As we left the park, a group of children accompanied us to the gate. The boys wore soccer jerseys, the older girls *abaya*s. They sang us a cheerful song bidding us—their beloved guests—farewell.

The final night of our stay in Jeddah, I was drawn to the balcony of my hotel by the call to prayer, the Isha prayer, which takes place after darkness has fallen and all trace of twilight has left the sky. Looking out over the city dimly lit below, I could see public swimming pools and basketball courts and enclosed yards surrounded by rows of tall palm trees. In the distance, at the end of a long avenue, stood a minaret framed between two even taller skyscrapers. Mounted on flat rooftops everywhere I looked were air conditioners, satellite dishes, and purple, red, and green neon lights—Magrebi Dental Center, Ramada Inn, al-Bustan Hospital, and Haifaa Mall. And off in the distance to the west I could see planes taking off from the King Abdulaziz International Airport and the white jet of water rising up from King Fahd's Fountain high above the Red Sea.

SEVEN

Who Can Go to Mecca?

CONVERSION AND PILGRIMAGE IN ISLAM

It is not the beard alone which proves a man to be a true Moslem.[1]

FOR ONE AND A HALF billion people, almost a quarter of humanity, Mecca, the birthplace of the Prophet Muhammad, is the most sacred city on earth. Performing the pilgrimage to Mecca is one of the Five Pillars of Islam, one of the supreme expressions of the Muslim faith. The Hajj is the largest and one of the oldest pilgrimages in the world; it has been performed for almost fourteen hundred years and now draws over two million pilgrims a year. All Muslims who are physically and financially able should perform the Hajj at least once in their lives, so powerful is the spiritual force that Mecca exerts over devout Muslims throughout the world. The city of Mecca is so sacred that under no circumstances are non-Muslims allowed to enter.

For centuries the prohibition against non-Muslims visiting Mecca has made the city a source of fascination—a dangerous and forbidden destination—for non-Muslim explorers and travelers. The Quranic sources of this taboo, as well as the moral and religious justifications for it, have been debated for centuries. Why are non-Muslims forbidden from visiting Mecca? Who decides who is a Muslim and who is not? Based on what criteria? And what does it mean to be a Muslim? Who, in other words, is allowed go to Mecca after all?

These questions are not only of interest to experts in Islam and sharia law, they are hotly debated on the Internet as well—on popular question-and answer sites like Yahoo Answers, Wiki Answers, and more specialized websites like American Bedu, Islam.com, and Islam Question and Answer.[2] The responses generated by these questions vary widely in tone and sophistication.

SHAMSIDEEN: Excluding non-Muslims from entering the Holy City of Makkah is a commandment from Allah: "O you who believe! The idolaters are unclean. So let them not come near the Inviolable Place of Worship after this year" (Quran 9, verse 28). The condition for entry to the sacred territory of Makkah has been laid down by the owner of that territory—Allah. Makkah and Madinah are religious places, not tourist attractions.

ROZAIBA: I feel this is an unfortunate example of Muslim bigotry. There are instances where Muslim bigotry defies logic and humanity. Don't try to find comfort in 7th century edicts for such grossly disgusting and inhumane regulations. Say it like it is! Muslim bigotry.

INVADER: In my opinion Mecca being out of bounds for non-Muslims has nothing to do with Islam. I believe it has to do with Saudi Arabia's government being run by NUT CASES. Did you read anywhere in Quran that woman can't vote? Did you read anywhere in Quran that woman can't drive? I bet your answer is NO. But these restrictions have been put in Saudi for political, not religious reasons.

LEA77: Non-Muslims cannot enter Makkah because it is the law in Saudi Arabia. But most rules are broken aren't they? (joke) SAPTCO [the Saudi Public Transport Company] uses Mercedes buses, and they employ German mechanics. Germans go in and out of Makkah under cover of darkness to fix buses and make sure that there are fewer traffic jams during Hajj.

JHYDER: In *The Saudis,* Sandra Mackey recalls trying to drive near Mecca (with her husband at the wheel of course): "Billboard-size blue and white signs in both Arabic and English appeared along the road, warning non-Moslems to turn back" [see fig. 15]. Eventually, she was "forced off the road by an angry policeman." She was fined about $100 and turned away. Mackey tells of the building of a hotel designed by a Western architect. The Saudis refused to allow him into the city and "insisted that he stand on a hill outside of town and direct the work through a telescope."

UMICH: I completely agree with the rule that non-muslims should not be allowed in makkah. after all, the highly pious wahhabi scholars (who are subservient to the even more pious saudi royal family) know best. There are many other shining examples of their intellect—such as barring women from driving, banning cartoons from cinemas for 30 years, and holding the zionists/infidels responsible for all the evils in the world from britney spears to earthquakes in pakistan.

INAYA: Imagine trying to make *tawaf* [the circumambulation of the Kaba] with a bunch of tourists taking pictures, standing in the way. And bored teenagers leaning against the Kaba smoking ciggies while they wait for their parents. Then maybe The Donald will come and build a few casinos for the tourists.

DIGITAL AKHI: I think people are getting too caught up on the labels "Muslim" and "non-Muslim." One can give lip service to the *shahada* [the Muslim testimony of faith], and technically be considered a Muslim and enter the city; which begs the question, "How do we know who is a real Muslim?" Frankly, that is not the point. God alone knows who is a true and sincere devotee of His versus a plain pretender.

SOUL: officially, no you can't enter mecca if you're a non-muslim. however, i personally took some of my non-muslim friends (i'm a saudi woman from jeddah btw). if you want to take the risk, try visiting with a local saudi during the off-season. please make sure your arms, legs, and hair are covered. avoid any problems [so] as to not attract police attention who of course will ask you for ID and papers. (Busted!)

BK: by law it is not allowed for non-muslims to enter mecca and madina, the two holy cities of islam in saudi arabia. if you get caught, you will face deportation and certainly lots of problems prior to that: jail, interrogation, etc. etc. if you are so fascinated by it, read about it, and learn—perhaps this could lead you to embrace this religion of ours. then you may be able to visit Mecca for a purpose and not only out of curiosity.

NOMAD: Well, strictly in Islam there is nothing that the Prophet (PBUH) has said to ban non-muslims from entering mecca. So if someone challenged this rule on theological grounds, the Saudis will find themselves on slippery grounds. However, rules are rules, and the Saudis as of now do not let any non-muslims enter mecca. Officially. Unofficially a lot of non-muslims go there for work and business. The check post is a joke! During the off-season they don't check at all. We have certainly never been stopped. Just blend in—cover your hair so it doesn't show, look firmly down, and avoid looking at anyone at the check posts. Chances are you'll be waved past. If caught, pretend you are a muslim and hope for the best!

AMERICAN BEDU: A non-muslim expat and a Saudi national worked together and became close friends. They both worked for a high profile institute. The expat accompanied his Saudi friend to Makkah. Back at work, the expat was sharing his experience of being able to see the Holy Mosque. Not surprisingly news of the trip made its way to a very senior official of the institution. Both the Saudi national and the non-muslim expat were called to the executive offices. They were both severely chastised on their poor judgment in violating the law, culture, and traditions of Saudi Arabia.

A LADY: To visit Makkah you need a special visa. That is: La ilaha ill Allah Muhammadur rasool Allah. There is no God, only Allah. Muhammad is the Messenger of Allah. If you say this, you can enter there.

NONO: sorry no way.

MOUHAMAD: Allah kills all Christians and their alliances. Insha'allah Allahu Akhbar!!!

AMERICAN BEDU: Shame on you Mouhamad. Allah (and Islam) is tolerant of all Ibrahamic faiths.

A STATE OF PURITY

The Kaba is a granite cube twelve meters on each side draped in a large black cloth embroidered in gold with passages from the Quran. It stands in the courtyard of the Holy Mosque in Mecca, the most sacred site in the Muslim world. According to Islamic tradition, a black stone inside the Kaba is part of the "primordial house" built by Adam as a place for humans to worship God. According to the Quran, God instructed Abraham to rebuild the Kaba with the help of his son Ishmael and declare it a pilgrimage destination for all mankind. For centuries the Kaba was the focus of the worship of the chief deity of a pre-Islamic pantheon. Then the Prophet Muhammad restored the Kaba to monotheism by purging the rituals performed there of paganism and proclaiming: "There is no God but Allah." In 632 C.E., the final year of his life, Muhammad performed a "farewell pilgrimage" and founded the Hajj. With the exception of a short period during World War I, the Hajj has been performed every year since then.

The Hajj takes place from the eighth to the twelfth day of Dhu al-Hijjah, the last month of the Islamic calendar. Because the date of the Hajj is determined by the lunar Hijri calendar, it cycles through the solar Gregorian calendar, which was developed in the Christian West and is now in widespread use as the international civil calendar. On the first day of the Hajj, before pilgrims reach Mecca, they enter a state of ritual purity known as *ihram,* when men wear two pieces of white seamless cloth (one around their waist and one over their left shoulder); women cover their hair (but not their face); and both men and women are forbidden from swearing, fighting, wearing perfume, having intercourse, cutting their hair or nails, and harming plants or animals in any way.

After their arrival in Mecca, pilgrims perform a series of rituals commemorating events in the lives of Abraham, his wife Hagar, and their son Ishmael. First they enter the Holy Mosque and perform the *tawaf,* circumambulating the Kaba seven times in a counterclockwise direction. Then they perform the *sai* by running or walking seven times back and forth between the hills of Safa and Marwa, reenacting Hagar's desperate search for water when she and Ishmael were abandoned by Abraham. Pilgrims then drink from the sacred Well of Zamzam, which Allah miraculously revealed to Hagar in her time of need.

After spending the night in Mina, a tent city five kilometers from the Holy Mosque, pilgrims proceed to the Plain of Arafat, another twelve kilometers east of Mecca. There at noon they gather at the Mountain of Mercy, a sixty-meter-high rocky hill, where Muhammad gave his last sermon. Pilgrims stand there until sunset reading from the Quran and praying to Allah for forgiveness. For many Muslims this vigil, known as *wuquf*—"the standing"—is a preview of the Last Judgment. It is usually considered the high point of the entire Hajj.

Pilgrims spend the night in the desert at Muzdalifah, where they pray and collect the pebbles they will use to stone the Devil the next day at the Jamarat. Early in the morning, they travel to Mina, where they throw seven pebbles at each of the three pillars representing the Devil. Then they reenact Abraham's sacrifice of the ram that God miraculously substituted for Ishmael with their own sacrifice at Mina.

Following the sacrifice, men shave their heads, women cut their hair, and all pilgrims change back into their everyday clothes. At this point, they leave the sacred state of *ihram* and are free from all the restrictions it entails. After traveling back to Mecca to circle the Kaba and run back and forth between the hills of Safa and Marwa once more, pilgrims return for the night to Mina. On each of the next two or three days, they stone the Devil at the Jamarat again. The final act of the Hajj is a farewell circumambulation of the Kaba. With this, the Hajj is complete, and pilgrims are now in a blessed state, spiritually renewed and free from sin. For the rest of their lives, they are permitted to use the title *hajji* (for men) or *hajja* (for women), a sign to all that they have performed their most sacred duty in the eyes of Allah.[3]

"A CROWD WHOSE NUMBER IS KNOWN TO GOD ALONE"

Throughout its fourteen-hundred-year history, management of the Hajj has been the responsibility of the custodian of the Two Holy Mosques, the title traditionally held by the caliph, the successor of Muhammad and leader of the *umma,* the world-wide Islamic community. This title was also adopted by the Ottoman sultans during the centuries the Hijaz was under their control. It is the custodian of the Two Holy Mosques who hosts the "guests of God," and it is he who must do everything possible to insure the health and safe passage of all the pilgrims who make the sacred journey to Mecca. In 1986, the title "Custodian of the Two Holy Mosques" was ceremoniously adopted by the king of Saudi Arabia, who now bears full responsibility for management of the Hajj. While it is first and foremost a religious event, the political dimensions of the Hajj should not be underestimated. The Hajj has long been a prominent stage on which the high drama of Muslim politics has been performed.

From the seventh until early in the twentieth century, Mecca, Medina, and the entire Hijaz were ruled by a succession of caliphs, sultans, and emperors from capitals throughout the Middle East: the Umayyads of Damascus in the seventh and eighth centuries, the Abbasids of Baghdad from the eighth to the thirteenth centuries, the Mamluks of Cairo from the thirteenth to the sixteenth centuries, and finally from the sixteenth century until the second decade of the twentieth, the Ottoman sultans in Istanbul.

Throughout the centuries, the Hajj was a spectacular event. Huge caravans with tens of thousands of pilgrims and as many as 130,000 camels set out every year from Damascus, Cairo, Baghdad, Persia, and North Africa, traveling for months across the deserts. They were mobile marketplaces, small traveling towns, with their own administrative, judicial, and religious officials, as well as their own poets, doctors, bakers, carpenters, and camel tenders. Major caravan routes were marked by fortified stations a day's march apart that provided water, supplies, and much-needed protection from raiding parties of nomadic Bedouins.

Ibn Jubayr, a twelfth-century traveler from Spain, offers an evocative portrait of a caravan of Hajj pilgrims.

> This assemblage of people ... made up a crowd whose number is known to God alone. ... a sea swollen with waves, whose waters were the mirages and whose ships were the camels, their sails the lofty litters and round tents. They all went forward gliding in and out of a great rising of clouds of dust, their sides colliding as they passed. ...
>
> This caravan travels at night to the light of torches, which people on foot carry in their hands, ... Thus people travel as it were among wandering stars which illuminate the depth of the darkness and which enable the earth to compete in brightness with the stars of heaven.[4]

During the eighteenth century, travel in Hajj caravans became increasingly dangerous. In 1757, some twenty thousand pilgrims died from heat, thirst, hunger, and Bedouin raids. As a result, Ottoman officials began to supervise the Hajj more closely. In the 1880s, authorities required all pilgrims to have passports and visas; they also began to collect taxes, customs duties, and other fees as well. With the increasing economic exploitation of pilgrims, the Hajj became an important source of revenue for the sultan. What Bedouin raiders had previously stolen Ottoman officials now collected legally as taxes.

An elaborate service industry grew up around the Hajj, and the economies of Mecca, Medina, and the entire Hijaz became dependent on it. Prominent Hijazi families formed guilds of guides that were responsible for the pilgrims' welfare. Known as *mutawwif*, they provided food, water, and shelter for pilgrims, as well as religious education and instruction for the proper performance of the Hajj. Each family of *mutawwif* specialized in recruiting and providing services for pilgrims from a specific region.

By the middle of the nineteenth century, the steamship had come to dominate Hajj travel. The trip from Suez to Jeddah was shortened from thirty days by sail to three by steam. The opening of the Suez Canal in 1869 made travel by steamship even more convenient. In addition, steamships made it much easier for Muslims from the Indian subcontinent and East Asia to participate in the Hajj. Inevitably it also led to a significant decline in overland travel; the last great caravan left Cairo for Mecca in 1883.

In 1922, Amin Rihani, a Syrian, witnessed pilgrims arriving in Jeddah both by land and by sea:

> At Yanbu and Jidda they land in multitudes of shifting squalor and picturesqueness. From every ship a scene, from every land a fashion. Takruri black, a giant with a rag around his loins; the fastidious Somali in florid gingham apron and white toga; the Javanese with their unveiled women in short skirts of gorgeous colors or just a piece of rich material clinging to their stunted forms; the gentlemen from India, in graceful folds of silk and cashmere, traveling third class with the multitude; the fellah of Egypt in red slippers and blue *gallabiyya*; the trans-Caucasian in a huge turban crowning a truculency of aspect unassuaged; and the Moroccan, graceful and stately and proud, in the ample folds of an immaculate white burnous—they are all brought together in the most democratic spirit by the faith that was born in the wilds of al-Hijaz. Zamzamward the caravan moves.
>
> Across the desert, through the Najd hills and the Great Nafud, they come from Persia and Arabistan, from Bukhara and Baghdad, in caravans that link the plateau with the plain and the desert with the hills. The leader gives the

word—a gun is fired—woh-haw!—the sun is setting—we start! And the camels grunt and gurgle and growl; and the pilgrims, after the sunset prayer, jam and hiddle and clamor for attention; and the copper utensils rattle in the pack; the sword of the Arab clatters at his side against his water can; ... thus the caravan, slowly and tumultuously composed, moves to the tinkling of bells and the squeaking of saddles and the rhythmic cry of Allah! Allah! It slowly moves into the shadow and soon out of it, in a generous moon, toward the Holy city.[5]

The change from camel to steamship was accompanied by a shift from Ottoman to British control. By the late nineteenth century, so many pilgrims were subjects of the British Empire that the Hajj was on the verge of becoming "a ritual of the British Empire."[6] In the 1880s, Thomas Cooke became the official travel agent for pilgrims from British India. The expansion of the lands from which Muslims could travel to Mecca for the Hajj had serious negative consequences for the health of the pilgrims. After thirty-three thousand pilgrims died in a cholera epidemic in 1893, Britain and France insisted that quarantine stations should be set up in Jeddah and other Red Sea ports. Authorities in some Arab countries resented this development as just another example of European interference in Muslim affairs.

During the first decade of the twentieth century, overland pilgrimages made a brief comeback. In an effort to link Istanbul and Mecca—both to facilitate Hajj travel and to bring the Hijaz more firmly under his control— the Ottoman sultan ordered the construction of the Hijaz Railway. Work was carried out by Turkish soldiers under the supervision of German engineers, who were not allowed to enter the Hijaz, since they were not Muslims. In 1908, the thirteen-hundred-kilometer line from Damascus to Medina was completed, but because of the outbreak of World War I, the link between Medina and Mecca was never finished. A thirty-day journey by camel had been reduced to a three-day journey by train. The Hijaz Railway was frequently attacked by Arab forces under the sharif of Mecca, who considered the line a threat to his control of the region. During the war, the railway was further damaged by Arab guerrillas led by T. E. Lawrence, and in 1918, with the defeat of the Ottoman Empire by the Allies, the Hijaz Railway ceased operations altogether. During the 1920s, travel by automobile, truck, and bus transformed the nature of Hajj travel forever.

Political events of the time affected the Hajj even more dramatically. With the collapse of the Ottoman Empire, the sharif of Mecca emerged as ruler of the short-lived Kingdom of Hijaz from 1916 until 1925, when Abdulaziz ibn Saud conquered the region. The first Hajj conducted under the rule of the

House of Saud took place in 1925. Wahhabi religious authorities, whose support provided the Al Saud dynasty with much-needed legitimacy, quickly imposed their conservative form of Islam on Mecca and Medina. They also began the process, which continues today, of destroying historical and archaeological monuments to prevent them from becoming sites of pagan and idolatrous practice. Saudi authorities even prohibited pilgrims from praying at the locations of ancient cemeteries and mosques that had long ago been destroyed.

Under Saudi rule, management of the Hajj was transformed from what one student of the Hajj has called the "zenith of unbridled laissez faire capitalism" into "a public utility industry."[7] Saudi steps to regulate the Hajj included introducing tighter passport controls in the form of a Hajj visa system; establishing a formal vaccination program; professionalizing the guide system; publishing fee rates for food, rent, and transportation; and providing increased measures for the safety and security of all pilgrims. These regulations were imposed gradually through a series of royal decrees and the establishment of a succession of committees, offices, and ministries all responsible for managing different aspects of the Hajj. Until World War II and the rapid growth of the oil industry, the Hajj remained the primary source of revenue for the newly established Kingdom of Saudi Arabia.

THE SACRED AND THE FORBIDDEN

Journeys to holy places are an important feature of many world religions. Pilgrimage sites, like Delphi, Bodh Gaya, Rome, Jerusalem, and Mecca, have a sacred geography frequently associated with striking natural landmarks, events that took place in the mythical past, or the accomplishments of important figures, human or divine. Pilgrims set out on what are often costly, difficult, and dangerous journeys with the hope of entering another, more sacred world; a different, higher order of reality. On at least two occasions during their travels, once going out and once returning home, pilgrims cross the boundary between the sacred and the profane, a boundary that is often ritually marked in a meaningful way.

Several concepts central to understanding the Hajj are expressed by Arabic words derived from the root *h-r-m*, whose basic meaning is "taboo." The word *haram* means "sacred" or "holy." It is used to refer to a sanctuary, a site that is consecrated and therefore sacrosanct; it designates a place that is protected or inviolate. The Kaba is the *Bayt al-Haram,* the "Holy House"; the cities of

Mecca and Medina are *al-Haramayn,* the "Two Holy Sanctuaries." A closely related word, *haraam,* means "forbidden," "prohibited," or "sinful." Actions that are *haraam* include idolatry, murder, adultery, premarital sex, eating pork, and drinking alcohol. The Holy Mosque in Mecca is the *Masjid al-Haraam,* literally the "Inviolable" Mosque, a mosque so sacred that entry is forbidden to all those who are not ritually pure.

The word *ihram,* derived from the same *h-r-m* root, denotes the state of ritual purity Muslims enter when they perform the Hajj. The act of putting on the white *ihram* garments, foreshadowing the act of being wrapped in a shroud at death, celebrates entrance into a sacred community in which all pilgrims, regardless of social or economic status, stand together as one and as equals before God. The exact geographical boundaries of the sacred space in which pilgrims must be in a state of *ihram* are marked by *miqat,* "stated places" or "stations," where pilgrims on their way to Mecca stop, pray, and change into their *ihram* garments. The Prophet designated five of these stations, one on each of the main pilgrimage routes from Iran and Iraq, Syria, Yemen, Medina, and the center of the Arabian Peninsula. With the advent of travel by steamship, a sixth station was added for pilgrims from the Indian subcontinent and points further east. Now pilgrims traveling by air enter *ihram* before they board the last leg of their flight to Jeddah or when the pilot notifies them that their plane is passing over one of the "stated places."

The division of humanity into two categories, Muslims and non-Muslims, is one of the fundamental distinctions in the Muslim world. The word *kafir* is used in a derogatory sense to refer to non-Muslims as "nonbelievers" or "infidels," people who deny, or more literally "hide" or "cover," the truth. The term "People of the Book," *Ahl al-Kitab* in Arabic, is used to designate non-Muslim followers of monotheistic, Abrahamic religions that predate Islam, namely Judaism and Christianity. In some contexts, Muslims show "People of the Book" greater tolerance and respect than other non-Muslims.

Non-Muslims are strictly forbidden from participating in the Hajj; they are forbidden from even entering the cities of Mecca and Medina, as well as the entire region marked by *miqat* that surrounds them. Two passages from the Quran are cited in support of these restrictions: "It is not for those who ascribe divinity to aught beside God to visit or tend God's houses of worship" (9:17); and, "Those who ascribe divinity to aught beside God are nothing but impure: and so they shall not approach the Inviolable House of Worship from this year onwards" (9:28). According to one commentator, these passages refer literally to the Kaba and, "by implication, the whole of the territory of Mecca."[8]

The key phrase here is "by implication." Precisely what this verse implies is, of course, open to interpretation. Some cite these verses to support the view that non-Muslims are forbidden from entering the entire region around Mecca and Medina; others quote the same passages to support the position that non-Muslims are *not* forbidden from entering the entire region or even the city of Mecca, but only the Holy Mosque itself. Here the Quran seems ambiguous at best, and the crucial issue of who can go to Mecca remains open to debate.

Because the Holy Mosque and the city of Mecca are "sacred" (*haram*) to Muslims, they are also "forbidden" (*haraam*) to non-Muslims. For centuries, therefore, Mecca has exerted a tremendous fascination over the imagination of European travelers and adventurers. Like the headwaters of the Nile and "the heart of darkest Africa," Mecca was one of the exotic and dangerous destinations that held such great allure for explorers seeking out places no European had ever been before. Traveling to Mecca was the ultimate Orientalist fantasy—lifting the veil on the mysterious East to discover the innermost secrets of Islam.

AN UNJUSTIFIABLE VIOLATION OF CONSCIENCE

An entire body of travel literature has grown up around the Hajj. Many works in this genre were written by Europeans who were not Muslims, but who traveled to Mecca disguised as Arabs and who presented themselves falsely as Muslims. This act of deceit created the sense of intrigue and suspense that was an essential element of this genre. Since any European who converted to Islam would be allowed to go to Mecca, the simple act of conversion would eliminate all the mystery, challenge, and danger of the journey. Many European explorers who went to Mecca thought that if they identified themselves as European converts they would be treated as untrustworthy foreigners, or even worse, spies.

The majority of Europeans who visited Mecca in the nineteenth century were engaged in a double act of deceit. Not only were they falsely claiming to be Muslims, they were falsely claiming to be Arabs or members of other cultures of the Middle East. They were claiming both a religious identity and a cultural identity that did not belong to them. Their goal was not simply to be accepted a Muslim, but to "go native," to *pass* as someone who belonged to a culture whose members were Muslim "by blood" or "by birth." This act of deceit was much more difficult; the sense of pride in accomplishing it much greater.

Sir Richard Burton's three-volume *Personal Narrative of a Pilgrimage to Al-Madinah and Meccah,* first published in 1855–56, is a classic of nineteenth-century British travel writing. It also served as a guidebook for future European travelers who sought to participate in what critics have called "the Hajj masquerade." After seven years in India, where he studied several different languages and cultures, and after publishing several books on his travels, Burton received the support of the Royal Geographical Society for an expedition to Arabia. While some biographers consider Burton's trip to Mecca and Medina "a smart career move," others suggest it also was the culmination of a genuine spiritual quest. Regardless of Burton's individual intentions, the tradition he inspired of "non-Muslim interlopers," "pseudopilgrims" traveling to Mecca in disguise, is certainly an egregious example of Orientalist presumption at its worst.[9]

In 1853, Burton sailed from England to Alexandria. After a stop in Cairo, he traveled to Suez, the Red Sea port of Yanbu, Medina, Mecca, and Jeddah, before returning to Egypt. During his journey, Burton traveled as "an incognito," disguised as different characters and using different aliases, each with its own elaborate costume: a Sunni gentleman, a Persian Shia, a Sufi dervish, and an Afghan doctor. Burton prided himself on his ability to pass successfully as a native by behaving in a convincingly "oriental manner." He was able to convince people, as he put it, that "the sheepskin covered a real sheep."[10]

Burton emphasized the fact that he did not convert to Islam—he did not "turn Turk," as he put it—in order to reach his destination. This, he wrote, would have been too degrading to endure. More importantly, this would have eliminated the very danger that made his journey to "the heart of Islam" such a worthy adventure.

> But to pass through the Moslem's Holy Land, you must either be a born believer, or have become one; in the former case you may demean yourself as you please, in the latter a path is ready prepared for you. . . . Moreover, it would have obstructed the aim of my wanderings. The convert is always watched with Argus eyes, and men do not willingly give information to a "new Moslem," especially a Frank: they suspect his conversion to be feigned or forced, look upon him as a spy, and let him see as little of life as possible. . . . Consequently, I had no choice but to appear as a born believer.[11]

Danger was a constant theme in Burton's narrative. He claimed to be "the only living European who has found his way to the Head Quarters of the Moslem Faith." He emphasized how easy it would be for local officials in Mecca or Medina "quietly to dispose of a suspected person by giving a dollar to a Badawi." On one occasion, Burton admitted that because he was an Englishman "neither the Pasha nor the Sharif would . . . dare to enforce . . . the old law, a choice thrice offered between circumcision and death." On another he claimed that, "the first Badawi who caught site of a Frank's hat would not deem himself a man if he did not drive a bullet through the wearer's head." In her preface to the 1893 memorial edition of the book, Burton's wife, Isabel, wrote that Mecca and Medina were "more jealously guarded than the 'Holy Grail,'" and that "no white man, European or Christian, could enter (save as a Moslem), or even approach, without certain death."[12]

In his own preface to the third edition of his *Personal Narrative,* published in 1880, Burton presented for his readers' consideration the charges that had recently been leveled against him and other European travelers who had visited Mecca under what his critics called the "unjustifiable fanciful disguise of a Mohammedan Pilgrim." One critic decried the immoral "violation of conscience" that travelers like Burton had committed, arguing that "the Christian, who conforms to Islamism without a corresponding persuasion of its verity" deserves the "odium all honest men attach to apostasy and hypocrisy." According to another critic, "to feign a religion which the adventurer himself does not believe, to perform with scrupulous exactitude, as of the highest and holiest import, practices which he inwardly ridicules," and to turn "the most sacred and awful bearings of man towards his Creator into a deliberate and truthless mummery . . . seems hardly compatible with the character of a European gentleman, let alone that of a Christian."[13]

Burton dismissed these charges as "invidious remarks," "truculent attacks," and "foul blows" directed against him and the memory of his predecessors. He warned his critics not "to cast the first stone," not to judge him from a position of ignorance.[14] In fact, Burton seems to have interpreted his critics as condemning him on the grounds that a Christian who performed the Hajj was engaging in behavior that was offensive to other Christians, rather than behavior that was offensive to Muslims.

The vast psychological and spiritual distance between Burton's experience of the Hajj and that of a Muslim is painfully obvious when after almost six hundred pages Burton's narrative reaches its climax and Burton sees the Holy Mosque in Mecca for the first time. "There at last it lay," he writes, "the bourn of my long and weary Pilgrimage, realizing the plans and hopes of many and many a year. . . . I may truly say that, of all the worshippers . . . none felt for the moment a deeper emotion than did the Haji from the far-north. . . . But, to confess humbling truth, theirs was the high feeling of religious enthusiasm, mine was the ecstasy of gratified pride."[15] Bluntly and honestly Burton acknowledges here the difference between the reaction of an ambitious British explorer, on the one hand—pride in his own worldly accomplishments—and the reaction of devout Muslims, on the other—spiritual unity with Allah and their fellow Muslim pilgrims.

"A VERY TERRIBLE CRIME"

Arthur Wavell, who visited Mecca in 1908, is generally considered to be the last "Western pretender,"[16] the last non-Muslim European author traveling in disguise to publish a first-person account of the Hajj. Wavell was also the first European writer to describe the journey from Damascus to Medina on the newly opened Hijaz Railway. A British intelligence officer, Wavell had multiple audiences for his account of the trip. He clearly understood the spiritual power that Mecca had for Muslim pilgrims, writing that Mecca was "a place hardly belonging to this world, overshadowed . . . by an almost tangible presence of the deity," a place where "the feeling is one of awe and reverence." Yet he also acknowledged that his trip would help advance his career: "The rank and reputation of a Hagi," he wrote "is useful to the traveller in Moslem countries."[17]

After obtaining a false Turkish passport in Marseilles—without offering a bribe—from an official who did not realize he was an Englishman, Wavell traveled to Alexandria, where he shaved his head "to look as 'un-European' as possible, and dressed in Arab clothes." Having assumed his "Muslim guise," Wavell continued on to Damascus, where he planned to stay long enough to convince himself that his "assumption of Eastern character was effective before entering the forbidden territory." There he told Arabic speakers he met that he was from Zanzibar and spoke Swahili, while he told Swahili speakers he met that he was from Oman and spoke Arabic. Wavell realized that it was "the multifarious customs and ceremonies" of Muslim life that constituted "the real obstacle to a European passing himself off as a Mussulman born and bred. . . . No matter how Eastern his appearance might be, how carefully he might be dressed, and how adept in the language." Wavell insisted that "a bad mistake when praying, visiting a tomb, or even in the responses during a service, might easily be fatal."[18]

In Medina, Wavell heard an old story told to justify the ban against non-Muslims entering the city. Once, a long time ago, two Europeans entered the city in disguise. They tried to tunnel from their house into the mausoleum in the Mosque of the Prophet, but they were caught and crucified.[19] Residents of the city also told Wavell that if a European imposter were unmasked there, he would immediately be put to death. Wavell, however, suspected that this was not the case. He thought that outside the pilgrimage season if the "imposter" just offered local officials a large enough bribe, he would simply be driven out of the city. But if the imposter were exposed during the Hajj season, the outcome would be very different: "All the sultan's horses and all the sultan's men, would not avail to save [him] . . . from the wild fury of the pilgrim mob. . . . A quick passage to a better world by a sword-thrust or bullet would probably be the best that could befall him, for a much more unpleasant end might well be feared. The only chance in such an emergency would be to repeat the Moslem profession of faith and endeavour to take refuge in the house of some influential person, such as the Sharif of Mecca."[20]

Wavell concludes his account of his pilgrimage to Mecca by offering advice to other non-Muslims who might try to follow in his footsteps. He recommends they assume their disguise before arriving in Jeddah, that they avoid associating with pilgrims from the country they claim to be from, and that no one try to visit Medina unless he is "very thoroughly at home in his Oriental character." Wavell then offers some final thoughts on the legality, if not the morality, of his journey. The Ottoman government claims the right to expel foreign travelers from the Hijaz, he writes, but representatives of foreign powers based in the Hijaz are "not supposed to 'give away' anyone making the journey in secret of whom they may come to have knowledge."[21]

Finally, Wavell claims, somewhat disingenuously I think, that he did "nothing illegal" in going to Mecca and that his trip there was "merely contrary to regulation." He admits, however, that his journey to Mecca did "to some extent involve defying the 'wishes and express injunctions' of the authorities, which . . . is regarded in some quarters as a very terrible crime."[22]

CONVERSIONS OF FAITH OR
CONVERSIONS OF CONVENIENCE?

When pilgrims pass one of the five stations, on their journey to Mecca, they literally cross the boundary between profane and sacred space. When non-Muslims convert to Islam, they cross the equally significant, but invisible boundary between two categories of people, non-Muslims and Muslims. Religious conversion can take many forms. It may be a powerful spiritual experience in which a person's psychological and social worlds are dramatically transformed; it may be accompanied by an altered state of consciousness that is interpreted as a message from a divine source calling a person to follow a sacred path. It can occur suddenly without warning or after a long period of preparation and study. And finally, it can involve the renunciation of one religion and the exclusive adoption of a new one in its place.

There are also many other, very different types of conversion. Some conversions do not involve intense emotional states. They may be much more mundane experiences that involve practical considerations, strategic planning, or even the cold calculation of self-interest and material gain. These less religious, or less spiritual experiences include marital conversions, forced conversions, and what could be called conversions of convenience.

In much of the Muslim world, conversion *from* Islam *to* another religion is treated very differently from conversion *from* another religion *to* Islam. The former, conversion *from* Islam *to* another religion, is considered apostasy, an act that some Muslim scholars believe is punishable by death according to sharia law. This is the case in Saudi Arabia. The latter, conversion *from* another religion *to* Islam, is accomplished by what seems to be the simple act of reciting the Muslim declaration of faith, the *shahada:* "There is no God but Allah, and Muhammad is his Prophet."

According to many Muslim authorities, the *shahada* must be uttered aloud and in front of witnesses. New converts must also fully understand and sincerely believe their declaration of faith. If the *shahada* is not uttered honestly—if it is not spoken "with the heart"—it is without value or meaning. In some cases, converts must also state that they believe in the Holy Books (the Torah, the Old and New Testaments, and the Quran), all the prophets of Allah (Abraham, Moses, Jesus, and Muhammad), and the angels (spiritual beings created by Allah from light).

From this perspective, which sets what could be considered a high bar for conversion, it is "intention," *niyya,* that determines the validity of all religious acts. The mechanistic utterance of the declaration of faith alone is insufficient to bring about a real conversion. It is only with conviction, sincerity, and purity of intention that reciting the *shahada* can transform a non-Muslim into a Muslim. As a Muslim judge told J. L. Burckhardt, another early nineteenth-century British explorer who traveled to Mecca in disguise, "It is not the beard alone which proves a man to be a true Moslem."[23]

There are situations, however, when the bar for conversion is set much lower and the simple act of uttering the *shahada* alone, regardless of intention or belief, is sufficient to transform an aspiring convert into a Muslim. A story in the hadith presents a striking example of this type of conversion. Usama ibn Zayd, a soldier of the Prophet Muhammad, captured an enemy soldier, a non-Muslim. Ibn Zayd then killed his prisoner, even though he had cried out "There is no God but Allah, and Muhammad is his Prophet." The Hadith continues: "The Prophet (peace be upon him) admonished him, saying: 'You killed him after he said "There is no God but Allah?" What are you going to do on the Day of Resurrection with this man who said "There is no God but Allah"?'"[24] Another passage from the hadith makes this point more explicitly: "If an unbelieving prisoner of war accepts Islam, he acquires inviolable rights." If he recites the *shahada*, his "blood and wealth become forbidden."[25] These texts present clear evidence that Muhammad accepted the legitimacy of conversions that consist of the simple utterance of the *shahada*.

Charles Doughty, author of *Travels in Arabia Deserta*, first published in 1888, was one of the few European explorers who did not disguise the fact that he was both an Englishman and a Christian, and who did not attempt to go to Mecca or Medina. Doughty encountered this same willingness to accept the profession of faith alone as evidence of conversion to Islam. Some Arabs Doughty met called him a *kafir*, threatened his life, and attacked him violently. Others defended him as a guest or protected him like a brother. On several occasions, Doughty's Bedouin hosts encouraged him to convert to Islam. All he had to do, they said, was to recite the testimony of faith.

"Only become a Moslem," said one. "It is a little word and soon said."

"What are two little words?" asked another. "Pronounce them with us and it shall do thee no hurt."[26]

THE DOUBLE LIFE OF H. ST. JOHN PHILBY

Unlike Burton, Wavell, and other nineteenth-century European travelers, who succeeded in reaching Mecca by means of dishonesty and deceit, during the twentieth century there were many examples of westerners who converted to Islam and performed the Hajj in good faith, or at least in what could pass as good faith. One of the most interesting of these twentieth-century converts is H. St. John Philby, a career officer in the British Foreign

Service, who served in India and Iraq before being sent to Riyadh in 1915 to lead the British mission there. Philby's primary assignment was to establish contact with Abdulaziz ibn Saud, whose Arab forces were threatening the sharif of Mecca for control of the Hijaz.

In his autobiography, *Arabian Days,* Philby presents an account of his "double life," as an Englishman and an Arab, as a Christian and a Muslim. Early in the book, Philby admits that he, like many "giants of Arabian adventure," had a tendency to "fall foul of [his] own folk." He writes: "I suppose I was born a Christian" and admits that during his youth he "was certainly a Christian." But then when he attended Cambridge as a young adult, he writes, "I came to doubt the justice of my convictions" and "discarded them without remorse or bitterness."[27]

Over the decades that followed his posting to Riyadh, Philby developed a close personal and professional relationship with King Abdulaziz ibn Saud and dedicated his life to promoting the king's economic, political, and military interests. Philby also devoted himself to expanding his knowledge of the Arabic language and Bedouin culture. He was the first European traveler to explore much of the vast desert interior of the Arabian Peninsula. Near the end of his autobiography, Philby confesses that for him there was "no escape from the lure of the desert."[28] While some British officials considered him a traitor and some Arabs suspected he was a British spy, Philby maintained the trust of King Abdulaziz through both the First and the Second World Wars.

In 1930, Philby was living with his "growing collection of Arabian baboons" in a mansion in Jeddah on the shore of the Red Sea. Increasingly frustrated with the difficulties of managing the Ford Motor Company concession there, he was torn between returning to England and remaining in Saudi Arabia. He understood that he could never expand his "sphere of activity" in Arabia because of the king's policy "of protecting his realm rigorously from European penetration and the economic and political exploitation" that would inevitably follow.[29]

But Philby realized that there *was* an alternative, an alternative he had actually been contemplating for many years:

> Ever since my early days in India I had been greatly attracted by Islam. . . . I had long ceased to be a Christian and become a philosopher without anything in the nature of religions feelings or convictions. . . . So it was not until I went to Arabia that I came into contact with what seemed to me undeniably a pure form of Islam . . . a religion which one could accept without intellectual

dishonesty as a guide to life and conduct, and whose ethical standards seem to conform better than those of other religions—Christianity for instance—to the basic needs of humanity.[30]

One hot, humid July afternoon in Jeddah, Philby fell asleep at his desk while working on one of his many books. "My head went down on the table like a log, and the world seemed to be turning summersaults about me. I suppose it was an ordinary fainting fit, but being unaccustomed to that sort of thing I thought it was a stroke, and managed to crawl to a sofa, where I lay for some hours in a stupor.... It was then that I made my decision."[31]

Philby immediately telephoned King Abdulaziz to inform him that he had at last decided "to come into the fold of the faithful." The king was delighted and sent him a document to sign "in token of" his acceptance of Islam, a document that was "required for the satisfaction of the ecclesiastical authorities at Mecca." The next day, August 7, 1930, Philby put on his "Arab garments" and drove off in his green Ford "out of the old life into the new." In the company of several Saudi officials sent by the king, Philby traveled to Mecca to perform the Umrah, the lesser pilgrimage, and confirm his conversion to Islam.

"I seemed to be living in a dream," Philby wrote that evening, "and I was content to relax in an orgy of intellectual and spiritual self-surrender—at least for that one unforgettable night.... I felt like some disembodied spirit restored by accident or miracle to its proper environment. For the first time for many years I felt strangely at peace with the world."[32]

The next day King Abdulaziz welcomed Philby to his court in Taif in the mountains sixty-five kilometers southeast of Mecca. There the king gave Harry St. John Bridger Philby a new Muslim name, Abdullah. Philby performed the Hajj for the first time the next year and did so every year after that for the next decade.[33] All this time, Philby writes, he never accepted an official position in the Saudi government, so no one could claim he had benefited financially from his conversion to Islam. It was enough that after completing the Hajj he could feel "the spirit of Arabia coursing through the veins of Islam."[34]

The account of his conversion Philby presents in his autobiography is somewhat idealized. His diaries and letters reveal a much more complicated process. While there clearly was a significant spiritual component to Philby's conversion, other factors also played an important role. Philby understood the considerable professional advantages he would gain as a result of his conversion to Islam. Improved access to the king would help greatly in his business dealings with western automobile manufacturers, oil companies, and arms dealers. It would also increase the chances that King Abdulaziz would grant him permission to explore the Rub al-Khali Desert in the Empty Quarter and other unmapped areas of the Arabian Peninsula. Over subsequent years, Philby benefited tremendously from the king's generosity. Abdulaziz rewarded him for his long years of loyal service with a variety of gifts: large amounts of money, a house in Riyadh, and a sixteen-year-old odalisque—a concubine or slave girl—who lived with Philby for the rest of his life and bore him several children, much to the dismay of his English wife, Dora.[35]

In her biography, *Philby of Arabia*, Elizabeth Monroe argues that Philby's conversion to Islam was not a sincere one. She cites a letter in which one of his colleagues wrote that Philby never made any "pretense whatever that his conversion was spiritual"; then she concludes baldly that Philby "needed Islam not as a faith, but as a convenience."[36] Monroe's claim, however, is no more convincing than Philby's claim that he enjoyed no material advantage at all from his conversion.

The most revealing account of Philby's conversion to Islam is contained in a letter he wrote to an old friend in Cambridge at the time:

> My future is irrevocably bound up with that of Arabia and Ibn Saud. . . . I was as it were between two doors both closed on me, my own people (Government etc.) having turned me adrift for my uncomfortable opinions on matters eastern and Arab, while the Arabs were ready with a welcome (and a very genuine one) if only I would put off my old clothes (for to them I was a Christian!) and adopt theirs. Anyway the deed is finally and irrevocably done, and I shall die in perfect equanimity in the Muslim faith for which (especially on its ethical side) I have a very real admiration.[37]

MALCOLM X AND THE TRUE MESSAGE OF ISLAM

One of the most famous American converts to Islam was Malcolm X, the African-American leader whose forceful advocacy of black supremacy made him a controversial figure during the civil rights movement of the early 1960s. In 1946, at the age of twenty-one, after an early life of foster care, drug use, poverty, and crime, Malcolm Little was sent to prison for seven years on charges of theft. There he had the first of two conversion experiences that would lead him in the last years of his life to become a devout follower of Sunni Islam.

In his autobiography, Malcolm describes himself prior to his conversion as "deaf, dumb, and blind," "a brainwashed black Christian," a sinner who had "sunk to the very bottom of the American white man's society." His nickname was "Satan." When Malcolm was introduced to the teachings of Elijah Muhammad and the Nation of Islam, he struggled to understand this new view of the world. He stopped eating and just sat in his cell staring at the walls. He describes being "struck numb" and seeing "a blinding light." He lay awake all one night praying to Allah for relief from his confusion. The next night, as he lay in bed, he saw a man sitting beside him in a chair. This man disappeared as suddenly as he had come.[38]

The difficult years of Malcolm's life came to an end with his conversion to Islam. "I found Allah and the religion of Islam," he wrote, "and it completely transformed my life. . . . I still marvel at how swiftly my previous life's thinking pattern slid away from me like snow off a roof. . . . I would be startled to catch myself thinking in a remote way of my earlier self as another person."[39]

After his release from prison in 1952, Malcolm changed his name from Malcolm Little to Malcolm X in order to mark the loss of his original African family name. He was appointed to serve as a minister in the Nation of Islam. Malcolm soon became the controversial public face of the Black Muslims. Later in his life he realized that the religion of Islam "had reached down into the mud," lifted him up, and saved him from an early, violent death or a long life in prison. He now understood that Allah had blessed him "to remain true, firm and strong in his faith in Islam."[40]

In 1964, after a bitter falling out with Elijah Muhammad, Malcolm left the Nation of Islam. At this point in his life, he decided to immerse himself more fully in Sunni Islam and travel to Mecca to perform the Hajj. In order to obtain a visa from the Saudi consulate in New York, Malcolm had to obtain the approval of the director of the Federation of Islamic Associations of the United States and Canada. When he arrived in Jeddah, he was also required to appear before the Hajj Committee Court, the official Saudi government body responsible for examining the cases of pilgrims whose conversion to Islam might not have been authentic.

After questioning him about the sincerity of his conversion, the judge was still hesitant to approve Malcolm's Hajj certificate because he was not convinced that Malcolm had completely rejected the teachings of the Nation of

Islam, which the judge knew were inconsistent on many counts with the beliefs of Sunni Islam. Twice during the hearing, the brother-in-law of Prince (and future King) Faisal, who had accompanied Malcolm to the hearing, intervened on his behalf, telling the judge, "The man says, *la ilaha illa Allahu,* 'There is no god but God,' and says he is Muslim. What more do you want?" That night, after being accepted by the judge as a "true Muslim," Malcolm left Jeddah by car for the Holy City of Mecca to perform the Hajj.[41]

During his time in Saudi Arabia, Malcolm was overwhelmed not only by the lack of racism he encountered, but also by the absence of even the most basic racial categories of "black" and "white" that had so completely dominated his life until then. Malcolm somewhat naively believed that he had entered a new world of racial equality. The sense of racial harmony and unity he experienced during his pilgrimage to Mecca had blinded him both to the important role that Muslim Arabs had played in the African slave trade and to the fact that slavery in Saudi Arabia had been abolished only three years earlier.

On the plane to Jeddah, Malcolm saw "white, black, brown, red, and yellow people, blue eyes and blond hair, and my kinky red hair—all together, brothers! All honoring the same God Allah, all in turn giving equal honor to each other." When he landed in Jeddah, he felt he was part of a scene from the pages of *National Geographic.* Describing a Saudi man who came to meet him the next morning, Malcolm wrote: "In America, he would have been called a white man, but—it struck me, hard and instantly—from the way he acted, I had no *feeling* of him being a white man. . . . That morning was when I first began to reappraise the 'white man.' . . . That morning was the start of a radical alteration in my whole outlook about 'white' men."[42] Malcolm attributed this experience to the power of Allah and the "colorblindness" of the Muslim world, where the distinction between "blacks" and "whites" was irrelevant and everyone was simply Muslim.

For Malcolm, as for many pilgrims, the climax of the Hajj was the afternoon he spent praying on Mount Arafat. "There were tens of thousands of pilgrims, from all over the world. They were of all colors from blue-eyed blonds to black-skinned Africans. But we were all participating in the same ritual, displaying a spirit of unity and brotherhood that my experiences in America had led me to believe never could exist between the white and the non-white."[43]

During his prayers, Malcolm swore to Allah that when he returned to the United States he would "spread the true message of Islam" and "eliminate racism from the American Moslem movement." Over the course of the next few days, as he tried to make sense of the behavior of "white" Muslims, Malcolm realized that "their belief in one God had removed the 'white' from their *minds,* the 'white' from their *behavior,* and the 'white' from their *attitude.*"[44]

When he returned to the United States, Malcolm adopted a new name for the second time. His new name, his Muslim name, el-Haji Malik el-Shabazz, marked his new status as a pilgrim; it suggested the increased legitimacy he now enjoyed in the Muslim world. For the second time in his life, Malcolm had undergone a conversion experience. This time he had converted from the Nation of Islam, with its ideology of racial separatism and violence, to Sunni Islam, with its idealized vision of racial unity, equality, and brotherhood.

After completing the Hajj, Malcolm was no longer "the angriest Negro in America." Free from the sickness of racial hatred; he had moved "from the deepest darkness" to the "greatest light." This was the "truth" that Malcolm preached during the short time that remained before his assassination in February 1966.[45]

ADAM TRAVEL'S HAJJ PACKAGE 1A: *MAKKAH FIRST,* FOUR NIGHTS AT THE HILTON MAKKAH STARTING AT $11,900

In the decades after World War II, the rapid growth of international air travel and the oil revenue that flooded the Saudi economy transformed both the Hajj and the Holy City of Mecca itself. In the early 1950s, 100,000 pilgrims a year performed the Hajj, and Mecca's traditional Ottoman architecture was still very much intact. In the first decades of the twenty-first century, two million pilgrims a year perform the Hajj, modern skyscrapers dominate Mecca's horizon, and luxury hotels tower over the Holy Mosque.

By the 1970s, all major Arab airlines were operating Hajj charter flights to Jeddah from cities around the world. The Hajj no longer drew pilgrims primarily from Arab countries; it had become a truly global phenomenon. The Hajj had also come under the control of the Organization of Islamic Cooperation (OIC), formerly the Organization of the Islamic Conference, a group of fifty-seven Muslim countries founded in 1969 and dedicated to managing the affairs of the Muslim world.

The most important accomplishment of this international political regime has been the imposition of a quota system to control the overwhelming growth of the Hajj. The OIC has frozen the number of pilgrims allowed to perform the Hajj at the 1998 level of two million a year, a limit that corresponds to approximately one person for every thousand Muslims in each country that sends pilgrims to Mecca. This quota has had significant political ramifications. It has stopped Iran from flooding Mecca with huge numbers of Shia pilgrims, who had repeatedly demonstrated against policies of the Sunni Saudi state; it has also enabled governments of Muslim countries around the world to manipulate the allocation of Hajj visas for their own political purposes.[46]

Since King Abdulaziz seized control of the Hijaz from the sharif of Mecca in 1925, the Saudi government has been responsible for managing all domestic aspects of the Hajj. Now, virtually every agency of the Saudi government is involved in regulating some part of what has been called "the Hajj service industry."[47] While pilgrims are still "guests of God," they are now also guests of the Saudi state.

The Directorate-General of Hajj Affairs was established under the Ministry of Finance in 1930; it became the Ministry of Hajj in 1962. The Supreme Hajj Committee was formed in 1966 to assume responsibility for providing pilgrims with much-needed services. And in 1975, the Hajj Research Center was set up to furnish the government with an interdisciplinary team of expert consultants under the leadership of Dr. Sami Angawi, an internationally known architect and urban planner.

Among the most important tasks facing Saudi authorities have been the modernization and expansion of facilities to accommodate the ever-increasing number of pilgrims who come to Mecca ever year on Hajj. These responsibilities include providing millions of pilgrims each year with food, housing, sanitation, security, and emergency medical care during the two-week period they are in the country. In addition, the Saudi government has constructed facilities capable of handling the hundreds of thousands of sacrificial animals that are ritually slaughtered and butchered each year. The government has also licensed several thousand barbers to shave the heads of male pilgrims when they have completed the Hajj.

The Saudi government has spent freely from its vast oil revenues to develop the international airport at Jeddah and the mosque complexes in both Medina and Mecca. These huge, ongoing public works projects have transformed the Hijaz into one of the most cosmopolitan areas in the Muslim world. Occupying an area of over a hundred square kilometers, the new Hajj Terminal at the Jeddah airport, constructed in 1981, is widely regarded as one of the world's busiest and best airport terminals in the world. During the two-week period of the Hajj, six thousand flights pass through the Hajj Terminal, while fifteen thousand buses transport pilgrims along the four-lane highway from Jeddah to Mecca. Tunnels have been dug through the mountains to improve the roads between Mecca and Medina. And in 2010, the elevated Mecca Metro was built to ease local traffic congestion, because during the Hajj it was taking some pilgrims nine hours to travel fourteen kilometers from Mecca to Arafat by bus.[48]

Since its first major expansion in the 1950s, the Holy Mosque has been rebuilt and enlarged many times. In the process, valuable archaeological sites and important examples of early Islamic architecture have been destroyed. In 1989, another multibillion-dollar program to expand the Holy Mosque was begun. New minarets, domes, and gateways have been added; pedestrian walkways, escalators, and elevators have been built. An air-conditioning system and heated floors have also been recently installed. Now the Holy Mosque, one of the largest public buildings in the world, can hold over a million worshipers.[49]

Critics accuse the Saudi government of "cultural vandalism" for transforming the most sacred space in the Muslim world into a commercial zone dominated by boutiques, hotels, and shopping malls. In 2002, the Saudi government demolished an eighteenth-century Ottoman fortress in order to construct a huge new luxury hotel right across the street from the Holy Mosque. The Turkish minister of culture condemned the destruction of the fortress as an "act of barbarism."

The Mecca Royal Clock Tower Hotel, at 601 meters and 120 floors is one of the tallest buildings in the world. It dwarfs the minarets of the Holy Mosque (see fig. 16). The hotel can accommodate a hundred thousand people a night; it has two heliports and a parking lot for 10,000 cars. Its health club sports both a sauna and a jacuzzi. Detractors have begun to refer to Mecca as a new Las Vegas.[50]

Several disastrous accidents have marred the Hajj over the past twenty-five years. In 1990, over fourteen hundred people died when a crowd of pilgrims panicked inside a pedestrian tunnel leading from Mecca to the Plains of Arafat. And in 1997, 343 people were killed in a fire that destroyed seventy thousand tents in Mina. More recently, on September 11, 2015, just ten days before the beginning of the Hajj, a huge construction crane fell onto the Holy Mosque when a powerful sand storm moved through the area. The crane crashed through the roof of the Holy Mosque, killing over a hundred people and injuring several hundred more. Less than two weeks later, on September 24, 2015, during the Hajj itself, the deadliest Hajj disaster in history took place. In what experts described as a "progressive crowd collapse," rather than a "stampede," two large groups of pilgrims moving toward the Jamarat Bridge from different directions converged onto the same street with tragic results. While the official announcement of the Saudi government put the death toll at 769, according to other estimates the final death toll was over 2,100, with more than a thousand pilgrims still missing.[51]

The Saudi government has spent vast sums of money to improve the safety and comfort of its guests. In Mina, a hundred thousand air-conditioned, Teflon-coated tents have been set up, and in the Plain of Arafat sprinklers have been placed on top of thousands of ten-meter poles to spread a fine mist over the pilgrims who spend the day praying there. An enclosed, air-conditioned concourse has been built between the hills of Safa and Marwa, where pilgrims can perform the *sai*, running back and forth between the hills seven times. Even more impressive is the five-story walkway, a thousand meters long with dozens of exits and entrances, that pilgrims now use to stone the three curved walls that have replaced the pillars at the Jamarat. Three hundred thousand pilgrims an hour can now stone the Devil with much less danger of being crushed to death by a collapsing crowd.

To point out that the Hajj in its present form is an example of mass religious tourism in no way diminishes the religious significance it has for the millions of pilgrims who perform it. The Hajj is without a doubt the most important religious *and* commercial event in the Saudi year. While the revenue it provides the Saudi treasury—over 16 billion dollars a year—pales in comparison to the country's oil royalties, it nevertheless makes an important contribution to the economy of the country in general and the Hijaz in particular.

The website of the Ministry of Hajj lists over three hundred approved travel agencies in over thirty countries that are licensed by the Saudi government to make travel arrangements for pilgrims planning to visit Mecca. Many of these agencies are clearly trying to take advantage of the booming market in Hajj tourism by offering an impressive variety of Hajj packages to suit budgets of all kinds. Adam Travel is a full-service travel agency that specializes in Hajj travel. It has thirty offices in the United States, and its website features two video feeds streaming live footage from the Holy Mosque in Mecca.

Adam Travel's Hajj Package 1A: *Makkah First* features five-star accommodation for four nights in the Hilton Makkah, which is located at the

Haram boundary—four people per room with breakfast included. Accommodation at Mina and Arafat are in the North America Camp in air-conditioned tents with mattresses and boxed food. Transportation from Jeddah to Mecca, on to Medina, and back to Jeddah is in government provided, air-conditioned buses. Well-respected Muslim scholars and professional guides accompany each group. Visits to historic sites in Medina are also available. *Mecca First* programs start at $11,900—the sacrifice fee of $150 is not included. Hajj packages offered by other government-approved travel agencies include Hajj education seminars, religious advisors fluent in English, Arabic, and Urdu, complementary *ihram* clothing for men and prayer rugs for women, SIM cards with local Saudi numbers, and Zamzam water to bring back to relatives.

The website of the Ministry of Hajj also offers a wealth of information for pilgrims. It presents an account of the history of the Hajj, a description of its ritual components, and advice on preparing for "your journey of a lifetime." It also provides detailed information on how to apply for a Hajj visa, as well as a variety of "useful contacts" in Saudi Arabia. The website's frequently-asked-questions page contains suggestions on finding accommodations, performing the sacrifice, traveling with disabilities, and a host of other health and safety issues.

In two films available on its website, the ministry welcomes "our brothers and sisters, the pilgrims" to Mecca and asks them in the name of the Prophet Muhammad to be "peaceful, orderly, kind, and understanding." It warns pilgrims to avoid wickedness, wrangling, jostling, and crushing. The Jamarat safety film requests that "our brothers and sisters, the pilgrims" carefully follow the instructions of their guides and comply with the directions of all wardens and security personnel. It emphasizes the fact that the Ministry has developed a detailed schedule according to which each group of pilgrims has been assigned a specific time to perform this portion of the Hajj, and it warns that noncompliance with this timetable will result in people being returned to the site of their encampment. Most importantly the film urges pilgrims to please be on time when they "go to stone the Devil at the Jamarat."

The Saudi government strictly controls who is allowed to perform the Hajj. In addition to more common travel documents—passport, extra photographs, proof of vaccination, and nonrefundable round-trip ticket—several additional documents must be provided by applicants for a Hajj visa. Women over the age of forty-five must submit a notarized letter from their male guardian, or *mahram,* giving them permission to participate in the Hajj with an organized tour group. Women under forty-five may not perform the Hajj unless they are accompanied by their *mahram*. If applicants for Hajj visas have non-Muslim names or have converted to Islam, they must also submit a notarized certificate from the imam of their mosque or Islamic center stating that they are Muslims. On this document, called a "Declaration of Conversion to Islam," which is available on the websites of approved travel agents, an applicant's imam certifies that the applicant has converted to Islam, become a Muslim, and is recommended for travel to Mecca on the Hajj.

The al-Taqwa Mosque on Bedford Avenue in Brooklyn, New York, is open seven days a week for all five prayer services. Its imam offers classes in Quran recitation, Islamic studies, Arabic, and martial arts. He also offers "New *Shahada* Orientation" classes for people interested in converting to Islam. According to a mosque official I spoke with, when the imam is asked to fill out a *shahada* certificate for someone, he inquires when and where the applicant "took *shahada*" and what community "the brother or sister is a member of." If the imam doesn't know an applicant, I was told, he would ask the applicant some questions "just to see if he was playing around." But the mosque official acknowledged that a person's sincerity "is known only to Allah." The imam at the Tri-State Islamic Center on Flatbush Avenue in Brooklyn told me that if someone he didn't know asked him to fill out a *shahada* certificate, he wouldn't do it without first getting to know the person.

"I don't know what's in a person's heart," he said. "No one can judge that. But if you break God's law, then God will punish you."

WHO CAN GO TO MECCA?

Dr. Sami Angawi is a descendent of the Prophet Muhammad, a prominent Sufi leader of the Hijaz, a public intellectual, and a highly respected architect. He has a Ph.D. in Islamic architecture from the School of Oriental and African Studies at the University of London and has been a fellow at the Graduate School of Design at Harvard.[52] He has dedicated his life to the preservation of traditional Hijazi architecture and material culture. Angawi, who describes himself as a "Hajjologist," a student and scholar of the Hajj, founded the Hajj Research Center in 1975 and served as its director until he resigned in 1988 to protest the Saudi government's long-standing practice of destroying ancient sites and historical buildings in Mecca and Medina.

Angawi is one of the strongest critics of what he and many others consider the Saudi government's disastrous mismanagement of the architectural heritage of the two holy cities. Seeing this destruction, he once said, is like seeing his children killed every day.[53] Saudi officials defend their practice—building new parking lots, luxury hotels, and high-rise apartment buildings—as necessary to meet the needs of pilgrims, but it's also clear that conservative Wahhabi religious authorities are afraid that the preservation or restoration of ancient buildings and historical sites will inevitably lead to idolatry and polytheism.

On a warm, humid evening near the end of our stay in Saudi Arabia, we visited Dr. Angawi at his home on a very ordinary looking street on the outskirts of Jeddah. The Angawi family home is an extraordinary example of modern Hijazi architecture. It is as if one of the decaying houses of al-Balad, the old city of Jeddah, had been meticulously restored and miraculously transported out of the center of the city. An exterior of latticed balconies and carved stone gives way through an ornately carved dark wooden door to a spectacular interior constructed around a three-story atrium with a shallow blue pool, green plants, stained-glass windows, marble arches, and airy domes. Off the atrium are several *diwaniya,* or sitting rooms, with inlaid wooden floors and oriental carpets surrounded by low cushioned benches, or divans, after which the rooms are named.

Dr. Angawi received us on the top floor of his house in an open area that had a wonderful view of the setting sun out over the Red Sea to the west. His face was framed by a thinning gray beard, wire-rimmed glasses, and a traditional gold-and-white Hijazi turban. His self-effacing smile conveyed both a sense of intense passion and gentle wisdom. As we sat on cushions on the floor around him, Dr. Angawi shared with us his thoughts on freedom, humanity, Islam, and Allah.

"My architecture and my life," he told us, "are based on the principal of balance—*mizan.*" He held his black cane out in front of him balanced on a finger to illustrate his point. "The Bill of Rights, the Ten Commandments, and the Quran are our points of reference. They are the tools we use to create balance and order in society. Unity in diversity is an example of balance. Jews and Christians and Muslims share a great deal. The minor differences that separate us are a matter of faith, and faith cannot be proved or disproved."

Angawi went on to criticize conservative Muslims who say that only Muslims will go to heaven. "If you have an atom of belief in God, you'll reach heaven. The goal is to find God. It's not our business to discuss who goes to

Heaven and who goes to Hell. Islam is the most flexible religion I've ever experienced. Islam is the religion of freedom. Allah is the God of everyone, even people who don't believe in Him. We are trying to share love with you now—Muslims and Christians, Saudis and Americans. We're not angels. Angels do good naturally; we humans have to struggle. God made us so that we come back to Him through love."

The evening call to prayer sounded above the noise of the traffic below. Dr. Angawi left us to pray in the next room. Later, when it was time for us to go, Dr. Angawi walked downstairs with me. He told me he would be happy to take me to Mecca if I wanted. "I'll tell you what to say; I'll give you the password so you can go. Anyone can go to Mecca. Islam is very open. I'm a servant, not a judge. I'll take you to Mecca myself. I have a cane; I'll use it to enable you to go. I can get you the official forms you need so you can travel to Mecca safely."

I was stunned. I thought only Muslims could go to Mecca. I *knew* only Muslims could go to Mecca. "That would be a great honor," I said. "Thank you. But I don't feel it would be appropriate for me to go to Mecca. I'm not a Muslim."

"Do you believe in one God?" Dr. Angawi asked. "Do you believe in the Holy Books? In the Prophets?"

Dr. Angawi was offering me such an inclusive definition of what it meant to be Muslim that it could almost accommodate me, an anthropologist who had long since drifted away from a liberal Protestant upbringing.

I thanked Dr. Angawi again, and again I politely declined his offer.

"You know how I feel," he continued. "If you keep quiet or tell other people, if you keep it to yourself or write about it, that's between you and God. If you want to go to Mecca, you can. If you don't, that's up to you. But I will take you to Mecca."

On the bus ride back to our hotel, I discussed Dr. Angawi's offer with Ahmed, the young Saudi accompanying us on our trip. "That's weird," Ahmed said. "It's against the law. He's not the government. Who's he to say that? It's not up to him to decide who can go to Mecca."

Ahmed mentioned the huge sign above the main highway from Jeddah to Mecca that marks the route to Mecca for "Muslims Only." Non-Muslims are directed to take the next exit off the highway.

"That's the government," said Ahmed. "That's the law. There's no other place in the world where you can go and feel as a Muslim spiritually. All the people there are the same religion; it doesn't matter how rich or how poor they are. But if you're not a believer, it's not the same. Someone watching me gets in the way of my contacting God. It's an invasion of my privacy. It loses spiritual meaning if nonbelievers go; it becomes less holy. It becomes a tourist circus."

Ahmed's argument that non-Muslims should not go to Mecca reminded me of an earlier conversation we'd had about whether non-Muslims were allowed to touch the Quran. I told him I thought I should be able to touch—and read—the Quran. Ahmed disagreed; he said I should not be allowed to touch the Quran because I was unclean. I assured him that I washed my hands regularly and asked him if Muslims with dirt on their hands were cleaner than Christians who had just washed their hands. Ahmed clarified his position; he said that I wasn't spiritually clean. I told him that I tried to lead a good life and that I considered myself fairly clean from a moral, even spiritual point of view. Ahmed paused and tried to clarify his position further. I was not clean in a Muslim way. I smiled, shook his hand, and told him that I understood his position, but that I still disagreed with him.

At this point, an older Saudi man who was standing nearby and who had overheard our conversation about whether non-Muslims could go to Mecca, told Ahmed in Arabic, "Of course they can't go, they're *kafir*."

Ahmed was furious. "Don't use that word!" he said.

"Why?" the man asked. "If they aren't Muslims, they're *kafir*."

"You shouldn't call anyone a *kafir*. That's offensive." Ahmed replied angrily.

The man apologized and claimed he didn't know it was offensive. Ahmed didn't believe him.

The next morning several students returned to Dr. Angawi's house to discuss the possibility of going to Mecca. That afternoon three students told me they were going to go to Mecca with Dr. Angawi.

I couldn't believe it. I knew they weren't Muslims. I knew that their Saudi visas stated clearly that they weren't Muslims; I had filled out their visa applications myself. When I told the three students that they couldn't to go to Mecca because they weren't Muslim, they were very upset. They insisted that Dr. Angawi's plan was perfectly legal. Before they left Jeddah, they said, they would go to the office of the Islamic Educational Foundation, where they would say they believed in God, the Holy Books, and the Prophets. Then they would go to Mecca.

I told the students that this constituted conversion to Islam. They were converting to Islam; they were becoming Muslims. They disagreed; they didn't see it that way at all. Neither did Dr. Angawi, they said. He told them that a Christian could recite the *shahada* and not convert to Islam. Natasha said that signing the form was no big deal. She was an agnostic, but she felt perfectly comfortable reciting the *shahada*. Natasha didn't see a contradiction between being an agnostic and saying she believed in Allah. Anyway, she said, if Allah existed, He wouldn't care whether she recited the *shahada* or not. And He certainly wouldn't object to her going to Mecca.

I decided to call the Islamic Educational Foundation myself. A young American Muslim who worked there told me that the process was perfectly legal and that the "formalities" did constitute conversion to Islam, but only "nominally," only "on paper." He said that about thirty people a month came to his office, recited the *shahada,* and went to Mecca. That was it.

"It's not our business to ask questions," he said. "We have no right to ask if they're going just to see Mecca as tourists or photographers. We have no authority to question their sincerity; it's enough for them to say the *shahada*.

"They'll receive an official document saying they converted to Islam. If they say they're Muslims because they want to go to Mecca, that's between them and God. They're human beings on a spiritual journey. Their parents may be upset that they converted to Islam, but there has been no proselytism, no influence, from us. It's their decision. We're in no way responsible."

At this point I felt extremely conflicted. On the one hand, I was responsible for the students' safety; I also had a responsibility to Bates College. On the other hand, as an anthropologist and a teacher, I didn't think it was appropriate for me to forbid students from converting to Islam and going to Mecca. I did, however, feel an obligation to convey to them the implications of their actions, at least as I understood them.

I supported them in their spiritual quest, but I wanted them to understand the process of religious conversion. I appreciated, with great discomfort, the irony of the fact that I was endorsing a more conservative, more restrictive, approach to conversion to Islam than the Saudi government. I was also rejecting the more liberal and inclusive position articulated by Dr. Angawi, a position that I respected and admired and that was much closer to my own personal religious beliefs than the position I felt forced to impose on the situation facing me. After much thought, I decided I would try to explain to the students the seriousness of their planned course of action and then leave the final decision up to them.

My meeting with Emma was very difficult. I challenged her to articulate her religious beliefs and defend her desire to visit the most sacred city in the

Muslim world, a city that non-Muslims have been forbidden from entering for fourteen hundred years. At the end of our conversation, Emma was extremely angry. She'd been insulted by my questions; she felt they were demeaning and disrespectful. She was angry that I hadn't asked Adnan the same questions, that I hadn't challenged Adnan's right to go to Mecca.

Adnan was a Nepali student on our trip who had a Muslim father and a Hindu mother. He had identified himself as a Muslim on his Saudi visa and had gone to Mecca with a Saudi friend several days earlier. But Emma was right about the inconsistencies in my position. That evening, another student whose plans to visit Mecca I had challenged confronted Adnan with some hostile questions—"Are you Muslim? Have you read the Quran?" Adnan was taken completely by surprise; he didn't understand what was happening. He told her that he was partly Muslim, that he was agnostic.

The next morning I spoke with Elva. This conversation was even more difficult than my conversation with Emma. I asked Elva if she would be converting to Islam if she didn't have the chance to go to Mecca. I suggested she go back home, study the Quran, convert to Islam, and *then* visit Mecca. I asked Elva if she believed in the Holy Books. She had never even heard of the Torah. Then I asked Elva what for me was the crucial question. I asked her if she was a Muslim? Not if she was partly Muslim, not if she might be a Muslim, and not if there was a possibility that she might become a Muslim. I asked her if she was a Muslim.

I apologized to Elva for confronting her this way, but I felt it was my responsibility. Elva in turn apologized to me for making me confront her this way. We understood each other; we respected each other. And we were both in tears.

NOTES

PREFACE

1. DeBuys 2015, 3.

INTRODUCTION

1. Pogrebin 2013.
2. CBS News 2009; BBC News Middle East 2011b, 2002; Hopkins 2012.
3. House 2012, 33; and Lippman 2012, ix.
4. Geertz 1973b, 5.
5. Geertz 1973b, 23.
6. Marcus 1986.
7. This brief overview of the history of Saudi Arabia is intended to provide background material for the individual chapters that follow. It draws on the following valuable sources: Hammond, *The Islamic Utopia* 2012; Hegghammer, *Jihad in Saudi Arabia* 2010; Hertog, *Princes, Brokers, and Bureaucrats* 2010; T.C. Jones, *Desert Kingdom* 2010; Lacroix, *Awakening Islam* 2011; Lacy, *Inside the Kingdom* 2009; Long and Maisel, *The Kingdom of Saudi Arabia* 2010; Menoret, *The Saudi Enigma* 2005; and al-Rasheed, *A History of Saudi Arabia* 2010.
8. While the term *Wahhabism* is sometimes used interchangeably with the term *Salafism,* and while some people object to any use of the term *Wahhabism,* I follow Esposito 2011, 144–46; and al-Rasheed 2013, 15–22, in using Wahhabism to refer to a distinctly Saudi revivalist movement that exists in the wider context of Salafism.
9. See al-Rasheed 2010, 139; Menoret 2005, 110; Trofimov 2007, 25–34; and R. Wright 1985, 152.
10. Lippman 2012, 16.
11. Human Rights Watch 2011.
12. Lippman 2012, 105; Hertog 2009, 18; and Middle East Institute n.d.

13. Lippman 2012, 105; and UNESCO 2006–7.

14. Lippman 2012, 130–32.

15. International Crisis Group 2005.

16. International Crisis Group 2005.

17. Huntington 1996.

CHAPTER ONE. CAN OIL BRING HAPPINESS?

1. A Saudi's description of the Aramco compound.

2. CBS News 2008.

3. Saudi Aramco 2015.

4. Clark and Tahlawi 2006, xxii.

5. Nawwab, Speers, Hoye 1980, 188.

6. Stegner 1971, 28.

7. Clark and Tahlawi, 2006, 223.

8. Field 2000, 25.

9. Stegner 1971, 202.

10. Clark and Tahlawi, 2006, 219.

11. Nawwab, Speers, and Hoye 1980, 245.

12. Nawwab, Speers, and Hoye 1980, 249.

13. Nawwab, Speers, and Hoye 1980, 235.

14. Nawwab, Speers, and Hoye 1980, 238.

15. Clark and Tahlawi, 2006, 284 and 289.

16. Vitalis 2009, x.

17. Cheney 1958, 125.

18. Cheney 1958, 31.

19. Vitalis 2009, xi and xvi.

20. Stegner 1971, 223.

21. Vitalis 2009, 28 and 62.

22. Vitalis 2009, xiii.

23. Cheney 1958, 125.

24. Vitalis 2009, xvii.

25. B. Thompson 2007.

26. Stegner 1971. For more information on the *Discovery!* controversy, see Leff 2007; Lippman 2007; Matthews 2007; B. Thompson 2007; and Vitalis 2009, 194–99.

27. Vitalis 2009, xvii.

28. Vitalis 2009, xviii.

29. Cheney 1958, 215; Barnes 1979, 6; and Vitalis 2009, xii.

30. Cheney 1958, 25, 38, 43, and 53.

31. O'Connor 1971, 325.

32. Johnson 1982, 42–44, 72, and 76.

33. L. Kennedy 1969, 332.

34. Barnes 1979, 37 and 43.
35. Vitalis 2009, 26 ff.; and Johnson 1982, 49.
36. Kimball 1956, 469–84, 477.
37. Kimball 1956, 470.
38. Kimball 1956, 484.
39. Cheney 1958, 222 and 225.
40. Vitalis 2009, 157.
41. Lackner 1978, 98.
42. Vitalis 2009, 136.
43. Brown 1999, 372.
44. Barnes 1979, 169.
45. Brown 1999, 137.
46. Simmons 2005, 50.
47. Brown 1999, 266.
48. Simmons 2005, 294.
49. Brown 1999, 367.
50. Brown 1999, 267.
51. Aramco Brat Media 2007.

CHAPTER TWO. DRIVING WHILE FEMALE

1. A Saudi opponent of the women's right to drive campaign.
2. M.I.A. 2012.
3. Menoret 2014.
4. Noisey 2012.
5. Jones 2012.
6. Noisey 2012.
7. Hermes 2012.
8. For a valuable account of the position of women in Saudi Society, see al-Rasheed 2013. On Muslim women more generally, see Abu-Lughod 2013.
9. Haussman, Tyson, and Zahidi 2009.
10. Geertz 1973a.
11. Hausman, Tyson, and Zahidi 2009.
12. Lippman 2012, 156.
13. For a valuable compilation of material on women driving in Saudi Arabia, see Campbell 2009–13.
14. Jawhar 2009.
15. Wagner 2011.
16. MacFarquhar 2011a.
17. Ibn Baz n.d.
18. Bloxham 2011.
19. My Right to Dignity 2012.
20. Reuters 2010.

21. *Al-Arabiya News* 2010.

22. ABC News 2005.

23. BBC News Middle East 2011a.

24. *Emirates 24/7* 2013b.

25. Shane 2013.

26. Milani 2012.

27. Al Jazeera English 2011.

28. Mackey 2011.

29. Al-Suwaidan 2012.

30. Kiefer 2011.

31. *Guardian* 2011.

32. Al-Nafjan 2011a.

33. Al-Suwaidan 2012.

34. Mackey 2011.

35. Shubert 2011.

36. Akeel 2011.

37. MacFarquhar 2011a.

38. Ahmari 2013; and MacFarquhar 2011b.

39. Ahmari 2013.

40. Ahmari 2013.

41. *Los Angeles Times* 2011.

42. Saudi Jeans 2012.

43. *Emirates 24/7* 2012.

44. Baker 2012.

45. Al-Sharif 2012

46. Ahmari 2013.

47. Jensen 2012.

48. *Emirates 24/7* 2013a.

49. ANSAmed 2012.

50. Al-Sharif 2013.

51. *Khaleej Times* 2013.

52. Jamjoom 2013.

53. Nelson 2013.

54. Amnesty International 2013.

55. Jamjoom and Smith-Spark 2013.

56. Reilly 2014.

57. Lu 2013.

CHAPTER THREE. SAUDI MODERN

1. Hussein al-Mohasen, a Saudi Artist.

2. The following discussion of Arab and Islamic art, as well as the survey of Saudi art that follows, draws on the following sources: Ali 1989, 1997; Amirsadeghi,

Mikdadi, and Shabout 2009; Eigner 2010; Porter and Caussé 2006; Shabout 2007; Sloman 2009.

3. Appadurai 1996, 33.
4. Ali 1997, 158.
5. Khaleejesque 2011.
6. Stapleton et al. 2012.
7. Bharadwaj 2012.
8. Stapleton et al. 2012, 95.
9. Al-Dowayan 2012.
10. Al-Dowayan 2011.
11. Quoted in Bailey and Van Gorder 2007, 35.
12. Stapleton et al. 2012, 95.
13. Mater 2010, 49.
14. Ahmed Mater, "Ibn Aseer (Son of Aseer)," http://ahmedmater.com/about/background/ (accessed October 18, 2015).
15. Detour Film 2012.
16. In 2005, Mater filed a lawsuit against the Swatch Group seeking to prevent them from using the image of an Omega watch surrounded by a ring of iron filings in an advertisement. The Swatch Group argued that the ad was designed to highlight their watch's antimagnetic properties. Mater charged that it was a blasphemous appropriation of a religious image for commercial purposes (http://blogs.artinfo.com/artintheair/2015/02/18/artist-files-suit-against-swiss-watchmaker-over-ad/ [accessed September 19, 2015]).
17. Mater 2009.
18. Mater 2009.
19. Wheeler 2006, 248–65.
20. *Shift* 2011.
21. Batrawy 2014.
22. Pellerin 2008.
23. *Saudi Gazette* 2013b.
24. Hemming 2011, 53–54.
25. Simcox 2009, 86.
26. Wasil and Jeraidi 2012.
27. Manjal 2012.

CHAPTER FOUR. FINDING SCIENCE IN THE QURAN

1. Yahya 2006, 158.
2. Gould 1999, 5.
3. Gould 1999, 193.
4. Gould 1999, 84 and 170.
5. Gould 1999, 81–82 and 124.
6. Edis 2007.

7. Iqbal 2007, 309.

8. The preceding discussion of attitudes toward Darwinian evolution in different Muslim societies draws on the work of Edis 2007; Iqbal 2007; and E. Burton 2010, 2011.

9. Grove 2008.

10. Krajeski 2013.

11. Poyrazlar 2013.

12. Yahya 2006, 154, 229, and 236.

13. Yahya 2006, 41.

14. Yahya 2006, 613; and the Quran (39:62–63).

15. Brasseur 2007; and Dean 2007.

16. Bucaille 1978, 3–4.

17. Golden 2002.

18. CNN Wire Staff 2011.

19. International Commission on Scientific Signs in the Quran and Sunnah 2011, 115–16.

20. "What Scientists Really Think of the Quran: William Hay; This Is the Truth UNCUT," produced by *The Rationalizer,* n.d., uploaded by JesusOrMuhammad, December 15, 2011, www.youtube.com/watch?v=6YNkSc8jZsc (accessed October 10, 2015).

21. International Commission on Scientific Signs in the Quran and Sunnah 2011, 87.

22. Quoted in Golden 2002.

23. "Holy Quran: Top Scientists Comments on Scientific Miracles in the Quran #Faith and Science#," n.d., uploaded by OurBestLife, July 26, 2008, www.youtube .com/watch?v=FUUPYsogElU (accessed October 10, 2015).

24. Moore 1986, 15–17.

25. Golden 2002.

26. Myers 2010.

CHAPTER FIVE. ROADS OF ARABIA

1. President of the Saudi Commission for Tourism and Antiquities, Sultan bin Salman bin Abdulaziz Al Saud.

2. Ham 2008.

3. The translation of this inscription on Tomb IGN 44 is from an informational plaque at the site of the tomb itself.

4. Doughty 1923, 1: 96.

5. Saudi Commission for Tourism and Antiquities 2009.

6. Saudi Commission for Tourism and Antiquity 2013c.

7. Fowler 1987, 229–48; 229 and 241.

8. Trigger 1984, 355–70; 358 and 360.

9. Luke 2002, xiii and xiv.

10. Body 1999, 22–29.

11. *Travel Magazine* 2010.

12. O'Brien 2012.

13. *Smithsonian* 2012a.

14. Abu-Nasr 2009.

15. Swami 2011b.

16. Down 2010.

17. Langfeldt 1994, 32–60.

18. Hume and Ayish 2013; and Swami 2011a.

19. Abu-Nasr 2009.

20. Quoted in Covington 2012.

21. Allsop 2010.

22. Langly 2012.

23. The Saudi government has recently adopted the spelling "Makkah" in response to derogatory metaphorical misuses of the old spelling in phrases like "Auto Mecca" and "Gambling Mecca."

24. Al-Ghabban et al. 2010, 512.

25. Camp 2012, 10–11.

26. *Smithsonian* 2012b.

27. *Saudi Voyager* 2012, 24.

28. Sullivan 2012.

29. Quoted in Covington 2012, 5.

30. Shea 2013.

31. Hawting 1999.

32. Saudi Commission for Tourism and Antiquities 2013a.

33. O'Brien 2012.

34. Al-Ghabban, Ibrahim, and Weber 2012.

35. Abraham 2010.

36. Juvin 2010, 491 (emphasis added).

37. Scholler 2004, 9.

38. Scholler 2004, 28, 202, and 250.

39. The Arabic name of the Kingdom of Saudi Arabia, *al-Mamlaka al-Arabiyya al-Saudiyya,* literally means "the Arabian Kingdom of the Sauds."

40. Franke and Gierlichs 2011, 16 (emphasis added).

41. Al-Simari 2010a, 566; and 2010b, 569, 572, and 573.

42. L. Lawrence 2012.

43. Abraham 2010.

44. Langly 2012.

45. Evin 2011.

CHAPTER SIX. SAVING JEDDAH

1. Dr. Adnan al-Yafi, former deputy director-general of the Hajj Research Center, Mecca.

2. Farsi 1991, 12.

3. Pesce 1977, appendix 5.

4. Quoted in Buchan 1980, 221.

5. Wavell 1912, 120.

6. Lawrence 1935, 72.

7. Buchan 1980, 53.

8. This discussion of the public art of the Corniche and its restoration draws on Farsi 1991; and Loyd 2012.

9. Elwi 2011.

10. Dunne 2008.

11. Byron 2011.

CHAPTER SEVEN. WHO CAN GO TO MECCA?

1. Burckhardt 1968, 71.

2. Wiki Answers: "Why Can't Non-Muslims Enter Mecca?" www.answers .com/Q/Why_can%27t_non-Muslims_enter_Mecca (accessed October 15, 2015); Yahoo Answers: "Can Christians Go to Mecca?" https://answers.yahoo.com/question/index?qid=20100913144549AAl2FkQ (accessed October 15, 2015); "Can I Go to Mecca If I'm Not a Muslim?" https://answers.yahoo.com/question/index?qid=20111209231917AAEsLCv (accessed October 15, 2015); "Why Cannot Non-Muslims Go to Mecca?" https://answers.yahoo.com/question/index?qid=20120702093101AAsjHoz (accessed October 15, 2015); American Bedu: http://americanbedu.com/2008/09/30/non-muslims-go-to-makkah/, posted on September 30, 2008 (accessed October 15, 2015).

3. This account of the Hajj is based on Peters 1994; and Porter 2012.

4. Peters 1994, 75.

5. Rihani 1930, 53–55, as cited in Peters 1994, 339–40.

6. Porter 2012, 204.

7. Long 1979, 28.

8. Asad 1984, 261.

9. Wolfe 1997, xxxviii and xxxi.

10. Rice 1990, 181.

11. R. F. Burton 1893, 1: 23.

12. R. F. Burton 1893, 1: xvii, xxiii, and 2: 57 and 240.

13. R. F. Burton 1893, 1: xx and xxi.

14. R. F. Burton 1893, 1: xx and xxi.

15. R. F. Burton 1893, 2: 160–61.

16. Wolfe 1997, 295.

17. Wavell 1912, 28 and 126.

18. Wavell 1912, 30 and 41.

19. Wavell 1912, 76.

20. Wavell 1912, 77.

21. Wavell 1912, 179.

22. Wavell 1912, 179.

23. Burckhardt 1968, 71.

24. Al-Bukhari 1980, 25; and Muslim 1971–75, 21, as cited in al-Ouda 2004.

25. Al-Bukhari 1980, 25; and Muslim 1971–75, 21, as cited in al-Ouda 2004.

26. Doughty 1923, 1: 507 and 2: 48.

27. Philby 1948, xvi and 15.

28. Philby 1948, 324.

29. Philby 1948, 277–78.

30. Philby 1948, 278.

31. Philby 1948, 279–80.

32. Philby 1948, 281.

33. Wolfe 1997, 386.

34. Wolfe 1997, 405.

35. Monroe 1973, 243.

36. Monroe 1973, 164.

37. Monroe 1973, 170.

38. Malcolm X 1965, 39, 70, 151, 165, and 188.

39. Malcolm X 1965, 151 and 171.

40. Malcolm X 1965, 199 and 290.

41. DeCaro 1996, 206.

42. Malcolm X 1965, 328, 331, and 336–39.

43. Malcolm X 1965, 345.

44. DeCaro 1996, 345–46.

45. Malcolm X 1965, 336.

46. Bianchi 2004, 40–50.

47. Long 1979, preface.

48. Porter 2012, 232.

49. Porter 2012, 88.

50. Chehata 2014.

51. Gambrell 2015 and Benedictus 2015.

52. Amiruddin 2010.

53. Sciolino 2002.

BIBLIOGRAPHY

ABC News. 2005. "Transcript: Saudi King Abdullah Talks to Barbara Walters." Abcnews.go.com, October 14.

Abraham, Heather. 2010. "Greetings from the Louvre's 'Roads to Arabia' Exhibition." Religionnerd.com, August 11.

Abu El-Haj, Nadia. 2001. *Facts on the Ground: Archaeological Practice and Territorial Self-Fashioning in Israeli Society.* Chicago: University of Chicago Press.

Abu-Lughod, Lila. 2002. "Do Muslim Women Really Need Saving? Anthropological Reflections on Cultural Relativism and Its Others." *American Anthropologist* 204 (3): 783–90.

———. 2013. *Do Muslim Women Need Saving?* Cambridge, MA: Harvard University Press.

Abu-Nasr, Donna. 2009. "Digging Up the Saudi Past: Some Would Rather Not." *US News and World Report,* August 31.

Acharya, S., and D. M. Murdock. 2009. "Islam Is against Our Past, Present, and Future." Islam-watch.org, September 1.

Agence France Presse. 2009. "Saudi Floods Kill 77, Leave Scores Missing." November 26.

———. 2014. "US Backs Rights of Women in Ally Saudi Arabia to Drive." October 29.

Ahmari, Sohab. 2013. "Manal al-Sharif: The Woman Who Dared to Drive." *Wall Street Journal,* March 22.

Akeel, Maha. 2011. "Women's Driving a Nonevent." *Arab News,* July 7.

Ali, Wijdan, ed. 1989. *Contemporary Art from the Islamic World.* London: Scorpion Publishing.

———. 1997. *Modern Islamic Art: Development and Continuity.* Gainesville: University Press of Florida.

Allsop, Laura. 2010. "Pre-Islam Saudi Treasures on Show for the First Time." CNN.com, July 29.

Amirsadeghi, Hossein, Salwa Mikdadi, and Nada M. Shabout. 2009. *New Vision: Arab Contemporary Art in the 21st Century.* London: Thames and Hudson.

Amiruddin, Sayyid A. 2010. "Visiting the Angawi Mansion Al Makkiyya." Ahmedamiruddin.wordpress.com, August 29.

Amnesty International. 2011. "Saudi Arabia Urged to Release Woman Arrested Following Driving Campaign." Amnesty.org, May 24.

———. 2013. "Saudi Arabia: Threats and Cyber Attack Will Not Deter Women from Driving." Amnesty.org, October 25.

ANSAmed. 2012. "Saudi Arabia: Women to Drive, a Battle for Dignity." Ansamed. info, October 8.

Appadurai, Arjun. 1996. *Modernity at Large: Cultural Dimensions of Globalization.* Minneapolis: University of Minnesota Press.

al-Arabiya News. 2010. "Women's Driving Issue Needs No Fatwa: Saudi Cleric." Alarabiya.net, May 25.

Aramco Brat Media. 2007. *Home: The Aramco Brats' Story.* www.bratstory.com (accessed October 7, 2015).

Asad, Muhammad. 1954. *The Road to Mecca.* New York: Simon and Schuster.

———. 1984. *The Message of the Quran.* Gibraltar: Dar al-Andalus.

Assyrian International News Agency. 2008. "4th Century Assyrian Church in Saudi Arabia." Aina.org, August 28.

Bailey, Natalie Elaine, and Sally Van Gorder. 2007. *Self-Representation in the Arabian Gulf: Perspectives in Photography and Video.* Doha, Qatar: Virginia Commonwealth University in Qatar.

Baker, Aryn. 2012. "Manal al-Sharif." *Time,* April 18.

al-Banawi, Itidal. n.d. *Modern Science as Revealed in the Qur'an and Traditions of the Prophet.* Jeddah: International Commission on Scientific Signs in the Qur'an and Sunnah.

Barbour, Ian. 1990. *Religion in an Age of Science.* New York: Harper Collins.

Barnes, Larry. 1979. *Looking Back over My Shoulder.* Petersborough, NH: Larry Barnes.

Batrawy, Aya. 2014. "Saudi Artists Cautiously Push against Redlines." Yahoo News, April 3.

BBC News Asia. 2013. "Sri Lankan Maid Rizana Nafeek Beheaded in Saudi Arabia." January 9.

BBC News Middle East. 2002. "Saudi Police 'Stopped' Fire Rescue." March 15.

———. 2011a. "Viewpoint: Saudi Women Should Not Drive." Bbc.co.uk, October 3.

———. 2011b. "Saudi Woman Executed for 'Witchcraft and Sorcery.'" Bbc.co.uk, December 12.

———. 2013. "Saudi Woman Makes History by Reaching Everest Summit." Bbc. co.uk, May 18.

Benedictus, Leo. 2015. "Hajj Crush: How Crowd Disasters Happen, and How They Can Be Avoided." *Guardian,* October 3.

Bennett, Drake. 2009. "Islam's Darwin Problem: In the Muslim World, Creationism Is on the Rise." *Boston Globe,* October 25.

Bharadwaj, Vinita. 2012. "Contemporary Artists Rock the Boat Gently in Saudi Arabia." *New York Times,* January 18.

Bianchi, Robert B. 2004. *Guests of God: Pilgrimage and Politics in the Islamic World.* New York: Oxford University Press.

Bigliardi, Stefano. 2011. "Snakes from Staves? Science, Scriptures, and the Supernatural in Maurice Bucaille." *Zygon* 46: 793–805.

Bloxham, Andy. 2011. "Allowing Women Drivers in Saudi Arabia Will Be 'End of Virginity.'" *Telegraph,* December 2.

Body, Trevor. 1999. "History's New Home in Riyadh." *Aramco World* 50 (5) (September–October): 22–29.

Brasseur, Anne. 2007. "The Dangers of Creationism in Education." *Report: Committee on Culture, Science, and Education.* Parliamentary Assembly, Council of Europe, assembly.coe.int, September 17.

Brown, Anthony Cave. 1999. *Oil, God, and Gold: The Story of Aramco and the Saudi Kings.* Boston: Houghton Mifflin.

Bucaille, Maurice. 1978. *The Bible, the Quran, and Science: The Holy Scriptures Examined in Light of Modern Knowledge.* Indianapolis: American Trust Publications.

Buchan, James. 1980. *Jeddah, Old and New.* London: Stacey International.

Bukhamsin, Aqeel. 2011. "Challenging Jeddah's Floods." Alarabiya.net, July 15.

al-Bukhari, Muhammad. 1980. *Sahih al-Bukhari: The Translation of the Meanings of Sahih al-Bukhari: Arabic-English.* N.p.: Dar AHYA Us-Sunnah al Nabawiya.

Burckhardt, John Lewis. 1968. *Travels in Arabia: Comprehending an Account of Those Territories in Hedjaz Which the Mohammedans Regard as Sacred.* 1829. Repr., New York: AMS Press.

Burton, Elise. 2010. "Teaching Evolution in Muslim States: Iran and Saudi Arabia Compared." *National Center for Scientific Education Reports* 30 (3): 25–29.

———. 2011. "Evolution and Creationism in Middle Eastern Education: A New Perspective." *Evolution* 65 (1): 301–4.

Burton, Richard F. 1893. *Personal Narrative of a Pilgrimage to Al-Madinah and Meccah.* 2 vols. London: Tylston and Edwards.

Byron, Katy. 2011. "Flooding in Saudi Arabia Kills 10." CNN.com, January 29.

Camp, Beatrice. 2012. "Unique Museum Tour: Smithsonian Detail Opens Door to New Opportunities." *State Magazine,* June 10–11.

Campbell, Kay Hardy. 2009–13. "Saudi Women Driving: News and Thoughts about Saudi Women Driving." Saudi Woman Driving, www.saudiwomendriving.blogspot.com/ (accessed October 18, 2015).

Casserly, Meghan. 2011. "Fifteen Minutes of Power: Women Who (Briefly) Rocked 2011." *Forbes,* August 25.

CBS News. 2008. "The Oil Kingdom." *60 Minutes,* December 7.

———. 2009. "Saudi Rape Victim Gets 200 Lashes." Cbsnews.com, February 11.

Chehata, Hanan. 2014. "Saudi 'Cultural Vandalism' of Muslim Heritage Continues." *Middle East Eye,* April 14.

Cheney, Michael Sheldon. 1958. *Big Oil Man from Arabia.* New York: Ballantine Books.

Clark, Arthur P., and Muhammad A. Tahlawi, eds. 2006. *A Land Transformed: The Arabian Peninsula, Saudi Arabia, and Saudi Aramco*. Dhahran: Saudi Arabian Oil Company.

CNN Wire Staff. 2011. "Yemeni Leader Lashes Out at U.S. as Protests Continue." CNN.com, March 1.

Comaroff, John L., and Jean Comaroff. 2009. *Ethnicity Inc*. Chicago: University of Chicago Press.

Cook, Terry, ed. 2011. *Controlling the Past: Documenting Society and Institutions*. Chicago: Society of American Archivists.

Coppola, John. 2005. "A Price of Museums in the Desert: Saudi Arabia and the 'Gift of Friendship' Exhibition." *Curator* 48 (1) (January): 90–100.

Covington, Richard. 2012. "Roads of Arabia." *Saudi Aramco World*, www.saudiaramcoworld.com/issue/201102/roads.of.arabia.htm (accessed October 18, 2015).

Danforth, Loring M. 1995. *The Macedonian Conflict: Ethnic Nationalism in a Transnational World*. Princeton, NJ: Princeton University Press.

Dean, Cornelia. 2007. "Islamic Creationist and a Book Sent Round the World." *New York Times*, July 17.

DeBuys, William. 2015. *The Last Unicorn*. New York: Little, Brown.

DeCaro, Louis A., Jr. 1996. *On the Side of My People: A Religious Life of Malcolm X*. New York: New York University Press.

Desert Designs World. "Welcome to Desert Designs World." Desert Designs, www.desertdesigns.com/index.php (accessed October 18, 2015).

Destination Jeddah. 2011. "Jeddah: The Jewel of the Red Sea." Destinationjeddah.com, March 16.

Detour Film. 2012. "Detour-Saudi Art Movement Teaser." Uploaded January 12, www.youtube.com/watch?v=SmfCJOzqdlQ (accessed October 18, 2015).

Doughty, Charles M. 1923. *Travels in Arabia Deserta*. 2 vols. London: Jonathan Cape.

al-Dowayan, Manal. 2011. "Suspended Together." Personal website, http://manaldowayan.com/suspended-together.html (accessed October 17, 2015).

———. 2012. "Esmi (My Name)." Cuadro Fine Art Gallery, http://cuadroart.com/en/exhibitions/esmi.html (accessed October 17, 2015).

Down, Kendall K. 2010. "Saudi Archaeology: A Contradiction in Terms?" Digging Up the Past, www.diggingsonline.com (accessed October 17, 2015).

Dunne, Michele. 2008. "Women's Political Participation in the Gulf: A Conversation with Activists Fantin Bundagji (Saudi Arabia), Rola Dashti (Kuwait), Muniar Fakho (Bahrain)." Carnegie Endowment for International Peace, August 12, http://carnegieendowment.org/sada/?fa=20516 (accessed October 14, 2015).

"Edge of Arabia Jeddah: We Need to Talk." 2012. Edge of Arabia, http://edgeofarabia.com/exhibitions/we-need-to-talk-jeddah (accessed October 17, 2015).

Edis, Taner. 2007. *An Illusion of Harmony: Science and Religion in Islam*. Amherst, NY: Prometheus.

———. 2008. "Harun Yahya's Legal Troubles." *National Center for Science Education* 28 (3) (May–June): 4–5.

Edis, Taner, and Saouma BouJaoude. 2014. "Rejecting Materialism: Responses to Modern Science in the Muslim Middle East." In *International Handbook of Research in History, Philosophy, and Science Teaching*, ed. Michael Matthews, 1663–90. New York: Springer.

Egyptian Independent Staff. 2011. "Prominent Islamic Cleric Urges Saudi King to Let Women Drive." *Egyptian Independent*, October 31.

Eigner, Saeb. 2010. *Art of the Middle East: Modern and Contemporary Art of the Arab World and Iran*. London: Merrell.

Elwi, Yousra. 2011. "Jeddah's Who's Who: Fatin Bundagji: A Lady with a Message." Destinationjeddah.com, June 15.

Embassy of Saudi Arabia. "Preserving Jeddah's Historic Buildings." *Saudi Arabia* 15 (4) (Winter). Saudiembassy.net, www.saudiembassy.net/files/PDF/Publications /Magazine/1999-Winter/preserving.htm (accessed October 17, 2015).

Emirates 24/7. 2012. "Saudi Set to Reject Woman's Plea to Drive Car." Emirates247. com, February 9.

———. 2013a. "Saudi Women Will Take the Right to Drive Cars." Emirates247. com, January 3.

———. 2013b. "Saudi Women Should Not Drive Cars: Female Activist." Emirates247.com, May 9.

Epatko, Larisa. 2011. "Saudi Arabia: Women Can Vote, Starting in 2015." *PBS Newshour*, www.pbs.org, September 26.

Esposito, John L. 2011. *Islam: The Straight Path*. New York: Oxford University Press.

Evin, Florence. 2011. "Le Louvre reçoit l'Arabie, Etat riche à l'art riche." *Le Monde*, November 18.

Farsi, Hani M. 1991. *Notes from Jeddah: City of Art; The Sculptures and Monuments*. London: Stacey International.

Field, Michael. 2000. *From 'Unayzah to Wall Street: The Story of Suliman S. Olayan*. London: John Murray.

Forbes. 2011. "Fifteen Minutes of Power: Women Who (Briefly) Rocked 2011." August 25.

Fowler, David. 1987. "Uses of the Past: Archaeology in Service of the State." *American Antiquity* 52 (2): 229–48.

Franke, Ute, and Joachim Gierlichs, eds. 2011. *Roads of Arabia: The Archaeological Treasures of Saudi Arabia*. Tübingen: Wasmuth Verlag.

Friends of Jeddah Parks. 2008. At Jeddah Economic Forum. Uploaded December 16, 2010, www.youtube.com/watch?v=VTsus6gNx70 (accessed October 17, 2015).

Gambrell, Jon. 2015. "Saudi Arabia Hajj Disaster Death Toll at Least 2,177." Associated Press, October 19, www.businessinsider.com/ap-new-tally-shows-at-least-1621-killed-in-saudi-hajj-tragedy-2015-10 (accessed October 20, 2015).

Geertz, Clifford. 1973a. *The Interpretation of Cultures*. New York: Basic Books.

———. 1973b. "Thick Description: Toward an Interpretive Theory of Culture." In *The Interpretation of Cultures*, 3–30. New York: Basic Books.

————. 1983. "From the Native's Point of View: On the Nature of Anthropological Understanding." In *Local Knowledge: Further Essays in Interpretive Anthropology*, 55–70. New York: Basic Books.

al-Ghabban, Ali Ibrahim, and Stefan Weber. 2012. "Roads of Arabia—Introduction." Roads of Arabia in Berlin, universes-in-universe.org, January 29–April 9.

al-Ghabban, Ali Ibrahim, et al., eds. 2010. *Roads of Arabia: Archaeology and History of the Kingdom of Saudi Arabia*. Paris: Somogy Art Publishers.

al-Ghamdi, Jassim. 2011. "True Friends of Jeddah's Parks." *Saudi Gazette*, December 29.

Golden, Daniel. 2002. "Western Scholars Play Key Role in Touting 'Science' of the Quran." *Wall Street Journal*, January 23.

Gould, Stephen Jay. 1997. "Nonoverlapping Magisteria." *Natural History* 106 (2) (March): 16–22.

————. 1999. *Rock of Ages: Science and Religion in the Fullness of Life*. New York: Ballantine Books.

Graan, Andrew. 2013. "Counterfeiting the Nation? Skopje and the Politics of Nation Branding in Macedonia." *Cultural Anthropology* 28 (1): 161–79.

Grove, Thomas. 2008. "Turkish Islamic Author Given 3-Year Jail Sentence." Reuters, May 9.

Guardian. 2011. "Hillary Clinton Backs Saudi Arabia Women's Right-To Drive Campaign." June 21.

————. 2013. "Dozens of Saudi Arabian Women Drive Cars on Day of Protest against Ban." October 26.

Haerich, Donna. 2009. "The Hijab and Women's Ordination." *Spectrum Magazine*, October 12.

Ham, Anthony. 2008. "Inside the Hidden Kingdom." *Sydney Morning Herald*, November 13.

Ham, Anthony, Martha Brekhus Shams, and Andrew Madden. 2004. *Saudi Arabia*. London: Lonely Planet Publications.

Hameed, Salman. 2008. "Bracing for Islamic Creationism." *Science* 322 (5908): 1637–38.

Hammond, Andrew. 2012. *The Islamic Utopia: The Illusion of Reform in Saudi Arabia*. London: Pluto Press.

Hammoudi, Abdellah. 2006. *A Season in Mecca: A Narrative of a Pilgrimage*. New York: Hill and Wang.

Hausmann, Ricardo, Laura D. Tyson, and Saadia Zahidi. 2009. *The Global Gender Gap Report, 2009*. Geneva: World Economic Forum, www3.weforum.org/docs /WEF_GenderGap_Report_2009.pdf (accessed October 17, 2015).

Hawting, G. R. 1999. *The Idea of Idolatry and the Emergence of Islam: From Polemic to History*. Cambridge: Cambridge University Press.

Hegghammer, Thomas. 2010. *Jihad in Saudi Arabia: Violence and Pan-Islamism since 1979*. Cambridge: Cambridge University Press.

Hemming, Henry. 2011. *Abdulnasser Gharem: Art of Survival*. London: Booth-Clibborn Editions.

Hermes, Will. 2012. "M.I.A. 'Bad Girls.'" *Rolling Stone,* February 6.

Hertog, Steffen. 2009. "A Rentier Social Contract: The Saudi Political Economy since 1979." In *The Kingdom of Saudi Arabia, 1979–2009: Evolution of a Pivotal State,* 16–18. Washington, DC: Washington Middle East Institute, www .voltairenet.org/IMG/pdf/Kingdom_of_Saudi_Arabia_1979-2009.pdf (accessed October 17, 2015).

―――. 2010. *Princes, Brokers, and Bureaucrats: Oil and the State in Saudi Arabia.* Ithaca, NY: Cornell University Press.

Hopkins, Curt. 2012. "Malaysia May Repatriate Saudi Who Faces Death Penalty for Tweets." *Christian Science Monitor,* February 10.

House, Karen Elliott. 2012. *On Saudi Arabia: It's People, Past, Religion, Fault Lines—and Future.* New York: Alfred A. Knopf.

Hoyland, Robert G. 2001. *Arabia and the Arabs: From the Bronze Age to the Coming of Islam.* London: Routledge.

Hudson, John. 2011. "Saudi Women Driving Cars with Relative Impunity." *Atlantic Wire,* June 17.

Human Rights Watch. 2008. "Saudi Arabia: Male Guardianship Policies Harm Women." April 20, www.hrw.org/news/2008/04/20/saudi-arabia-male-guardianship-policies-harm-women (accessed October 17, 2015).

―――. 2011. *World Report, 2011: Saudi Arabia.* N.d., www.hrw.org/world-report-2011/saudi-arabia (accessed October 17, 2015).

Hume, Tim, and Samya Ayish. 2013. "Mecca Redevelopment Sparks Heritage Concerns." CNN.com, February 7.

Huntingon, Samuel P. 1996. *The Clash of Civilizations and the Remaking of World Order.* New York: Simon and Schuster.

Ibn Baz, Abd al-Aziz. n.d. *Fatwas: Ruling on Driving a Car by a Woman.* Kingdom of Saudia Arabia, www.alifta.com (accessed October 17, 2015).

Ibrahim, I. A. 1997. *A Brief Illustrated Guide to Understanding Islam.* Houston: Darussalam.

International Commission on Scientific Signs in the Qur'an and Sunnah. 2011. *This Is the Truth: Scientific Miracle in the Qur'an and Sunnah.* Jeddah: Dar Jeyad.

International Crisis Group. 2005. *The Shiite Question in Saudi Arabia: Middle East Report No. 45.* September 19, www.crisisgroup.org/~/media/Files/Middle East North Africa/Iran Gulf/Saudi Arabia/The Shiite Question in Saudi Arabia.pdf (accessed October 17, 2015).

Iqbal, Muzaffar. 2002. *Islam and Science.* Aldershot, England: Ashgate.

―――. 2007. *Science and Islam.* Westport, CT: Greenwood Books.

―――. 2010. "Darwin's Shadow: Evolution in an Islamic Mirror." *Islam and Science* 8 (1): 11–32.

Islam Web. n.d. Islamweb.net English,www.islamweb.net/en/ (accessed October 17, 2015)

Jamjoom, Mohammed. 2013. "Saudi Cleric Warns Driving Could Damage Women's Ovaries." CNN.com, September 29.

Jamjoom, Mohammed, and Laura Smith-Spark. 2013. "Saudi Arabian Women Defy Authorities over Female Driving Ban." CNN.com, October 26.

Jausen, A., and R. Savignac. 1914. *Mission archéologique en Arabie*. Vol. 2. Paris: Libraire. Repr., Cairo: Institute Français d'Archéologie Orientale, 1997.

Jawhar, Sabria. 2009. "Let Rural Women Drive, As They Always Have in Past." *Saudi Gazette,* October 14.

al Jazeera English. 2011. "Saudi Woman Campaigns for Right to Drive." Uploaded May 21, 2011, www.youtube.com/watch?v = gkeiCYaKVOY (accessed October 17, 2015).

Jeddah Flood. 2009. "God's Own Country-Kerala." Kerala Tourism, November 30, www.youtube.com/watch?v = xYAjyQvnMUI (accessed October 18, 2015).

———. 2011. "January 26th 2011 Wednesday (People Being Saved) Part 1." Uploaded by deadasred, January 26, https://www.youtube.com/watch?v=qB_R3CJsqFo (accessed October 17, 2015).

Jensen, Rita Henley. 2012. "Saudi Driving Star Pays a High Personal Price." *Forbes,* June 14.

Jesi. 2011. "In the Name of Freedom: A Saudi Woman's Struggle for Her Rights." Carbonated.tv, June 8.

Johnson, Nora. 1982. *You* Can *Go Home Again: An Intimate Journey*. Garden City, NY: Doubleday.

Jones, Lucy. 2012. "Watch: M.I.A.'s Middle Finger to Saudi Arabia's Insane Driving Laws Trumps Madonna's Sexy Pop." *Telegraph,* February 3.

Jones, Toby Craig. 2010. *Desert Kingdom: How Oil and Water Forged Modern Saudi Arabia*. Cambridge, MA: Harvard University Press.

Juvin, Carine. 2010. "The Tombstones from the Al-Ma'la Cemetery in Mecca." In *Roads of Arabia: Archaeology and History of the Kingdom of Saudi Arabia,* ed. Ali al-Ghabban et al., 490–521. Paris: Somogy Art Publishers.

Kennedy, Hugh. 2012. "Journey to Mecca: A History." In *Hajj: Journey to the Heart of Islam,* ed. Venetia Porter, 68–135. Cambridge, MA: Harvard University Press.

Kennedy, Ludovic. 1969. *Very Lovely People: A Personal Look at Some Americans Living Abroad*. New York: Simon and Schuster.

Khaleej Times. 2013. "Saudi Women Driving Ban Not Part of Shariah." Khaleej-times.com, September 19.

Khaleejesque. 2011. "Graphic Design Goes Bedouin!" Khaleejesque.com, July 4.

Khan, Ghazanfar Ali. 2013. "Shoura May Discuss Women Driving Issue." Arab-news.com, March 18.

Kiefer, Francine. 2011. "Honk If You Support Saudi Women Drivers." *Christian Science Monitor,* June 6.

Kimball, Solon T. 1956. "American Culture in Saudi Arabia." *Transactions of the New York Academy of Sciences* 18 (5): 469–84.

Krajeski, Jenna. 2013. "The Versace Harem." Slate.com, May 2.

Lackner, Helen. 1978. *A House Built on Sand: A Political Economy of Saudi Arabia*. London: Ithaca Press.

Lacroix, Stéphane. 2011. *Awakening Islam: The Politics of Religious Dissent in Contemporary Saudi Arabia*. Cambridge, MA: Harvard University Press.

Lacy, Robert. 2009. *Inside the Kingdom: Kings, Clerics, Modernists, Terrorists, and the Struggle for Saudi Arabia*. New York: Viking Press.

Langfeldt, John A. 1994. "Recently Discovered Early Christian Monuments in Northeastern Arabia." *Arabian Archaeology and Epigraphy* 5 (1): 32–60.

Langly, Julia. 2012. Review of *Roads of Arabia @ The Arthur M. Sackler Gallery*. Dcist.com, November 12.

Lawrence, Lee. 2012. "Gold Frankincense and Trade." *Wall Street Journal*, December 5.

Lawrence, T. E. 1935. *Seven Pillars of Wisdom: A Triumph*. Garden City, NY: Doubleday, Doran.

Leff, Lisa. 2007. "Dispute over Long-Buried Stegner Book." *Crossroads Arabia*, December 4, http://xrdarabia.org/page/6/?s = aramco (accessed October 18, 2015).

Lippman, Thomas W. 2007. Foreword to *Discovery! The Search for American Oil*, by Wallace Stegner. Vista, CA: Selwa Press.

———. 2012. *Saudi Arabia on the Edge: The Uncertain Future of an American Ally*. Washington, DC: Potomac Books.

Long, David Edwin. 1979. *The Hajj Today: A Survey of the Contemporary Makkah Pilgrimage*. Albany: State University of New York Press.

Long, David Edwin, and Sebastian Maisel. 2010. *The Kingdom of Saudi Arabia*. 2nd ed. Gainesville: University Press of Florida.

Lord, Barry, and Gail Dexter Lord. 2001. *The Manual of Museum Exhibitions*. Lanham, MD: Altamira.

Los Angeles Times. 2011. "Saudi Arabia: Reforms Will Allow Women to Vote But Not Drive." September 25.

Louvre. 2010. "Exhibition: Roads of Arabia; Archaeology and the History of the Kingdom of Saudi Arabia." July 14–September 27, www.louvre.fr/en/expositions /roads-arabia-archaeology-and-history-kingdom-saudi-arabia (accessed October 18, 2015).

Loyd, Christopher. 2012. "Notable Public Art Pieces in Jeddah to Undergo Restoration." *National*, April 3.

Lu, Anne. 2013. "'No Woman, No Drive' Parody of Saudi Female Drive Ban Goes Viral." *International Business Times*, October 29.

Luke, Timothy W. 2002. *Museum Politics: Power Plays at the Exhibition*. Minneapolis: University of Minnesota Press.

MacFarquhar, Neil. 2011a. "Saudis Arrest Woman Leading Right-to-Drive Campaign." *New York Times*, May 23.

———. 2011b. "In a Scattered Protest, Saudi Women Take the Wheel." *New York Times*, June 17.

Mackey, Robert. 2011. "Saudi Woman's Driving Video Preserved Online." *New York Times*, May 24.

Malcolm X. 1965. *The Autobiography of Malcolm X*. New York: Grove Press.

Manjal, Adnan Z. 2012. "The Story of One Saudi Sculptor Who Took a Chance and Made 'Un-art.'" Hyperallergic.com, September 18.

Marcus, George. 1986. "Contemporary Problems of Ethnography in the Modern World System." In *Writing Culture,* ed. James Clifford and George E. Marcus, 165–93. Berkeley: University of California Press.

Marshall, Paul A. 2005. *Radical Islam's Rules: The Worldwide Spread of Extreme Shari'a Law.* Lanham, MD: Rowman and Littlefield.

Masry, Abdullah H. 1994. "Archaeology and the Establishment of Museums in Saudi Arabia." In *Museums and the Making of "Ourselves": The Role of Objects in National Identity,* ed. Flora E. S. Kaplan, 125–67. London: Leicester University Press.

Mater, Ahmed. 2009. Interview by Waël Noureddine and Catherine David, for ADACH Platform for Visual Arts, https://vimeo.com /23904664 (accessed October 10, 2015).

———. 2010. *Ahmed Mater.* London: Booth-Clibborn Editions.

Matthews, Charles. 2007. "Rediscovering Discovery." *Houston Chronicle,* October 14.

McConnell, Philip C. 1985. *The Hundred Men.* Peterborough, NH: Currier Press.

McVeigh, Tracy. 2012. "Saudi Arabian Women Risk Arrest As They Defy Ban on Driving." *Guardian,* June 16.

Melikian, Souren. 2010. "'Routes of Arabia' Exhibition at Louvre Is Startling." *New York Times,* July 23.

Menoret, Pascal. 2005. *The Saudi Enigma: A History.* London: Zed Books.

———. 2010. "Rebels Without a Cause? A Politics of Deviance in Saudi Arabia." In *Being Young and Muslim: New Cultural Politics in the Global South and North,* ed. Asef Bayat and Linda Herrera, 77–94. Oxford: Oxford University Press.

———. 2011. "Development, Planning, and Urban Unrest in Saudi Arabia." *Muslim World* 101 (2): 269–85.

———. 2014. *Joyriding in Riyadh: Oil, Urbanism, and Road Revolt.* Cambridge: Cambridge University Press.

M.I.A. 2012. "Bad Girls." Official video, Uploaded February 2, 2012, www.youtube .com/watch?v = 2uYsogJD-LE (accessed October 18, 2015).

Middle East Institute, n.d. *The Kingdom of Saudi Arabia, 1979–2009: Evolution of a Pivotal State.* Washington, DC: Middle East Institute.

Milani, Farzaneh. 2012. "Saudi Arabia's Freedom Riders." *New York Times,* June 12.

Ministry of Hajj. 2015. "The Ministry of Hajj Portal: Kingdom of Saudi Arabia." Available at: http://haj.gov.sa/en-us/pages/default.aspx (accessed October 18, 2015).

Mirza, Mohammed. 2013. "The Historical District: The Jewel of Jeddah." Destinationjeddah.com, February 1.

Monroe, Elizabeth. 1973. *Philby of Arabia.* New York: Pitman Publishing.

Moore, Keith. 1983. *The Developing Human: Clinically Oriented Embryology with Islamic Additions.* Jeddah: Dar al-Qiblah for Islamic Literature.

————. 1986. "A Scientist's Interpretation of References to Embryology in the Qur'an." *Journal of the Islamic Medical Association of North America* 18 (January–June): 15–17.

————. 2013. *The Developing Human: Clinically Oriented Embryology.* 9th ed. Philadelphia: Saunders/Elseviers.

Muslim ibn al-Hajjaj. 1971–75. *Sahih Muslim.* Lahore: Sh. Muhammad Ashraf.

Myers, Paul Z. 2010. "Islamic Apologetics in the *International Journal of Cardiology.*" November 3, http://scienceblogs.com/pharyngula/2010/11/03/islamic-apologetics-in-the-int/ (accessed October 18, 2015).

My Right to Dignity. 2012. "Lawsuit Filed against the General Directorate of Traffic." Women2Drive, February 4, http://right2dignity.wordpress.com (accessed October 18, 2015).

al-Nafjan, Emam. 2009. "My Guardian Knows What's Best for Me." Saudiwoman's Weblog, September 3, http://saudiwoman.me/2009/09/03/my-guardian-knows-whats-best-for-me/ (accessed October 18, 2015).

————. 2011a. "Update on Manal al-Sharif." Saudiwoman's Weblog, May 22, http://saudiwoman.me/2011/05/ (accessed October 18, 2015).

————. 2011b. "Manal al-Sharif: For Putting Women in the Driver's Seat." *Foreign Policy,* November 28.

————. 2012. "Translation of My Right to Dignity Petition." Saudiwoman's Weblog, June 11, http://saudiwoman.me/2012/06/11/translation-of-my-right-to-dignity-petition/ (accessed October 18, 2015).

Naseef, Fatima. 1999. *Women in Islam: A Discourse on Rights and Obligations.* Cairo: International Islamic Committee for Woman and Child.

Nawwab, Ismail I., Peter C. Speers, and Paul F. Hoye, eds. 1980. *Aramco and Its World. Arabia and the Middle East.* Dhahran, Saudi Arabia: Aramco.

Nehme, Laila. 2010. "Hegra of *Arabia Felix.*" In *Roads of Arabia: Archaeology and History of the Kingdom of Saudi Arabia,* ed. Ali al-Ghabban et al., 286–307. Paris: Somogy Art Publishers.

Nelson, Sara. 2013. "Saudi Women Urged to Protest Against Driving Ban by Getting behind the Wheel on October 26." *Huffington Post,* September 23.

Noisey. 2012. "M.I.A.—'Bad Girls' (Official behind the Scenes): Noisey Specials. #8." March 19, www.youtube.com/watch?v = m6-sNTOhYnU (accessed October 18, 2015).

O'Brien, Jane. 2012. "Uncovering the Hidden Bodies in Saudi Art." BBC.com, November 17.

O'Connor, Richard, 1971. *The Oil Barons: Men of Greed and Grandeur.* Boston: Little, Brown.

Orwell, George. 1949. *1984.* New York: Harcourt, Brace.

al-Ouda, Salman. 2004. "Islamic Law and Prisoners of War." Sunni Forum, August 8, www.sunniforum.com/forum/showthread.php?875-Islamic-Law%20 and-Prisoners-of-War (accessed October 16, 2015).

Peer, Basharat. 2012. "Modern Mecca: The Transformation of a Holy City." *New Yorker,* April 16.

Pellerin, Ananda. 2008. "Abdulnasser Gharem." *Wheel Me Out* 2 (December), http://abdulnassergharem.com/background/interviews/wheel-me-out/ (accessed October 18, 2015).

Pesce, Angelo. 1977. *Jiddah: Portrait of an Arabian City*. 1974. Rev. ed. N.p.: Falcon Press.

Peters, F. E. 1994. *The Hajj: The Muslim Pilgrimage to Mecca and the Holy Places*. Princeton, NJ: Princeton University Press.

Philby, H. St. John B. 1948. *Arabian Days: An Autobiography*. London: Robert Hale.

Pint, John, and Susy Pint. 2005. "Discovering Old Jeddah: An Enchanting Jewel on the Red Sea." Updated September 2013, www.saudicaves.com/saudi/oldjeddah .html (accessed October 18, 2015).

Pizano, Pedro. 2012. "Where Driving Is a Crime and Speaking about It Leads to Death Threats." *Huffington Post*, June 6.

Pogrebin, Robin. 2013. "Qatari Riches Are Buying Art World Influence." *New York Times*, July 23.

Porter, Venetia, ed. 2012. *Hajj: Journey to the Heart of Islam*. Cambridge, MA: Harvard University Press.

Porter, Venetia, and Isabelle Caussé. 2006. *Word into Art: Artists of the Modern Middle East*. London: British Museum Press.

Poyrazlar, Elcin. 2013. "Creationism, with a Side of Eye Candy." *Vocativ*, November 14.

Quan, Kristene. 2013. "Saudi Women Can Now Ride Bicycles in Public (Kind of)." *Time*, April 3.

Rabinow, Paul. 1977. *Reflections on Fieldwork in Morocco*. Berkeley: University of California Press.

al-Rasheed, Madawi. 2010. *A History of Saudi Arabia*. Cambridge: Cambridge University Press.

———. 2013. *A Most Masculine State: Gender, Politics, and Religion in Saudi Arabia*. Cambridge: Cambridge University Press.

al-Rashid, Saad A. 2005. "The Development of Archaeology in Saudi Arabia." *Proceedings of the Seminar for Arabian Studies* 35: 207–14.

Reilly, Jill. 2014. "'No Woman, No Drive': Satirical Video Mocking Women Drivers in Saudi to the Tune of Bob Marley Classic Goes Viral." *Daily Mail*, October 31.

Reuters. 2010. "Senior Saudi Cleric Questions Women's Driving Ban." Reuters.com, November 30.

Rice, Edward. 1990. *Captain Sir Richard Francis Burton: The Secret Agent Who Made the Pilgrimage to Mecca, Discovered the Kama Sutra, and Brought the Arabian Nights to the West*. New York: Scribner's.

Richmond, Anthony. 1994. *Global Apartheid: Refugees, Racism, and the New World Order*. Oxford: Oxford University Press.

Rihani, Amin. 1930. *Around the Coasts of Arabia*. Translation of *Muluk al-Arab*. Beirut, 1929. 2nd ed., London: Constable.

Robin, Christian Julien. 2010. "Languages and Scripts." In *Roads of Arabia: Archaeology and History of the Kingdom of Saudi Arabia*, ed. Ali al-Ghabban et al., 118–31. Paris: Somogy Art Publishers.

Ross Solberg, Anne. 2013. *The Mahdi Wears Armani: An Analysis of the Harun Yahya Enterprise*. Huddinge: Södertörns Högskola.

Saffarini, Reema. 2004. "Fatin Bundagji Hopes to Participate in Future Elections." Gulfnews.com, October 18.

Said, Edward. 1979. *Orientalism*. New York: Vintage Books.

Saudi Aramco. 2015. History page, www.saudiaramco.com/en/home/about/history.html (accessed October 18, 2015).

Saudi Commission for Tourism and Antiquities. 2009. "Sites in Saudi Arabia." March, www.scta.gov.sa/en/Antiquities-Museums/InternationallyRegistered Sites/Documents/English.pdf (accessed October 18, 2015).

———. 2011. "Tourism Investment in Saudi Arabia." March 26, www.scta.gov.sa/en/TourismInvestment/SupportTourismInvestment/Documents/Touristic_investment_eng.pdf (accessed October 18, 2015).

———. 2012. Newsletter. 8th ed. March 15, www.scta.gov.sa/en/newsletter/v8/1902012_en.html (accessed October 18, 2015).

———. 2013a. "The Cultural Dimension of the Kingdom of Saudi Arabia." November 10, www.scta.gov.sa/en/eBook/Documents/Archive/TheCultruralDimension/TheCultruralDimension.pdf (accessed October 18, 2015).

———. 2013b. Roads of Arabia exhibition poster, www.scta.gov.sa/ebooks/Documents/Others/CarnegiPoster.pdf (accessed October 18, 2015).

———. 2013c. "Sheikh Bin Manin and al-Motlak Pay a Visit to Madain Saleh." February 10, www.scta.gov.sa/en/mediaCenter/News/GeneralNews/Pages/z-g-3-10-2-13.aspx.

———. 2015. "Archaeological Masterpieces," www.scta.gov.sa/en/Antiquities-Museums/ArcheologicalMasterpieces/Pages/Photogallery.aspx (accessed October 18, 2015).

Saudi Gazette. 2013a. "ALJCI, Jeddah Municipality Working to Restore Corniche Sculptures." Saudigazette.com, February 10.

———. 2013b. "Art Is an Effective Tool for Positive Criticism." Saudigazette.com, August 9.

Saudi Jeans. 2009. "Time to Wake Up." November 21, http://saudijeans.org/2009/11/21/fawzia-albakr/ (accessed October 18, 2015).

———. 2012. "Saudi Women Driving: Shifting Gears." February 5, http://saudijeans.org/2012/02/05/saudi-women-driving-shifting-gears/ (accessed October 18, 2015).

Saudi Voyager. 2012. "Cultural Masterpieces on Display." Saudi Commission for Tourism and Antiquities, Autumn, www.scta.gov.sa/ebooks/Pages/Voyager/10/index.html (accessed October 18, 2015).

Scholler, Marco. 2004. *The Living and the Dead in Islam: Studies in Arabic Epitaphs*. Vol. 2, *Epitaphs in Context*. Wiesbaden: Harrassowitz Verlag.

Sciolino, Elaine. 2002. "Where the Prophet Trod, He Begs, Tread Lightly." *New York Times*, February 15.

Shabout, Nada M. 2007. *Modern Arab Art: Formation of Arab Aesthetics*. Gainesville: University Press of Florida.

Shane, Daniel. 2013. "Women Drivers Would Cause Crashes—Saudi Grand Mufti." Arabianbusiness.com, May 27.

al-Sharif, Manal. 2012. "The Drive for Freedom." Oslo Freedom Forum, May 10, www.youtube.com/watch?v = 0PXXNK-3zQ4 (accessed October 18, 2015).

———. 2013. "My Talk in Ted: Global." Official blog, June 11, http://manal-alsharif. com/2013/06/16/tedglobal-2013/ (accessed October 18, 2015).

Shea, Nina. 2013. "The Saudis' PR 'Roads' Show." *National Review,* January 9.

Shift. 2011. "Art Dubai 2011." April 13, www.shift.jp.org/en/archives/2011/04/art_ dubai_2011.html (accessed October 18, 2015).

Shubert, Atika. 2011. "Saudi Woman Claims She Was Detained for Driving." CNN. com, May 27.

Silberman, Neil. A. 1989. *Between Past and Present: Archaeology, Ideology, and Nationalism in the Modern Middle East.* New York: Henry Holt.

al-Simari, Fahd A. 2010a. "The Kingdom of Saudi Arabia." In *Roads of Arabia: Archaeology and History of the Kingdom of Saudi Arabia,* ed. Ali al-Ghabban et al., 564–67. Paris: Somogy Art Publishers.

———. 2010b. "King Abdulaziz (Ibn Saud): 1902–53." In *Roads of Arabia: Archaeology and History of the Kingdom of Saudi Arabia,* ed. Ali al-Ghabban et al., 568–73. Paris: Somogy Art Publishers.

Simcox, Robin. 2009. *A Degree of Influence: The Funding of Strategically Important Subjects in UK Universities.* London: Centre for Social Cohesion.

Simmons, Matthew R. 2005. *Twilight in the Desert: The Coming Saudi Oil Shock and the World Economy.* Hoboken, NJ: John Wiley.

Sloman, Paul. 2009. *Contemporary Art in the Middle East.* London: Black Dog Publishing.

Smithsonian. 2012a. "Q+A: Saudi Arabia's Sultan bin Salman on 'Roads of Arabia.'" Around the Mall, December 3.

———. 2012b. "'Roads of Arabia' Presents Hundreds of Recent Finds That Recast the Region's History." Around the Mall, November 15.

Stapleton, Stephen A., et al. 2012. *Edge of Arabia.* London: Booth-Clibborn Editions.

Stegner, Wallace. 1971. *Discovery! The Search for American Oil.* Vista, CA: Selwa Press.

Suffolk University. 2012. "Alumna Addresses Women's Rights in Art." Suffolk.edu, Sawyer Business School, March 14.

Sullivan, Kevin. 2012. "In 'Roads of Arabia,' Dusting Off Ideas about a Kingdom and Civilization." *Washington Post,* November 14.

al-Suwaidan, Mafaz. 2012. "Driving For Freedom." *McClungs,* Winter.

Swami, Praveen. 2011a. "Analysis: Saudi Arabia's War between God and Archaeology." *Telegraph,* February 4.

———. 2011b. "Google Earth Finds Saudi Arabia's Forbidden Archaeological Secrets." *Telegraph,* February 4.

Thompson, Bob. 2007. "Was This 'Discovery!' Meant to be Found?" *Washington Post,* November 29.

Thompson, Damian. 2012. "The Saudis Are Bulldozing Islam's Heritage: Why the Silence from the Muslim World?" *Telegraph,* November 2.

Time. 1928. "Arabia: Tomb of Eve." February 27.

Totten, Michael J. 2012. "Closed Kingdom." Review of *On Saudi Arabia,* by Karen Houses. *New York Times Book Review,* November 18.

Travel Magazine. 2010. "No More Tourist Visa for Saudi Arabia." September 4.

Trigger, Bruce. 1984. "Alternative Archaeologies: Nationalist, Colonialist, Imperialist." *Man,* n.s., 19 (3): 355–70.

Trofimov, Yaroslav. 2007. *The Siege of Mecca: The 1979 Uprising at Islam's Holiest Shrine.* New York: Anchor Books.

UNESCO. n.d. "Archaeological Site of al-Hijr (Saudi Arabia), No. 1293." N.d., http://whc.unesco.org/archive/advisory_body_evaluation/1293.pdf (accessed October 18, 2015).

———. 2006. "Historical Area of Jeddah." November 28, http://whc.unesco.org /en/tentativelists/5085/ (accessed October 18, 2015).

———. 2011. International Bureau of Education. *World Data on Education: Saudi Arabia.* Rev. version. August, http://www.ibe.unesco.org/fileadmin/user_upload/Publications/WDE/2010/pdf-versions/Saudi_Arabia.pdf (accessed October 18, 2015).

U.S. Department of State. 2011. "2010 Country Reports on Human Rights Practices: Saudi Arabia." April 8, www.state.gov/j/drl/rls/hrrpt/2010/nea/154472 .htm (accessed October 18, 2015).

———. 2013. "2012 Country Reports on Human Rights Practices: Saudi Arabia. Executive Summary." Available at: www.state.gov/documents/organization /204593.pdf (accessed October 18, 2015).

Vitalis, Robert. 2009. *America's Kingdom: Mythmaking on the Saudi Oil Frontier.* New York: Verso.

Von Uthmann, Jorg. 2010. "Saudi King a No Show as Treasures Glitter in Louvre Exhibition." Bloomberg.com, July 26.

Wagner, Rob L. 2011. "Away from the Cities, Saudi Women Take to the Roads." *Jerusalem Post,* February 10.

Wasil, Saddek, and Sami Jeraidi. 2012. *Saddek Wasil: "And They Will Not Cease to Differ."* Jeddah: Athr Gallery.

Wavell, A.J.B. 1912. *A Modern Pilgrim in Mecca and a Siege in Sanaa.* London: Constable.

Weinstein, Jamie. 2012. "Saudi Woman Driver: I Was Pressured Out of My Job for My Activism." *Daily Caller,* May 14.

Wheeler, Brannon. 2006. "Moses." In *The Blackwell Companion to the Qur'an,* ed. Andrew Rippin, 248–65. Malden, MA: Blackwell.

Wilson, Joy. 1977. "Raising Children in an American Oil Camp in Saudi Arabia." *Radcliffe Quarterly* (March): 8–9.

Wolfe, Michael. 1997. *One Thousand Roads to Mecca: Ten Centuries of Travelers Writing about the Muslim Pilgrimage.* New York: Grove Press.

Wright, Gwendolyn. 1996. *The Formation of National Collections of Art and Architecture*. Studies in the History of Art 47. Washington, DC: National Gallery of Art.

Wright, Robin. 1985. *Sacred Rage: The Wrath of Militant Islam*. New York: Simon and Schuster.

Yahya, Harun. (Pseudonym of Adnan Oktar.) 2006. *The Atlas of Creation*. Istanbul: Global Publishing.

INDEX

abaya, 2, 62, 95

Abdulaziz ibn Saud: Arabian Peninsula campaign of, 112, 168, 169–70, 172, 193, 203; Aramco aircraft used to transport, 50; Aramco Brat film portrayal of, 55; at CASOC opening ceremonies, 32–33; first Hajj conducted under rule of, 193–94; as founder of Kingdom of Saudi Arabia, 5, 24, 30, 96, 153; as guardian of the two holy mosques, 152; historic preservation efforts and, 141; museum exhibits honoring, 112, 113; oil concession agreement signed by (1933), 30–31, 41–42; Philby and, 203, 204; Roads of Arabia exhibit honoring, 153–54; during WWII, 34

Abdullah bin Abdulaziz ibn Saud Al Saud, 184; ascension to King, 8; as Crown Prince, 7, 32; as "King of Dialogue," 8, 156, 183; liberalization process under, 8, 80–81; Roads of Arabia exhibition not attended by, 150; Saudi artwork endorsed by, 102; *ulama* and, 7; #Women2Drive campaign and, 76–77, 84; women's rights and, 64, 70, 80–81, 84, 85

Abdul Latif Jameel Community Initiatives, 98, 178

Abha (Saudi Arabia), 98, 102–3, 106, 107

Abqaiq (Saudi Arabia), 34, 55

Accident! (sculpture; Lafuente), 177

Adam Travel, 211–12

adhan (call to prayer), 3

Afghanistan, 146, 173–74, 181

Afghanistan War, 7

al-Aghar Group, 182–83

Ahl al-Kitab (People of the Book), 195

Ahmed, Qamar, 89–91

air travel, 208, 209–10

alcohol, 45–46, 52–53, 60, 144, 212–13

Ali, Wijdan, 93

ALJ Company, 98, 178

American Bedu (website), 186–89

"American Invasion of the Near East, The" (Eddy), 39

American University of Beirut, 92

America's Kingdom: Mythmaking on the Saudi Oil Frontier (Vitalis), 41

Amira Park (Jeddah, Saudi Arabia), 184–85

Amnesty International, 77

Angawi, Sami, 148, 209, 213–15

anthropology, 4, 5

apostasy, 201

Appadurai, Arjun, 93

Arab art, 91–93, 176

Arabian Archaeology and Epigraphy (Langfeldt), 146–47

Arabian Days (Philby), 203–5

Arabian Peninsula: Abdulaziz's conquest of, 112, 168, 169–70, 172, 193, 203; map, xiv; as multicultural region, 156, 157; as multilingual region, 157; Ottoman influence on, 96, 169; as polytheistic region, 157–58

Arabic language/script, 93, 203
Arab-Israeli War (1948), 50
Arab-Israeli War (1967), 50
Arab modernism, 92
Arab popular culture, 136
Arab Spring, 10–11
Aramaic language, 157
Aramco (Arabian American Oil Company), 6, 34–36. *See also* Saudi Aramco
Aramco and Its World (Aramco company history), 30, 36–37
"Aramco Brats," 12, 53–58
Aramcons, 18, 21, 39, 53. *See also* "Aramco Brats"
"Aramco story," 11, 24
Aramco World, 40, 142
archaeological sites: Christian, 146–47; conservation of, 172; early Islamic, 147–48, 152–53; excavation of, 139, 141; pre-Islamic, 134–38, 141, 144–46, fig. 11; restricted access to, 146; Saudi destruction of, 210, 213–14; tourism and, 144–45
archaeology: critical, 139; nationalist, 139; politicization of, 14, 138–40, 146, 154–57; in Saudi Arabia, 13–14, 134–35, 140–41. *See also* Roads of Arabia (traveling exhibition; 2012–2013)
al-Arjoush, Madeha, 67, 68, 69, 86
Armstrong, Tom, 128–29
Arp, Jean, 176
al-Arrayed, Thuraya, 8
art: in the Middle East, 91–93; open-air monumental sculpture, in Jeddah, 176–78; patronage of, 178; in Saudi Arabia, 96–99; Wahhabi view of, as blasphemous, 148. *See also* Edge of Arabia (arts initiative)
Art Dubai (2007), 92
art exhibitions, 92, 98–99, 109
art galleries, 89–91, 94–96, 97, 109–11
art workshops, 109–11
Ashgar, Munira, 143
Asir region (Saudi Arabia), 102, 104, 106
Association for the Protection and Defense of Women's Rights in Saudi Arabia, 73
astronomers, Muslim, 177
astronomy, "scientific miracles" in, 126–27

Ataturk, Kemal, 121
atheism, 78, 119, 122
Athr Gallery (Jeddah, Saudi Arabia), 109–11
Atlal: The Journal of Saudi Arabian Archaeology, 141
Atlas of Creation, The (Oktar), 122–23, 130, fig. 9
Au Revoir (painting; al-Qahtani), 94
authenticity, 93

Bad Girls (music video; M.I.A.), 12, 59–60, 85, 87, 88, fig. 4
Baghdad (Iraq), 92, 191
Bahrain: Arab Spring unrest in, 10; King Fahd Causeway from, xiii, 17; oil discovered in, 30, 32
Baissa, Malik, 174–75
al-Bakr, Fawzia, 64, 68–69
al-Balad (Jeddah old city), 14, 170–75, fig. 14
Bangladesh, expatriate labor from, 4, 9, 19
al-Baqi Cemetery (Medina, Saudi Arabia), 162, 163
Barger, Thomas, 40, 41, 56
Barger, Tim, 40, 56
Basic Law of Governance (1992), 8
#Bates2Saudi educational program, xi–xv
Bates College (Lewiston, ME), xi, 72
Bayt Naseef (Jeddah, Saudi Arabia), 172
BBC, 20, 70–71, 144
Bedouins, 90; American stereotyping of, 23, 57; Aramco Brat memories of, 55–56, 57; in Aramco company histories, 42; artwork of, 89, 94–95; caravan raids of, 191–92; Doughty and, 202; in Jeddah, 181; during oil exploration, 31, 33–34; patriarchy of, 61; resettlement of, at Madain Saleh, 137; Roads of Arabia portrayals of, 164; women driving among, 65; during WWII, 33–34
Bedouins: The Trendsetters (painting series; al-Qahtani), 94–95
Bible, the Quran, and Science, The (Bucaille), 124–25
Biblical creationism, 117, 121
Bidoun (art magazine), 92

Big Bang theory, 112, 115
Big Oil Man from Arabia (Cheney), 38, 40, 41, 42–43
Bin Laden, Osama, 1, 2, 7, 83, 126, 130
Binladin Group, 17, 107
Binzager, Safeya, 142–43
biology, "scientific miracles" in, 127
Blue Flame, The (Aramcon alcohol-making guidebook), 46
Board of Grievances of the Eastern Province, 81–82
Brief Illustrated Guide to Understanding Islam, A, fig. 10
British Empire, 169, 193
British Foreign Service, 42, 170, 202–3
British Museum, 99, 102
Brown, Anthony, 41
Bucaille, Maurice, 124–25
Bukhari, Farid, 89–90
Bundagji, Fatin, 178–82
Burckhardt, J. L., 201
Burton, Isabel, 198
Burton, Richard, 15, 168, 197–99, 202

Cairo (Egypt), 105, 191, 197
Cairo International Exhibition of Art (1947), 92
Calder, Alexander, 176
California-Arabian Standard Oil Company (CASOC), 31–34. *See also* Aramco (Arabian American Oil Company)
caliph, 190–91
calligrafitti, 93, 95, 108
camels, 57, 112, 155, 191
caravans, 191–93
"caste system," 19, 23
Catholic Church, 53, 114
Cave Automatic Virtual Environment (CAVE; Saudi Aramco), 28
censorship, 9, 93, 95–96, 107–8
Cheney, Michael, 38, 40, 41, 42–43, 47
Chicago (IL), 150
child custody, 63
Choice, The (photograph series; al-Dowayan), 101–2, fig. 5
Christian archaeological sites, 146–47, 148–49
Christian concordism, 125–26

Christianity, 39, 45, 53, 114, 194, 195, 214. *See also* Judeo-Christian tradition
Christie's, 99
Christie's Dubai, 106
civil society organizations, 178–85
Clouds (sculpture; Lafuente), 177
CNN, 20, 78, 150
colonialism, 118–20
Committee for the Promotion of Virtue and Prevention of Vice (*hayah*), 7, 85
concordism, 123–26. *See also* Islamic concordism
Consultative Assembly, 64
Contemporary Art from the Islamic World (online magazine), 92
Convention on the Elimination of All Forms of Discrimination against Women (1979), 61
corporate histories, 37–38. *See also* Saudi Aramco—official company histories
corruption, 119
Country Reports on Human Rights Practices (US State Dept. report), 61, 64
creationism, 13, 114–15, 117, 121–23. *See also* Islamic creationism
critical archaeology, 139
Cuadro Fine Art Gallery (Dubai, UAE), 99
cultural imperialism, 124
cultural relativism, 132–33
cultural vandalism, 148, 210
culture shock, xv
culture wars, 140
Custodian of the Two Holy Mosques, 190–91

dallah (coffee pots), 109, 177
Dallah Fountain (sculpture; Lafuente), 177
Damascus (Syria), 92, 191
Dammam Dome, 31–32
Dammam Well Number 7 ("Prosperity Well"), 32, fig. 2
Damman (Saudia Arabia), 18, 31–32
Dark Face of Darwinism, The (Oktar), 121–22
Darwin, Charles, 117
Darwinism, 13, 106, 114–15, 119–23
Declaration of Conversion to Islam, 212
Dedan (archaeological site), 141, 152

gender mixing, 89, 182
gender segregation, xiii, 62–63, 70, 97, 143
General Petroleum and Mineral Organization (Petromin), 52
geology, "scientific miracles" in, 127
geosteering, 25–26
al-Ghabban, Ali Ibrahim, 149, 156
Gharem, Abdulnasser, 13, 98, 106–8, figs. 8, 15
Global Gender Gap Report (World Economic Forum; 2009), 60–61
globalization, 93, 94–95, 102
Goeringer, Gerald, 129
Golden Hour (photography; Mater), fig. 16
Gould, Stephen Jay, 116–17, 119, 122, 123–24
Great Britain, 41–42, 193
Guggenheim Abu Dhabi, 92
guide system, 192, 194, 212
Gulf War (1990–1991), 7, 54, 65–66, 67, 89

hadith, 69–70, 77, 202
Hajj: American convert participation in, 15, 206–8; artistic portrayals of, 103–4; concepts central to, 194–96; deaths during, 153; disasters during, 210–11; European convert participation in, 15, 202–5; in Five Pillars of Islam, 186; floods during (2009), 180; founding of (632), 189; history of, 15, 190–94; Jeddah as stop during, 168, 169, 170; management of, 190–91; in museum exhibits, 113; non-Muslims prohibited from participation in, 4, 14–15, 195–96; Orientalist travel literature involving, 196–200; "overstayers" (undocumented immigrants) from, 14, 173–74; quota system for, 208–9; rituals performed in, 15, 189–90, 200; service industry supporting, 171, 192, 209, 211; time of, 189; tourist packages, 211–12; transportation to, 137, 170, 191–93, 208, 209–10
Hajj Research Center (Mecca), 171, 209, 213
Hajj visas, 144, 194, 212
Hamilton, Lloyd, 30, 41–42
"al-Hamra cube," 152
haraam (forbidden; prohibited), 195, 196
haram (sacred; holy), 194, 196

al-Haramayn (Two Holy Sanctuaries), 194–95
Hay, William, 127–28
hayah. See Committee for the Promotion of Virtue and Prevention of Vice (*hayah*)
Hegra (Nabataean city), 134, 136–37, fig. 11. *See also* Madain Saleh (archaeological site)
hijab, 62, 72
Hijazi architecture, 214
Hijazi poetry, 177–78
Hijaz Railway, 137, 153, 154, 193, 199
Hijaz region (Saudi Arabia), 61, 96, 170, 191, 192, 193–94, 203
al-Hijr (Saudi Arabia), 134. *See also* Madain Saleh (archaeological site)
Hilton Makkah (Mecca, Saudi Arabia), 211–12
historic preservation, 14, 141, 175, 213–14
Hofuf (Saudi Arabia), xiv, 33
Holocaust Deception, The (Oktar), 121
Holy Mosque (Mecca, Saudi Arabia), 195, 196, 198–99, 210–11; animated history of, in Roads of Arabia exhibit, 152; Islamist siege of (1979), 82
Holy Quran: Top Scientists Comment on Scientific Miracles in the Quran (Islamic concordist video), 129
Home: The Aramco Brats' Story (documentary film), 54–56
homogenization, 93
homosexuality, Muslim perspective on, 13, 131–33
Houston (TX), 53, 55, 150
human form, prohibitions against depiction of, 90, 91, 97, 106, 148
human rights, 132, 155, 157
human rights activism, xiii
Human Rights Association, 76
Human Rights Watch, 9, 61
Hundred Men, The (McConnell), 41
Hussein, Saddam, 7, 54
Hussein, Sharif, 169
al-Huwaider, Wajeha, 73, 79

I Am (photograph series; al-Dowayan), 101
Ibn Baz, Abd al-Aziz, 69–70

Ibn Baz, Sheikh Ahmed, 70
Ibn Jubayr, 191
idolatry, 138, 145, 147, 168, 214
ihram (state of ritual purity), 189, 190, 195, 212
ikhtilat. See gender segregation
illegal immigration, 9, 14, 173–75, 181, 184, fig. 14
I Love Music (artwork; al-Mohasen), 96
"incense roads," 151, 152
India: British, Hajj travel from, 193; Buddhist pilgrimage sites in, 194; expatriates from, in Saudi Arabia, 9, 19; media from, in Saudi Arabia, 20
inheritance law, 65
intelligent design, 117, 121
interfaith dialog, 131, 183
International Commission on Scientific Signs in the Quran and Sunnah, 13, 126–30
International Islamic Committee for Woman and Child (Cairo, Egypt), 131
Internet, 83, 86, 186. *See also* Facebook; social media; Twitter; YouTube
Iqbal, Muzaffar, 119
Iran, 22, 120–21, 209
Iranian Revolution, 6, 61, 97
Iraq, 15
Iraq War, 7, 15
Islam: admission to Mecca and, 186; American Aramco employees' disrespect of, 44–46; American converts to, 15, 205–8; Arab Spring challenges and interpretations of, 11; call to prayer in, 3, 185; conversion from, as apostasy, 201; conversion to, 200–202, 212, 216–18; declaration of faith in (*shahada*), 201–2; European converts to, 15, 202–5; evolution and, 13, 114–15, 119–23; Five Pillars of, 186; golden age of, 113–14, 118; history of, in museum exhibits, 113; homosexuality and, 13, 131–33; influence of, in everyday Saudi life, 4; Philby as convert to, 42; pre-Islamic archaeological sites and, 138; science and, 13, 113–15, 118–19, fig. 10; women driving and, 69–70, 71; women's rights and, 61, 69; worldwide dissemination of, 142. *See*

also Shia Islam; Sunni Islam; Wahhabism
Islam and Science (Iqbal), 119
Islamic art, 91, 93, 149, 178
Islamic concordism, 131, fig. 10; Christian concordism vs., 125–26; criticism of, 130; early proponents of, 124–25; promotion of, 126; "scientific miracles" in, 125, 126–30
Islamic creationism, 13, 121–23, fig. 9
Islamic Education Foundation (Jeddah, Saudi Arabia), 13, 130–33, 216, 217
Islamic fundamentalism, 68, 105–6, 121; American stereotyping of, 1, 155. *See also* Wahhabism
Islamic nongovernmental organizations (NGOs), 126
Islamic State (ISIS/ISIL), 15, 105–6
Israel, 50, 52

Jahiliyya period ("Age of Ignorance"), 112–13, 134, 142, 145–46, 148
Jamarat (Hajj ritual stop), 190, 211
Jameel Gallery for Islamic Art (Victoria and Albert Museum, London, England), 178
Jarrar, Ziad, 182–85
Jeddah (Saudi Arabia), 35; architectural monuments in, 170, 185; art galleries in, 109–11; Bates College educational trip in, xv, 185; Burton's visit to, 197; civil society in, 178–82; establishment of, 169; floods in (2009/2011), 14, 180–82; during Hajj, 168, 169, 170, 208, 209–10, 212; Hajj Committee Court in, 206–7; historical overview, 168–70, 172; historic buildings/sites destroyed in, 168, 170, 171–72; Islamic concordist conference in, 127–29; location of, 169; museums in, 143; name of, 168; oil concession agreement in, 30–31; old city (al-Balad) in, 14, 170–75, fig. 14; open-air monumental sculpture in, 176–78; Ottoman influence in, 96, fig. 14; "overstayers" (undocumented immigrants) in, 14, 173–75, 181, 184; parks in, 182–85; tourism in, 175; women's rights in, 61
Jeddah Chamber of Commerce, 64, 179, 181, 183

religious freedom, 9, 23, 39, 53, 132, 144, 157
#Right2Dignity campaign, 84–85. *See also*
al-Sharif, Manal
Rihani, Amin, 192–93
riots, 10, 22
Riyadh (Saudi Arabia): Bates College
educational trip in, xiv–xv; "drifting"
in/near, 12; "driving while female" civil
disobedience in (1990), 65–68; women's
rights in, 61
Roads of Arabia (traveling exhibition;
2012–2013), 14; Christian artifacts
lacking in, 158–59; conception/curation
of, 149; early Islamic exhibit, 152–53, fig.
13; exhibition locations, 150; media
coverage of, 150; pre-Islamic exhibit,
150–52, 157–61, fig. 12; as rebranding
tool, 154–57; reviews of, 156–57; sponsorship of, 149–50
Road to Makkah (photography; Gharem),
fig. 15
*Rock of Ages: Science and Religion in the
Fullness of Life* (Gould), 116–17
Roosevelt, Franklin Delano, 154
Rub al-Khali desert, 112, 205

Sackler Gallery (Washington, DC), 150–
54, 156, fig. 12
Safaniya oil field, 34–35
sai (Hajj ritual), 190, 211
Salafism, 6, 219n8. *See also* Wahhabism
San Francisco Freedom Forum, 84–85
Saud, King, 48
Al Saud, Moudi al-Faisal al-Saad, 24
Al Saud dynasty, 5–9, 193–94, 225n39
Saudi Antiquities and Museums Ministry,
137, 140, 146
Saudi Arabia, 43; American stereotyping
of, 1–2, 3, 57–58, 155; Arabic name of,
225n39; Arab Spring and, 10–11; archaeological sites in, 134–38, 141; archaeology in, 13–14, 134–35, 140–41; art
exhibitions in, 98–99; art galleries in,
89–91, 94–96, 97, 109–11; art in, 96–99;
Bates College educational trip in, xi–xv,
2–3; dissidents in, 49; education in, 120;
expatriate influences in, 4–5, 9, 19–20;
flag of, 153; founding of (1932), 5, 24, 30,

96, 153, 169–70, 193–94; during Gulf
War (1990–1991), 7, 65–66; Hajj regulations, 194; history of, and Saudi
Aramco, 29–37; human rights record of,
157; Islam and, 4, 142; justice system in,
43, 75–76; king of, as Custodian of the
Two Holy Mosques, 191; legal system of,
63–64; liberalization process in, 6–7,
80–81; map, xiv; as monarchy, 1, 2, 8–9;
museums in, 13, 142–43, 148–49; name
of, 5–6; oil concession agreement signed
by (1933), 30–31, 41–42, 51; oil discovered in, 6, 17, 19, 31–32, 96–97; relations
with US, 154; Al Saud dynasty and
history of, 5–9; science museums in,
112–15; slavery banned in, 207; socioeco-
nomic problems in, 9–10; stability of,
15–16; State Dept. travel warnings on,
xii; tourism in, 14, 143–45; travel
restrictions in, 144–45; Wahhabism
and, 194; women's driving banned in,
65; women's position in, 12, 60–64;
during WWII, 33–34
Saudi Aramco: "Aramco stories" at, 24;
Core Area at, 25–29, fig. 1; corporate
culture of, 28–29, 46–47; Dhahran
residential camp, 11, 17–23, 55; education
system, 21, 27–29, 47; establishment of
(1988), 53; female employees, 29, 72, 73,
78–79, 83–84, 99; gender mixing at, 63;
housing allowances at, 48; HQs of, xiii,
34; Jeddah infrastructure improvements
by, 182; nationalization of, 51; production rates, 51, fig. 3; professional development at, 27–29; as Roads of Arabia
sponsor, 150; Saudi control of, 11–12,
50–53; Saudi employees, 43–44, 50–51;
Sunni-Shia tensions at, 23, 48; website
of, 30
Saudi Aramco—critical histories: CIA-
Aramco relationship in, 49–50; dissidents in, 49; economic exploitation in,
11, 47–48; Islam in, 44–46; labor unrest
in, 47–48; neocolonialism in, 11; racism
in, 11, 42–45, 47; residential compound
integration in, 48–49; Saudi control of
company in, 11–12, 50–53; Sunni-Shia
conflict in, 48

Shia Islam, xii, 6, 33, 209. *See also* Sunni-Shia conflict

Shura Council, 8, 80, 84

Siraat (conceptual artwork; Gharem), 107–8, fig. 8

Smithsonian Institution (Washington, DC), 154–55. *See also* Sackler Gallery (Washington, DC)

social activism, 178–82

social media, 9, 12, 73, 83, 84–85. *See also* YouTube

Somalis, 14, 173–75, fig. 14

Speedy the Camel (painting; al-Qahtani), 94–95

Standard Oil Company of California (SOCAL), 30–31, 41–42

Standard Oil Company of New Jersey (Exxon), 34

Standard Oil Company of New York (Mobil), 34

Stapleton, Stephen, 98

Stegner, Wallace, 31, 39, 40–41

Steineke, Max, 19, 32

Steineke Hall (Saudi Aramco residential facility), 19–20

strikes, 47–48

Suez Canal, 154, 169, 192, 197

Sultan bin Salman, Prince, 141, 144, 149, 155–56, 175

Sunni Islam, 183, 206; reformist movements in, 6. *See also* Sunni-Shia conflict

Sunni-Shia conflict: discrimination, 22–23; during Hajj, 209; Iranian Revolution and, 6; in Iraq, 15; need for dialogue in, 183; Saudi liberalization policies and, 8; unrest, 10

Suspended Together (artwork; al-Dowayan), 100–101

Tariki, Abdullah, 49, 51

tawaf (circumambulation of the Kaba), 189–90

Tayma (archaeological site), 141, 152

television, 20, 150

terrorism, 83; American stereotyping of, 1, 2, 3, 57, 155

This Is the Truth (Islamic concordist publication), 126–28

tourism: Aramco Brats and, 57; art, 108; domestic, at archaeological sites, 138, 141; foreign, Saudi Arabia closed to, 134; Hajj, 211–12; in Jeddah, 175; obstacles to development of, 143–45, 149; possible emergence of, 14

tourist visas, 134, 138, 144, 145

travel restrictions, 65, 100–101, 144–45, 212–13

Travels in Arabia Deserta (Doughty), 137, 202

Trigger, Bruce, 139

Turkey, 121–23, 148, 210

Twitter, 9, 12, 73, 83, 84–85

Two Holy Mosques Museum (Mecca, Saudi Arabia), 142

al-Ula (archaeological site), 141, 152

ulama (council of religious scholars), 6–7, 69–70

umma (worldwide Islamic community), 191

UNESCO World Heritage Sites, xv, 134, 137–38, 141, 175

United Nations General Assembly, 61

United States: civil rights movement in, 67, 205; colonialism of, 119; converts to Islam from, 205–8; creationism in school curricula of, 117; expatriates from, in Saudi Arabia, 4–5; Gulf War (1990–1991), 7; Hajj certificates in, 212; Iraq War, 7, 15; as Israel ally, 50; media from, in Saudi Arabia, 20, 44–45; oil embargo (1973), 52; relations with Saudi Arabia, 154; Saudi Arabia as stereotyped in, 1–2; Saudi protests against, 50; September 11 (2001) attacks in, 7, 57, 83, 96, 106, 122, 155; women's movement in, 67

United States Central Intelligence Agency, 39, 49–50

United States State Department, xii, 61, 64, 154

"Uses of the Past" (Fowler), 139

vaccination programs, 194, 212

Vaclav Havel Prize for Creative Dissent, 82–83

veiling, 1, 2, 88

Venice Biennale (2011), 108

Verse Boat (sculpture; Lafuente), 177
Victoria and Albert Museum (London, England), 108, 143, 178
visas, 134, 144, 145, 194, 212–13
Vitalis, Robert, 40, 41

al-Wahhab, Muhammad ibn Abd, 6
Wahhabism, 7–8, 10; archaeology and, 145–49, 194; art as blasphemy, 148; Hajj and, 194; historical sites destroyed because of, 168, 194, 214; human form depictions prohibited in, 90; influence of, on Islamic extremists, 105–6; oil and Saudi promotion of, 105; Saudi education policies in conformity with, 120; Saudi founding and, 96, 194; tourism and, 143–44; use of term, 6, 219n8; women's rights and, 77
Wasil, Saddek, 13, 109–11
Wavell, Arthur J. B., 15, 170, 199–200, 202
welfare state, 8, 9, 10–11
Well of Zamzan (Hajj ritual stop), 190, 212
"We Need to Talk" exhibition (Jeddah, Saudi Arabia; 2012), 97–98
westernization, 118–19, 121, 124
women: as Hajj participants, 212–13; labor force participation of, 63; social control of, artistic portrayals of, 93. *See also* Saudi women
#Women2Drive (social media campaign), 12; award received for, 82–83; driver's license campaign, 81–82; international support of, 77, 79, 80; launching of, 72–73; media coverage of, 78, 82; Saudi reactions against, 77–78, 80; social media role in, 84–85; turnout for, 79–80; YouTube

video promoting, 73–74, 77, 87, 88. *See also* al-Sharif, Manal
Women in Islam (Naseef), 131
women's education, 62–63
women's rights, 12, 60–64
women's rights activism, xiii
women's universities, 63
work visas, 144
World War I, 121, 189, 193, 203
World War II, 33–34, 194, 203, 208
wuquf (Hajj ritual), 190

x-ray paintings, 102, 106
XVA Gallery (Dubai, UAE), 96

al-Yafi, Adnan, 171–72
Yahya, Harun. *See* Oktar, Adnan
Yamani, Ahmed, 51, 52
Yellow Cow, The (conceptual artwork; Mater), 104–5
Yemen: Arab Spring unrest in, 10; expatriates from, in Saudi Arabia, 9; Houthi rebellion in, 15; media from, in Saudi Arabia, 20; "overstayers" (undocumented immigrants) from, 14, 173–74, 184, fig. 14
You Can Go Home Again (Johnson), 43
YouTube: Aramco Brat videos on, 54; Fageeh "No Woman, No Drive" video on, 86–87; Islamic concordist videos on, 127, 128; M.I.A. *Bad Girls* video on, 59, 60; popularity of, 9; al-Sharif's Oslo speech on, 82; #Women2Drive video on, 12, 73, 74, 77, 78, 84–85

al-Zindani, Sheikh Abdul Majeed, 126, 130